The Profit Prophet

Joshua Shafran

Copyright © MMV IP Breakthroughs, Inc. -
All rights reserved.
ISBN: 978-0-692-48672-6

This book contains educational material protected under International and Federal Copyright laws and Treaties. Any unauthorized reprint or use of this material is prohibited. Unauthorized duplication or distribution of this material in any form is strictly prohibited. Violators will be prosecuted to the fullest extent of the law. No part of this publication may be reproduced, stored in a retrieval system or transmitted in any form or by any means, electronic, mechanical, photocopying, recording or otherwise, without prior written permission from the author/publisher.

Joshua Shafran, the interviewees, guest experts, case-studies and IP Breakthroughs, Inc. or any of its affiliates (hereinafter "we" or "us" or "our") do not promise, guarantee or imply that you (or that your use of these resources) will improve your operation, raise your Internet profile or increase your revenues. As with any business, earnings potential and successful or unsuccessful use of our products and resources will vary widely among our users depending on many factors, including, but not limited to, the users' finances, knowledge and skill set, creativity, motivation, level of effort, individual expertise, capacity and talents, business experience, cost structure and the market in which they compete, and as such we do not guarantee their success or income level.

The information conveyed by Joshua Shafran and each of the case-studies, as well as the educational information otherwise conveyed in these resources, is intended to provide you with basic instruction regarding your business or operation. We do not guarantee any results or returns based on the information you receive. Past performance or examples of others' performance are no indication or guarantee of your anticipated future results, and individual results will vary.

Any perceived slights of persons, peoples or organizations are unintentional. The author, publisher, and/or affiliates assume no responsibility or liability whatsoever on behalf of any purchaser or user of these materials.

WHILST THE AUTHOR HAS FOUND GREAT SUCCESS FROM THE EDUCATIONAL MATERIALS PRESENTED HEREIN, THE

THE PROFIT PROPHET

READER UNDERSTANDS AND AGREES THEIR PERSONAL EXPERIENCE WILL VARY. THE AUTHOR'S RESULTS, EXPERIENCES, AND OPINIONS IS NOT A SUBSTITUTE FOR THE READER'S SOUND INDEPENDENT VERIFICATION AND PERSONAL EXPERIENCE WITH THE EDUCATION PRESENTED HEREIN.

We are not responsible for any success or failure of your business if you implement the information you receive from us. We provide a tool that you can use to try to improve the operations of your business. All information contained or received through the use of our materials is provided "as is" without warranty of any kind. We hereby disclaim all warranties with regard to the information contained in our materials, including without limitation all express, statutory and implied warranties of merchantability and fitness for a particular purpose. The reader/user assumes all responsibility for the use of the materials and information herein, including adherence to all applicable laws and regulations.

The author, publisher, and distributor of this product assume no responsibility for the use or misuse of this product, or for any physical or mental injury, damage and/or financial loss sustained to persons or property as a result of using this system. The liability, negligence, use, misuse or abuse of the operation of any methods, strategies, instructions or ideas contained in the material herein is the sole responsibility of the reader. *The material contained in this publication is provided for information & educational purposes only; and shall not be considered professional, legal, accounting, or tax advice!*

In other words, don't subordinate your judgment to Mr. Shafran's: it's up to the individual reader to adapt and adopt these educational materials for their specific needs and personal situation and reap the value that's right for them (or not).

> *"The two most important days in your life are the day you are born and the day you find out why."*
>
> ~ Mark Twain ~

DEDICATION

For the two most important (and influential) Profit Prophets I know: My incredible wife, Kathy, and brilliantly delightful daughter, Aimee. You guys bring balance, joy and laughter to my life beyond any serial entrepreneur deserves! Thanks for tolerating the highs and lows of this crazy (yet, never boring, and often fun) roller-coaster ride with a smile (and a loving kick in the ass as needed)! Your love empowers me with the courage to live a much, much bigger future.

CLIENT PRAISE

What's The BUZZ?
Rave Reviews Are In:

"...As a trainer and business person for nearly 30 years, I have been delighted an amazed from day one with Joshua. He says he takes you by the hand and leads you step by step through the process from assuring income right now, all the way up to assuring income for life -- and he goes far beyond what I had expected.

"Make no mistake, this is not a magic wand for income. It is a solid, practical, realistic course of study that you will need to commit yourself to. Follow it conscientiously and it will work for you. Stick it in a drawer or decide you're too lazy to use it, and for sure nothing will happen!

"However! If you will just put one foot in front of the other, and keep on making the steps, you will inevitably get the fabulous reward you deserve: priceless business acumen and a solid system for producing income for life."

~ Christine Sutherland

"Hi, I know this is you Joshua, I believe it, and therefore it will get to you. What fantastic, outstanding writing and ideas. I'm BLOWN AWAY. That short summary of life I just read is as good as, if not better than (Think & Grow Rich, Rich Dad, Anthony Robbins etc...)

Do I feel empowered to achieve my $million goal or what? Definately!!!!! Thanks, Thanks A Million $$$$$$

~ "MagicMark"

"...It took me like 1 minute to see that this book was the answer to my prayers. It answered so many questions I had and I just could not stop reading. It was 4am by the time I finished. I can't wait to get started!"

~ Julie Hilton

"Hi Joshua, I have just finished reading your 'Income For Life' ebook for the 2nd time (in one day) and wanted to send you my praise, I felt lost, not knowing which way I was heading but now I can see the exact steps I need to take to turn my life around, I haven't felt this clear headed for a long time. Your book provides me with a step by step guide allowing me to see where I need to start today to get to where I can see myself in the (hopefully near) future."

~ Adam Firminger

THE PROFIT PROPHET

"...Of the many things in it that impressed me, two stick out as being responsible for a significant difference in what I now do. 1. The part in your last lesson where you say Donald Trump is UNCOMFORTABLE *not* being a billionaire - and so he got back to becoming one!...

I'd been comfortable too long earning $200 checks each month. Why? Because translated into Indian rupees, it's the equivalent of Rs.10,000 - and that's just a bit below my 'salary' as heart surgeon. It's also average middle class income in India...I decided I was going to become UNCOMFORTABLE with this income level, and go for a bigger one. And then something strange happened. I found myself noticing bigger, better opportunities. Doing things differently. Feeling a new energy and purpose in everything I did...I made my first "$2,000 in a day" day...

Am I comfortable? No sir!....I'm well on my way to bigger things, Joshua. And I owe a great deal of it to you..."

~ Mani Sivasubramanian, M.D.

"Dear Joshua, Your IFL business development process is very powerful...I was living in Zimbabwe - a third world country, working towards a professional accounting qualification, hating it...At first I was skeptical, but as the information sank in, I realised the absolute incredible power...I made a massive decision. I quit my job - it was starting to stress me out and really effect my health. I borrowed US $ 2000 from my dad...and I've moved over to Australia...Tonnes of budding entrepreneurs need your IFL e-book and advice so they don't waste their time like I did."

~ Ryan Hough

"...I am happy that someone has finally shone light on the whole practical truth. This is a refreshing change from the elegant (but impractical) theories that are being tooted as the best, or even, the only ways to build wealth. Thanks."

~ Mohit Mago

"...I sincerely wish I had access to Income for Life 7 years ago. I wouldn't have had to go through the trial and error that I have been through. IFL is EXACTLY what a new person needs to succeed. It gives them the chance to learn everything they need to know. It not only helps them with their business, it helps them with "them"...Everyone tells you how to make money, but very few tell you how to KEEP the money, and also how to change "you" to enable you to gain the mentality that is necessary to stay motivated and moving along the journey to success...."

~ Tonya Pruitt

"Joshua, your efforts are extremely appreciated by myself and, no doubt, many others. It is a pleasure to learn from someone who relates to the world in a similar vein to myself. Yours in success and FUN!"

~ **Brett Tannahill**

"Many thanks for this ebook. It makes fascinating reading. It pulled together all aspects of business that I've sort of been doing over the last 25 years without realising it but now the path has been shown to me I'll hopefully be able to follow it in a straight line rather than meandering about all over the place. Thanks again."

~ **Derek Kewley**

"Hi Joshua. Thanks for all the time you've spent getting this training to other people...I really appreciate your ability to help me with my learning disabilities and I've learned from you that I have to systemize everything. It really works for me -- and if other people listen it will help them too, even those without attention deficits or learning disabilities."

~ **Glennys Moore**

"...Josha takes you from ground zero through the completion of your journey in a very well thought out manner. For those of us who are VERY DISORGANIZED, its a godsend. It should be a wonderful primer for your next product! 5K A MONTH IN 90 DAYS OR LESS!!!! I can't wait to give you more of my money!!!!"

~ **Frank Kelso**

"....I'm a business teacher and Joshua has done an excellent job at creating a real Home Study Course...I'm learning extremely fast and I'm confident that this will be very profitable. You kind of have to really want to fail for this stuff not to work."

~ **Mauricio Martinez**

CONTENTS

ACKNOWLEDGMENTS xv

WELCOME TO THE PROFIT PROPHET PARTY! 1

    WHAT TO EXPECT: 3

    A FEW WORDS OF CAUTION: 4

    1. QUO VADIMUS BLINDNESS (QVB). 7

    2. KNOWLEDGE & PERSONALIZED STRATEGY BLINDNESS (KPSB). 9

    3. CONFIDENCE BLINDNESS (CB). 11

        The Going Against Gravity Test: 13

        The Momentum Test: 14

        The Conviction Test: 16

BOOK ONE: LIFE VISION AND PERSONAL LEADERSHIP ...23

    CHAPTER 1: Deadbeats, Dads & Defining Moments! 25

        A WHOLE Lot MORE Than The Law Of Attraction: 28

    CHAPTER 2: The Yin And Yang Of Your Power, Control & Confidence 32

    CHAPTER 3: Bridging The Profit Prophet Gap 36

    CHAPTER 4: Your Recipe For Personal Power 41

        PERMISSION TO FAIL 50

    CHAPTER 5: The Zero Factor (Vision Vs Circumstances) 54

    CHAPTER 6: Knowledge In Action 67

CHAPTER 7: Risking ~~Your~~ FOR Life!..73

CHAPTER 8: WARNING! Skipping Book One Is Hazardous To Your Wealth..79

BOOK TWO: PACK LEADERSHIP AND VISION 81

CHAPTER 1: Charmed!...83

   YOU TOO CAN BE A "<u>VOODOO'er</u>"..85

CHAPTER 2: The "Oprah Effect"..86

   Creating Your Own "Oprah Effect"...87

CHAPTER 3: Mind Reading Voodoo (Marketing Telepathy).................92

   THEIR Mental Journey To YOUR Oprah-Like Powers 93

   Moving From Asshole To Advisor 95

CHAPTER 4: LEVEL 1 – The Fear Based, *"You're An Asshole"* Mental Conversation 98

CHAPTER 5: LEVEL 2 – The Fear Based, *"You're A Pest"* Mental Conversation 101

CHAPTER 6: LEVEL 3 – The Fear Based, *"You're On Probation"* Mental Conversation 104

   Curiosity marks the beginning of it being THEIR idea to pursue you! 105

CHAPTER 7: LEVEL 4 – The Trust Based, *"You're Like Me"* Mental Conversation 109

CHAPTER 8: LEVEL 5 – The Respect Based, *"You're An Authority"* Mental Conversation..113

   Manipulation <u>always</u> bites you in the ass..................................116

CHAPTER 9: LEVEL 6 – The Influence Based, *"You're A Leader"* Mental Conversation..119

More "WOW!" And Less "YUCK!" With Expectations Management 120

Using Unpredictability To YOUR Advantage (Or It Uses YOU) 121

How to turn the tables on sticky situations: 122

Creating & Molding Your Profit Prophet Influence 125

Rock Stars Only Hang With Other Rock Stars! 127

CHAPTER 10: LEVEL 7 – The Influence Based, *"You're My Advisor"* Mental Conversation 129

All of your success lives in their FUTURE! 131

CHAPTER 11: Confessions Of This Profit Prophet 136

THE "HOW-TO's" OF YOUR AUDIENCE ASCENSION PROCESS 145

CHAPTER 12: Your Magnetic Factor 147

Different Offer Structures: 154

Risk Reversal: 155

Communicating Your Offer Powerfully 158

    STEP 1: It's about THEM, not you 161

    STEP 2: Keep 'em curious and wanting more 163

    STEP 3: Give 'em a headache 168

    STEP 4: Crafting Your Best Audience Attraction and Ascension Process 169

    STEP 5: Add Posture and Stir 174

Helpful magnetic tips and tricks: 175

CHAPTER 13: The X-Factor 179

NEVER Propose <u>Before</u> The First Date..185

"Me-To-You"...186

The Bonding Power of Membership, Fraternities and Sororities 191

People Want What They <u>Can't</u> Have..192

The Grass Is ALWAYS Greener Syndrome 195

The "Super-Powers" Of Making YOURSELF The Idiot:..................201

    Two warnings about misusing your new "Super-Powers" 203

No One Ever "Wins" An Argument!..204

People Will Work For Money, But They'll <u>DIE</u> For A Ribbon!........205

Give 'em "Insider" Information..208

Let's Get Personal..210

BOOK THREE: BUSINESS MODEL PREEMINENCE............217

CHAPTER 1: The "Voodoo" That I Do, You Can Do <u>TOO</u>!..............219

CHAPTER 2: You Gotta *Go Direct*..222

    The Lifetime Value Of A Customer:..228

CHAPTER 3: The <u>Foundation</u> Of <u>All</u> Business Success 234

    The ONLY 3 Ways To Grow ANY Business: 236

CHAPTER 4: Creating Buying Cultures 242

    REPROGRAMMING THE MIND TO A NEW CONVERSATION!...245

    Fostering The Buying Conversation 246

    Buyers Remorse 252

CHAPTER 5: What IS Real?..254

Mind Control Powers? 256

ALL Desires Are Insatiable 263

CHAPTER 6: Selling Sucks, Marketers Are Manipulators & Capitalism Is Evil 265

CHAPTER 7: Shadowing Giants Of PREEMINENCE 269

CHAPTER 8: Inside Two Case Studies 281

CHAPTER 9: SHHSSSH, It's A Secret! 299

CHAPTER 10: Overwhelmed Much? 303

WHAT CAN "SHAFFY" DO FOR YOU? 311

VISIT SHADOWSUCCESS.COM FOR EXCLUSIVE OFFERS (And Advanced Profit Prophet Resources) 312

ACKNOWLEDGMENTS

As is always the case with any labor of love like this, it's never written in a vacuum. It's not a solo effort. Although I am the wordsmith, experience did the actual writing. It would take 100+ pages to thank every collaborator who helped significantly shape the experiences that made this book possible (and, even then, I'd probably forget to thank someone without whom you wouldn't have this resource). Therefore, first, a general acknowledgement to all my business partners, teams, clients, students, mentors and mastermind buddies…You've all had a HUGE impact on shaping my 30+ year entrepreneurial career. Hopefully, I've done a good enough job of showing my appreciation directly that you all know the tremendous impact you've had on my life (you'll quickly spot your influence in these pages).

However, there are 3 people I need to acknowledge specifically because without their help this book would *still* be among my ever growing (and already very long) of "someday maybe I will" projects list: Dan Kuschell, thanks for being a beacon of simplicity; for reminding me of my value when I forget; and for your uncanny clarity about the shortest path to impactful solutions & profits! Cindy Barajas, my COS, your experience, positivity, and can-do attitude not only keeps the train running on time, but brings me inner peace because of your commitment to completion (in excellence) and because of the way you *always* have your pack's back! John Zakens, thanks for the way you keep everyone laughing while making sure we craft the best audience centered messages that brings home the bacon AND delivers value beyond all expectations at the same time!

Finally, this book doesn't work without you, the reader! Anyone with the courage to reach for a bigger future gets major props in my book. Thanks for braving the front-lines of business (and for keeping the entrepreneurial spirit alive & expanding): Your vision helps us all grow exponentially!

WELCOME TO THE PROFIT PROPHET PARTY!

Let's be clear.

This is about YOUR Profit Prophet story. <u>Not</u> mine.

Sure, we'll be leveraging my experiences to help you create the results you're looking for. However, this is YOUR journey. It's about giving you the resources to go from where you are now to where YOU SAY you want to be (in the fastest, most direct way possible).

And, most importantly, it's about building the right environment (or conditions) that attracts business to you. It about leveraging the elements of the perfect storm that makes people stand in line and beg you to lead them to the results THEY want.

Now, not to be preachy, <u>the world needs a wake up call</u>: It's time to realize we *don't* need permission for financial freedom. It's our *birthright* (yet, most believe it's some cosmic game of *"Mother, May I?"*). The world is polarized, hemorrhaging and crying out for **each of us** to claim our prosperity NOW!

That's because when the population gets rich at a grass roots level, by creating value, the wealth tides rise for us all! If we ever want to *truly* shift the balance of power back to the people, **reigniting the entrepreneurial spirit has never been more critical (or urgent).**

It's time.

Now, here's what's really exciting (or sad, depending on your level of "success blindness"): No matter what being your own Profit Prophet looks like to you personally, there's NEVER been a better time in HISTORY to experience success on your terms! Right now there's MORE opportunity than there's EVER been. And, new opportunities are actually being birthed at an *increasing rate*!

Seriously.

Yet, at the same time, the majority of people feel stuck, frustrated, and powerless because they *can't see* the opportunity. Even seasoned business folk and entrepreneurs have resigned themselves to believe that profiting in business is harder today than it's ever been. They long for "the good 'ole days" when it was "easier," rather than learn the new rules.

You see, also like no other time in history, never has there been so many who've given up hope because they don't believe in a bigger future. Tomorrow holds no hope of being better than today. We've become a world of amputated spirits because we don't know how to take control back. Blinded by the pain of current life situations, many just can't see any other way.

For these poor blind souls, the oceans of abundant opportunities we're all swimming in, isn't just passing them by. **Quite literally, it's** *drowning* **them!** Just like the scuba diver who gets disorientated, panics, and instead of following their bubbles up to the surface, dives deeper into the darkness because they think down IS up.

Such a shame, because all it takes to turn things around is to give yourself a break. Take a breather. Simply stop struggling long enough to get your bearings and let your bubbles show you the way home again. Because *unless we fight against it* (and/or weight ourselves down) **our natural buoyancy always takes us upwards where we can see the endless opportunities we're** *already* **swimming in!**

WHAT TO EXPECT:

This book is actually 3 books in one. That's because there are 3 key pieces to building your own Profit Prophet story:

Book One is all about <u>YOU</u>.

(Specifically, your personal leadership; and the vision you have (or develop) for your life and the pack you want to lead. That's because people will only follow you if your vision for them is bigger than the one they can see before meeting you.)

Book Two is all about <u>THEM</u>.

(Specifically, the packs of people that want and need your solutions that **<u>solves their problems, fixes their pain and makes a positive impact on their lives.</u>** Once you truly understand the mental conversations "they" have about their fears and aspirations, then (and ONLY then) will they let you lead and influence them. BTW, <u>by "pack" I mean your audience</u>: The ideal tribe of prospects, clients, customers, students, distributors, franchisees, independent reps, etc. that make up your marketplace that you're looking to provide guidance and leadership to.)

Book Three is all about <u>BUSINESS PREEMINENCE</u>.

(Specifically, how to design the right business model and marketing that **<u>systematically communicates your vision for a bigger future to your pack; and emotionally engages them so powerfully that it becomes their idea to elect you as THEIR Profit Prophet.</u>** It's all about the structure that serves your pack best; that delivers superior value they can only get from YOU as their pack-leader. Your business preeminence is all about how you impact them by improving their lives **better than all the other options available to them.**)

Together, all 3 books are the ingredients you need to become The Profit Prophet (TPP) and make success chase you.

A FEW WORDS OF CAUTION:

Remember, while all success *starts* in your mind, thoughts alone ain't gonna pay the bills. All thoughts, beliefs, and burning desires are only *potential* riches. **It takes ideas AND** *implementation* **to** *reap* **your rewards.** Without action, someone else cashes in (how many times have you witnessed someone else making it big executing *your* million dollar idea?)…

That's why you've got to take TPP *beyond* just *learning*. It's about LIVING your Profit Prophet story! And, I think you'll be surprised by how quickly success comes gunning for you with only slight improvements to your success blind-spots.

In other words, you don't have to completely cure all 3 main levels of success blindness before the tables flip and freedom chases you (because, tiny hinges swing giant doors). Which is mighty fine news because you'll collect many wins along the way (which makes the curing process rewarding, fun, exciting, and pain-free).

And here's even *more* **good news:** Each time you *truly* "see" a previous blind-spot, you take a *permanent* step forward because you can't "unsee" it. *Any* breakthrough (no matter how small) triggers a chain reaction that, if uninterrupted, eventually roots out *all* your other blind-spots.

Why? How?

Simply because *any* small blindness breakthrough *experienced* (through *implementation*) increases your Profit Prophet momentum, *at an increasing rate*! Every small improvement packs massive leverage because you "see" bigger and bigger blind-spots. Success begets even more and bigger successes. The freer you get, the freer you get. It builds on itself.

Each breakthrough stands on the shoulders of your previous one. The bigger you grow, the more you *can* see; AND the more you see, the bigger you *can* grow!

You get sucked into a success vacuum that pulls you to ever greater heights…

Tempted to call bullshit on this success vacuum stuff? Understandable, if so. After all, if *any* breakthrough *really* puts us on the up escalator to success, **shouldn't we** *already* **be cured of all blindness?**

Yup! We all *should* be cured by now. But we ain't even close. How come the human race is *more* success blind than ever?

Well, there's a catch with blindness. You knew a catch was coming, right? Well, you were right and here it is: Our core animal instinctual needs for survival, safety, & security **makes us fight against and/or run** *from* **the breakthrough.**

Dead serious! We *don't* fight *blindness*.

It's the cure we fear!

Weird, yet true. Our caveman instincts protects us against anything we don't already understand. Anything unknown is assumed a threat. We instinctually fear and avoid all pain (physical, mental, real, or imagined). Fearing the unknown is now our number one unconscious survival mechanism (and ultimate controlling force). The slightest whiff of risk or danger (even if it turns out to be false) triggers our automatic "fight" or "flight" reactions.

So, what do you think happens the *first time* you get a glimpse of something you've never seen before? In other words, what happens when something invisible first comes into focus?

If you're like me, the first few times you experience the kind of breakthroughs that make you rethink everything you know/knew was/is "real," it is downright scary. It's like stepping into an alternate universe. Up is down. Hot is cold. Everything that use to make sense, *doesn't* anymore. But neither does your new paradigm because it's just starting to come into focus. Suddenly *nothing* fits.

It's a complete shock to your system: The old paradigm is shattered, but we're scared to let go of it because we don't understand the new one yet.

Trust and belief is in short supply. We doubt everything we see. You worry your eyes are playing tricks on you. **It takes courage to own new breakthroughs and let go of old paradigms** because it feels like an attack

<u>on our reality</u>.

However, remember, a breakthrough can't be a breakthrough WITHOUT breaking something!

See, by definition a *true* breakthrough *has* to render the old way obsolete.

So, of course, it triggers our natural defense instincts. It's completely normal. If you *didn't* feel the urge push back, then it means it wasn't *really* a breakthrough (or else you've gone through the process so many times before that you're now comfortable being uncomfortable). You've stepped into the unknown and you don't yet know what to expect. Any "fight or flight" urges are actually part of the blindness you're curing.

Until you adjust and regain your equilibrium inside this new paradigm, give yourself a break. If you approach this unfamiliar "no-man's-land" with the same wonder and curiosity as <u>a baby who hasn't *learned fear* yet</u>, you'll adjust really fast. Before you know it you'll find yourself inside that success vacuum where the better it gets, the better it gets.

Give in to your fears, however, and, you'll try to run back to the familiar comfort of blindness.

Only problem is you can't unsee the seen. You can *try*, but that's actually the source of all your unhappiness, pain, and suffering. See, you can't deny, fight, and ignore WHAT IS without *increasing* negative side effects like fatigue, disease, and powerlessness.

Sorry. But forewarned *is* forearmed.

The silver lining in all this is that freedom is an all powerful tractor beam. It's literally pulling us towards it all the time! When we stop fighting freedom's calls, life becomes fun, exciting, and fulfilling (and we get everything we want)!

All the freedom, power, and success you want lives in the unknown; in curing *blindness*.

OVERVIEW: THE 3-BARRIERS TO BECOMING A PROFIT PROPHET:

Unless you already have everything you want, we're all inflicted with varying degrees of success blindness.

So, I guess before we dive into book one, you need a solid foundation of what I mean by curing success blindness, right? Here, then, is a 100,000 foot view of the 3 major pieces of the master puzzle:.

1. QUO VADIMUS BLINDNESS (QVB).

Quo Vadimus is Latin for *"where are we going?"* and it goes WAY beyond goal setting!

Look, by now, I'm assuming you already know you'll never hit a target you can't see (or haven't picked). It's doubtful you'd be reading this if you didn't believe in the importance (and uncanny power) of setting big, compelling goals, yes?

You probably know all the goal setting rules by heart:

a. Goals must be <u>written down</u> in <u>specific</u>, <u>sensory rich</u>, and <u>emotionally engaging details</u> with a <u>deadline</u> for completion;

b. They get taped to your bathroom mirror, read aloud upon awakening and before sleep until they become so real you can't tell the difference between your imagined future and current reality; and

c. That big goals must be broken down into manageable bite-sized pieces you schedule, plan, and tackle step-by-step without getting overwhelmed.

Now, without a doubt, goal setting and visualization processes <u>unleash an unexplainable force</u>. **It mysteriously takes huge, impossible dreams and somehow makes them come true.** However, goal achievement *doesn't* necessarily bring us the kind of freedom, power, and prosperity we *really* want.

Often we get so lost in the pursuit and attainment of goals we actually get trapped (*not* freed) by them! When we work our asses off and still don't get what we want; or when we "win" the race only to discover we were running the wrong race, **Quo Vadimus Blindness (QVB) is the cause.**

For example, how many people want to be self-employed for freedom only to become a slave to a business that owns them? They're driven. And they DO accomplish big things, but balanced freedom ain't one of them. Their goals (both the ones they achieve and the ones they haven't yet) <u>consume, control, and *imprison*</u> them.

Addiction to goal accomplishment is NOT success.

And, yet, it IS the part of QVB that <u>turns us into workaholics</u> who can't ever take a break!

Quo Vadimus asks you to look at the *whole* **picture.** Not just where we *want* to go. It asks:

"Where <u>ARE</u> we going?"

What situations do our beliefs, goals, and actions create? Are those situations what we *truly* want? Have we stopped long enough to notice if where we ARE going is *really* the place we want to wind up?

Personally, I was completely blind to my Quo Vadimus Blindness until I was 42 because it didn't stop me from making *millions*. That's why it's tempting to write this area off, thinking you'll go back AFTER you get rich and address it. Mistake. *Big Mistake!*

Consider this before you decide to table curing your QVB in pursuit of great material wealth:

a) You can get rich a whole lot faster, with a lot more joy in the process, when QVB isn't working against you. It's actually easier to achieve freedom AND amass a fortune, together, at the same time!

b) QVB increases your lifestyle at the same rate (or faster) than your income. You might make millions but it becomes a **"have to"** because your obligations exceed earnings. Even if you're miserable, <u>it gets harder and harder to get off that gerbil wheel</u> (but at least you look good running with all your fancy stuff). Believe me, as hard it was for me to become a millionaire the first time, it was MUCH harder to break the cycle after I got addicted to achievement.

c) QVB makes you loose sight of what's really important to you. It turns healthy competition into an unhealthy need to prove you're better, smarter, and superior to everyone, all the time. **Unchecked, you'll sell your soul, sacrifice your values, and become consumed by how much everyone else has compared to you.** Life becomes about action for action's sake. We kill ourselves to tally up one more "credit" in the win column than the next guy.

Knowing what I know now, if I had it to do all over again, I'd spend all my time and efforts curing my Quo Vadimus Blindness, **FIRST** (instead of spending so much time on the second and third more obvious barriers to financial freedom).

It's *that* critical.

Whatever. Moving onwards...

2. KNOWLEDGE & PERSONALIZED STRATEGY BLINDNESS (KPSB).

The knowledge part of KPSB is the most obvious barrier to your Profit Prophet story because it's the one we've all been conditioned to work on the longest. And, unfortunately, **the information age we live in has** *increased* **our blindness, NOT improved it** (even though we believe otherwise).

We read all the books, listen to CD's, watch DVD's, and attend workshops, teleseminars, and webinars to improve ourselves. Which is great because our income, wealth, and success grows in direct proportion to how much we grow personally.

Access to the *right* information *is* crucial.

Fact.

However, without a *personalized* strategy to put that knowledge to work for you, you'll *always* be a spectator watching others cash in on that knowledge *without* you. After working with literally tens and tens of thousands people from all over the world, I can state with complete certainty:

We're stuck in professional student mode. We're getting *smarter*. We're accumulating more knowledge. BUT WE'RE NOT GETTING ANY WEALTHIER!

The problem is knowledge is mistaken for growth.

Vinegar and Baking Soda, separately, both will stay in the same state, right? But what happens when you mix the smallest amounts of each together? *Transformation* happens. And, that *transformation* creates overflowing growth.

Action without knowledge is the same as knowledge without action: <u>Stagnation</u>!

Personal growth requires, both, knowledge AND action. Combine small amounts of both and the chemical reaction of transformational growth starts instantly. The *experience* of *applying* new knowledge in our lives triggers the kind of growth that brings freedom.

The first step is transitioning from student to doer. Which requires a solid game-plan, right?

<u>Here's the next big KPSP blind-spot</u>: Almost all the plans we've focused on have been *tactical*, instead of strategic, in nature. Tactical plans have a shelf life, expire, and can only work under specifics conditions and circumstances. This, of course, automatically limits (or prevents) your results.

Without the right STRATEGIC plan, success is always short lived, if at all. That's because tactical plans makes you work like crazy looking for your gold eggs, but blinds you to the goose that lays 'em! We try every new technique, tactic, and method to detect where the eggs are hiding. And, if we're lucky enough to stumble on to an egg or two, it's only a matter of time before we have to find a new tactic to uncover more eggs (like, when Facebook, YouTube or Google make their next algorithm change).

Tactical plans are the leading cause of burnout. We're always searching. Can't stop, *ever*. The second we find a new egg or two, we know we will have to start all over again from zero tomorrow: Rinse. Lather. Repeat.

Fear drives our actions. Fear we won't find the right tactics to discover more eggs. Fear there are no more eggs to be found. Fear someone else will beat us to the limited egg supply. Fear the eggs we already have, will be stolen. And, once fear creeps in, it's just a matter of time before the crash 'n burn is *unavoidable*.

On the other hand, a good strategic plan directs us to look for the goose. It allows to stop that endless search for fresh eggs. And, <u>a brilliant, *personalized* strategic plan gives you the power to CREATE your own geese</u> (instead of trying to find 'em;-).

See, tactics are specific tools, resources, and methods you use in your hunt. Tactics only work as well as the person using them. *Personalized* **strategy determines** *who, what, when, where, why,* **and** *how* **you use those tactics.**

Now, even a strategic plan is likely to fail in the long run *if you never take the time to make it your own*. That's because it's vital that your strategy fits you, *personally*. Look, we're all different people with different goals, dreams, talents, and visions for ourselves. We all comprehend and learn differently. Which means the specific strategy that's right for you, might not work for me unless adapted to fit, right?

That's why the same strategic plan brings freedom to one person but not for another.

Okay, now, we're ready to talk about **the lynchpin in your journey to become The Profit Prophet of your business...**

3. CONFIDENCE BLINDNESS (CB).

Confidence is the power source freedom, success, and prosperity runs on. When confidence runs low (or is blocked), there simply isn't enough juice to power us. It takes confidence to start, to stick, and to complete your strategic plan.

Confidence blindness starts when we don't notice what drains and what recharges our power. *Life* controls our power levels because we don't understand how confidence works. Every single time you experience complexity, confusion, doubt, frustration, anxiety, fear, stress, rejection, regret, secretiveness, worry, failure, etc. you're making withdrawals from confidence accounts.

When your confidence runs on empty, CB takes over and we forget to make confidence deposits that fuels us. Things like vision, curiosity, fun, laughter, meaning, purpose, adventure, openness, passion, personal growth, appreciation, gratitude, perspective, love (*not* lust), welcoming, etc. all recharge your confidence batteries in minutes.

Blindness makes us fear "running out" of confidence. For some unexplainable reason, we think there's a *limited* supply. That's why we try to protect our self-confidence by avoiding the things that drain us all together. We don't see that the very act of protecting and holding on actually *depletes* our power even more.

It cuts off our power from flowing.

Oxygen is to your body as confidence is to your Profit Prophet journey. Because, what happens if you hold your breath for too long? Or, what happens if you exhale without ever inhaling? And, for that matter, what happens if you inhale without exhaling?

All 3 stop the natural in and out flow, cause light headedness, followed by unconsciousness and death if breathing doesn't resume, right?

Curing CB starts with the awareness that **your power comes from your FLOW of confidence**. Anytime we try to conserve our energy, we're actually choking ourselves off from the energy source. Confidence must be allowed to flow freely to power us. The deeper we inhale and exhale, the more that *can* flow.

Which is a damn good thing because it takes plenty of confidence to learn, plan, design, build, and operate financial freedom. You burn through an enormous amount of confidence every time you even *think* about venturing into anything unfamiliar.

It takes confidence to start. More confidence to face all the unexpected (and inevitable) obstacles along the way. And even more to create unprecedented results you've never lived before.

In fact, your Profit Prophet story requires you pass 3 specific tests of confidence before balanced success will hang out with you:

The Going Against Gravity Test:

This first test, without a doubt, is the hardest of them all because it sucks even the largest confidence reserves dry in a snap.

You've probably heard some version of Chinese philosopher, Lao-Tzu's advice: *"A journey of a thousand miles begins with a single step."* It's about not getting overwhelmed trying to swallow the elephant whole, right?

The problem is, taking that first step **feels like you're fighting gravity**.

Know what?

It feels that way because you *are*. The gravity of your *current* situation. Anytime you set out (mentally or physically) in a brand new direction, you're always going against the gravity of what is. Our comfort zones (that which we *know*, are *familiar* with, and *understand* the "rules" of) *always* **exerts a much stronger force on us** *because we're INSIDE its gravity field*.

Did you catch that?

If you don't understand this natural phenomenon you're doomed to failure no matter what else you try or do.

Why? Because you're always INSIDE your current situation. Therefore it's *always* exerting a more powerful force on you than any new, outside situation that you've yet to experience. That's why, **escaping the gravity of what is comes down to you exerting your own power from within the current situation.**

Just like a rocket blasting off burns through something like 90+% of it's fuel to escape earth's gravity, your first attempt to expand your comfort zone beyond your present reality, takes the majority of your confidence reserves. Because, oddly enough, even if your current situation *sucks*, it still has a stronger gravity than venturing into unknown waters (no matter how positive you anticipate and imagine the new situation will be).

But the good news in all this is that even though this first confidence test requires the most amount of energy, **your current situation <u>gives up it's hold on you really fast when you hit it with everything you've got</u>.**

When you feel the fear, doubts, and confusion... *and take those first few steps anyway,* before you know it, you will have escaped the gravity of what was. And, once free, now, you'll start feeling the brand new situation pulling you in slightly. It was always there, you just couldn't feel it because the gravity of the old situation was too strong. If you allow it, the gravity of the new situation you want, slowly, yet automatically, calls to you.

That's the misunderstood truth about how law of attraction *really* works. No amount of positive affirmations or visualization matters until you, first, break free of the gravity of what is (because you can't tune into the gravity of what you want to be AND what IS at the same time)!

The Momentum Test:

Until you gain a solid momentum towards what you want (but never experienced before), you're *always* in danger of having to retake the first confidence test all over again! Although you'll want to take a break in between the two tests, you *can't* because the instant you break through the main gravitational field of what was, the momentum confidence test starts *immediately*.

See, two things control the pulling power of any situation's gravity:

A. **INTENSITY:** The stronger a situation's emotional charge is for you, the more powerful is its gravity. But *gravity doesn't give any more weight to a positive emotional charge over a negative one.* That's why if you really, really, really want something, the burning desire of that situation <u>gathers the SAME GRAVITY as a situation you really, really, really hate!</u> **The more intensely we love or hate a situation (*both* real and imagined), the stronger its gravity pulling power.** *Period.*

B. **PROXIMITY:** The closer we "stand" to a gravity field, the stronger its influence on us. Each step closer increases the gravitational force exerted on us. Even if our emotional charge stays the same. However, "the closer" you get to an emotionally charged situation, the more it activates your intensity levels (that's because your excitement dials-up the closer you get to what you want; just like your fear levels dial-up as you get closer to a situation you DON'T want). In other words, the closer you stand to the fire, the hotter it feels no matter how intensely it's burning.

Get it?

Ponder this for a second: When you first enter the momentum phase, you're no longer inside your comfort zone; and NOR are you inside the new situation you want. However, which situation is almost always gonna be in a closer proximity to you at this point? Which holds a bigger emotional charge?

Remember, all emotions gather gravity equally.

See, even if the new situation has a stronger gravity, you're so far away from it compared to the gravity of your old situation. That's why its attractive powers are negligible until you move closer to its field (and, at the same time, move away from the gravity of the old situation).

Can you see how this is a major test of your confidence? If you lose focus here, you'll backslide into the familiar (and never understand the real reason why).

It's unconscious, yet before you gain enough momentum towards the success you want, you're stuck in limbo. It's that foreign place between the comfort of what you knew… and that uncomfortable, scary place where none of the "rules" seem to work anymore. You're in zero gravity (not actually zero, but it's so different from what we're use to, it might as well be).

See, you've escaped the gravity of your comfort zone but now you start to question what the hell you just did. Because, not only does it feel like you're drifting around in space, but if you don't keep your confidence levels strong, you'll loose sight why you took the leap in the first place.

It's like looking down and suddenly realizing how high up you are. And what does that fear do? Right: It adds to the gravitational pull of what was. Which shifts your focus back to what you understand. Before you know it, you're right back inside the old situation. Feeling like a failure. And wondering if you have it in you to get up off the mat one more time. Will you dare to go against gravity ever again, right?

You need a steady supply of confidence to remain focused when you don't have a clue (yet) how to gather enough gravity towards the new, unknown situation you want. It takes confidence to trust you can quickly gain the momentum that frees you from backsliding. It takes confidence to stick to your guns when lots of obstacles seem to block you.

Obstacles are a definite. Sorry, **that's a reality.**

In fact, there are usually MORE obstacles in the beginning, before gaining momentum. Not because there's it's some conspiracy to keep you from winning. Simply because the first time you attempt something you've never done before, you've gotta overcome inertia.

What's usually the inertia? It's almost always the learning curve of implementation. See, no matter how great a student we are, there's always a gap between learning and successfully doing. Simply put, <u>we make more mistakes the first time we try to do something we've never done before</u>.

But obstacles are your biggest momentum builders... *in disguise!*

Each obstacle is actually a mini launching pad that always propels motion. With confidence, you can direct that motion towards what you want. Without confidence, you recherché off one obstacle to the next, like a renegade pinball, until you get the shit kicked out of you and find yourself back where you started.

The point is, to successfully pass *this* confidence test you must use every challenge as an opportunity to move towards what you want: To increase your momentum forward!

The Conviction Test:

Conviction is the final test before success comes pouring into your experience in such staggering amounts it's almost spooky.

After you muster enough confidence to escape the gravity of what is, overcome the biggest barriers to motion towards what you want, and gain *some* forward momentum, you're still not there yet, right?

Conviction is the final piece of the confidence puzzle; it's what we all need to see things through to the end; the difference between wanting and *having*. Conviction is the ultimate confidence that allows us stay the course *until... until* we get where we're going... *until* desires become reality... *until* potential is actual!

Without conviction, all your ideas, beliefs, thoughts, visions, and positive affirmations NEVER becomes hard-core, real world reality!

Yes, passing the first two tests, makes those desires burn stronger *within* you. But holding a raging inferno inside *hurts*. You gotta let it out.

Making the leap from the intangible to tangible requires conviction to set your burning desires free. It's the missing ingredient that lets you pluck an idea from your mind and make it manifest in physical reality. It's the difference between imagining and actually driving your dream car.

It takes conviction to actually LIVE your dreams instead of wishing for 'em!

People who aren't yet living their dreams say, *"Show me. Prove it. When I see it, then I'll know it's true."* However, when you decide to take a stand for your beliefs (regardless if anyone else agrees or any outside "proof" supports your vision) and have the courage to draw your line in the sand, conviction super charges your personal gravity field.

Conviction sees the unseen; it knows the unknown BEFORE it's known; it *IS* the evidence of things not seen!

Read that again. It's the REAL secret of manifestation. Most miss its power because it's hidden in plain sight. See it? If not, don't worry, you will.

With conviction, no outside confirmation, verification, or approval is ever necessary. Impatience, insecurity, and doubt are replaced by a quiet, calm, centered (yet unlimited & unstoppable) power that makes everyone take notice without you saying a word. You're laser focused, but it's never forced because you know it's not *"if"* but *"when"* you'll get there; because you're confident you will figure out *all* the *"hows"* in between.

Conviction needs no guarantee of success to take the next step forward. It requires no promises that any individual step will work or not, because it *knows* the eventual outcome is 100% assured. It loves and embraces the zig-zag process that shows you how to make mid-course corrections that gets you there. It gives you confidence to stick to your guns no matter what (because YOU'RE the only one who gets to declare what's right for you).

Plus, conviction opens the door to ultimate freedom because <u>you never need to argue, justify, or convince anyone (or anything) opposing you</u>; there's *no* need to defend what you *know* to be true.

See, impatience is a sure sign fear has snuck in the backdoor. It points, with uncanny laser accuracy, exactly where your confidence needs recharging. Impatience is the fear something outside of you controls, influences, or has power over the situation. Impatience is always rooted in the fear of not getting what you want fast enough (if at all). **With conviction you don't worry about anything standing in your way because timing doesn't matter when your outcome is an absolute certainty.**

All setbacks and delays serve your purpose because all roads take you there (no matter how winding, scenic, or how fast you travel them). You relax in the confidence that comes from *knowing* sooner or later, it'll all work in your favor.

If you truly *knew* there was an infinite number of ways to get the outcome(s) you want, would ever be attached to one specific path? Would you force your experience along the way to look a certain way to make you happy? Or would you go with the flow and not sweat things like which path you take, challenges encountered, pitfalls foreseen and avoided, support given (or withheld), mistakes you made, how long the journey is taking, etc.?

If you *knew* each obstacle is a stepping-stone to your desires, would you fear or *welcome* it? Would you rush the process or savor each breakthrough for the confidence building power it gives you?

You'd go with the flow of your confidence.

It's the difference between playing to win and playing not to lose. Conviction plays to win. Fear plays not to lose.

Conviction gives you the open-minded flexibility to see solutions when everyone else is distracted by the problems. You stay focused without the forced action that comes when you fear *not* getting what you want. No new bright shinny object ever captures your attention long enough to distract you when conviction keeps you focused on your mission.

Funny thing happens when you calmly make up your mind to stand by your convictions; the universe backs you up and helps you get there (because **you're already there** emotionally, mentally, and spiritually). Why, how, you ask?

Gravity, of course.

Did you notice the first two confidence tests are about the gravity of outside situations (the current one you want to change and the new one you want to replace it with)?

Well, conviction builds your own <u>internal</u> personal gravity field!

Remember the two factors that control the pulling power of *any* gravity field (p-14)? Intensity and Proximity, right? Conviction super charges you with the emotional intensity of peaceful confidence. And, since it takes place inside you, no outside influence ever has a closer proximity to you!

The stronger your conviction, the stronger your personal gravity field. The stronger your personal gravity, the stronger you pull other masses to you… See, with conviction and momentum you actually close the gap from both sides! The stronger your gravity field grows the more it pulls other similar situations towards it.

You're moving towards the new situation you want AND it's actually being pulled into you!

Think about that for a second. It's a profound revelation!

That's how success becomes unavoidable. It's the difference between pursuing something that's always just outside your grasp and making success chase you!

Pass the first two tests and you CAN *still* create massive success, however, *without* conviction, it will always be fleeting, accidental, and a string of one-hit-wonders leaving you wondering, doubtful, and impatient about your future.

Fact!

LET'S ENJOY THE PROCESS OF BECOMING A PROFIT PROPHET, OKAY?

Looking at how deep each of the 3 levels of success blindness goes, it's easy to get lost in the process. Yes, there's lots of moving parts involved. Each level has so many potential blind-spots it *can* be overwhelming at times.

However, remember, what you look for, you <u>*will*</u> see.

If you make up your mind to have fun with this, you'll discover the process is a whole bunch easier (and simpler) than you've probably been telling yourself (that's what success blindness does). On the other hand, if you go into this process assuming it's going to be heavy, difficult, complex, and gonna take a long time, **then it WILL be (because that's what your internal gravity will pull to you)!**

That's why I strongly suggest you have fun with all this:

Be easy. Become an explorer again. Approach it with childlike wonder. Get excited about discovering your next blind spot because that's the breakthrough that takes you to the next level. Bless any confusion, fear, frustration, or impatience for showing you where your blind-spots are hiding.

I'm speaking from personal experience here…

Experiences I'd rather help you shortcut. It took me over 30 years to become a millionaire for the *first* time. Then it took loosing it all and rebuilding my financial empires (*not* once, *not* twice, *but <u>three</u> more times*) over the next 12 years to see the bigger pieces of the puzzle I completely missed.

For 40 something years, I believed making money was "SUPPOSED" to be hard. It was "SUPPOSED" to be a struggle. "SUPPOSED" to take a long time to learn. And even longer to master.

I wore those experiences like a badge of courage <u>to prove I paid my dues</u>. However, with the advantage of hindsight, now I can connect the dots backwards and see how I was blind to the truth. I was trapped in the gravity of what was. All my struggling, fighting, and pursuing success added more gravity to attract more of the same type of situations to me. Only I was blind to how hard I made it on myself. I fought for my blindness. Never saw how easily (and fast) things change when we know how to use gravity in our favor.

Now I *know* lasting success, joy, fulfillment, happiness, freedom, income, and prosperity is NOT hard and won't take forever unless you insist on clinging to your blindness.

So, if you find yourself resistant to any of these new ideas, then I only ask that you reserve your final judgment a while. At some point you'll experience that blinding flash of the obvious where confusion gives way to clarity.

The easier you are with this process, the faster you'll experience real, tangible progress; the kind of instant results the rest of the world thinks you can only get by winning the lotto!

You'll *see* (get it ;-)

BOOK ONE:

LIFE VISION AND PERSONAL LEADERSHIP

(How To 10X Your Future And <u>BE</u> The PROFIT PROPHET Of Your Life)

CHAPTER 1: Deadbeats, Dads & Defining Moments!

The day after Christmas, my Dad gave me a check for $125 and says…

"I got a Christmas Eve 'gig' that I wasn't expecting and I want you to have it since I never got you a birthday present for the last few years."

My dad was a professional musician and had played with such greats as John Lennon, Tito Puente, Count Basie, Bob Dylan, and The Band (if you're over 35 years old he's probably on some records in your collection right now). A New York Times critic had even called him a *"dazzling trumpeter."*

Now, in spite of all his musical talent and potential, he always struggled. Struggled with success, relationships, self-control, personal power, confidence, and, of course, _money_. He struggled to get it. Struggled to keep it. He was a deadbeat who constantly disappointed those closest to him.

So when my dad handed me that check in a gesture of kindness, I knew it wouldn't last. *"Thanks Dad,"* I told him, *"but you should keep it because you need it more than I do."*

He insisted, so I took it although I didn't deposit it for a couple of weeks because that little voice inside told me not to. Then, about a month later I get *"The Call"* from dear old dad. He said, *"Remember when you told me that I should keep that check because I needed more than you did? Well, you were right and I need it back."*

That really sucked!

I was crushed. But by a strange twist of fate, his broken promise actually helped write my Profit Prophet story (and might just help you write yours too).

See, that was a defining moment for me. I vowed I was either going to figure out how to take my power, freedom, and control back **or *die* trying**! (And if I ever had kids, I vowed I would always keep my word with them and empower them above everything else in the world.) My obsession with getting rich started before that defining moment, but dad poured gasoline on my burning desire and turned it into a raging inferno that fateful day!

That's when the cold harsh reality hit me. **I had no frigg'in clue how to find the power, control, and wealth I had to have!**

Because, I wasn't *just* broke. I was desperate. So I did what any self-respecting kid from the streets did. I looked for the *shortcuts*.

Here's a dangerous (yet seductive) trap you have to watch out for with shortcuts: When you have *"desperation"* written all over your face, every shortcut you'll find will be crap! But that's not the dangerous part. You see, **when you find yourself in** *"desperation mode,"* **you'll talk yourself into believing** *anything*.

Suddenly the most cockamamie fairytales, snake oil scams, schemes and outright cons seem to make complete sense, even when you *know* you're being lied to.

Desperation robs us of clear thinking. I tried EVERYTHING. Answered every ad in the back of those magazines. Ordered everything I could afford (and whole lot more I couldn't) from those 3:00 AM infomercials. Went to every "free" seminar (and found out they weren't so free as I ran to the back of the room to spend thousands of dollars).

You name it, I tried it -- Real Estate Investing, flipping discounted mortgages, direct marketing, stock trading systems, bi-weekly mortgages, MLM's, Internet marketing, etc.

If it said I could get rich with it, I tried it, even the scummy ones that had no chance on God's green earth of ever working. And, after 10+ years of banging my head against one wall after another and throwing away tens of thousands of dollars on worthless money making programs, I was 27 with a failed marriage, depressed, and totally alone in a very hot, sticky Florida apartment (because I couldn't afford the power bill).

When I woke up and realized that **everything I tried had <u>one fatal flaw</u>** (which meant they set me up to lose)! However, before we address this fatal flaw, you need to know the truth about taking control back over *any* area of your life (how to reclaim your power and LIVE *balanced* success).

Ready?

<u>The simple truth is:</u> Creating all those things in your life is just a <u>*skill*</u>. Like any skill (like dancing, singing or running), you must follow a very specific process *before* mastering that skill.

Take walking for a familiar example. Today, it's natural and automatic, yes? Yet as a baby, you learned to walk through a very specific process of first learning to crawl before walking, right? Once you got your crawling and walking skills down you learned to run.

Crawl... Walk... Run... is always the process of mastering *anything*.

Each step in the process leads to the next step. You can't skip crawling and go straight to walking or running. Crawling *always* comes FIRST (all success *starts* there).

Okay, now, pay very close attention to what I'm gonna say next.

The reason you don't have everything you want in life, right this very second, is *only* because you haven't yet mastered the crawl, walk, run skills that will bring them to you!

See, everything I tried addressed a small part of the walking or running process (and almost always assumed you already knew and mastered crawling). And, I don't care how much knowledge, training or how many books you read, even the best resources in the world can't work for you until you get your head straight.

<u>Meaning</u>: You must have a compelling vision for your future that's much bigger than your current situation. And, you've got to mentally **"OWN"** your bigger future *before* you will truly commit to mastering the new skills it'll take to create that vision. It's what's known as your *"Prosperity Consciousness"* (also called your *"Abundance Awareness"*).

A WHOLE Lot MORE Than The Law Of Attraction:

This is *more* than mindlessly parroting positive affirmations like, *"I'm driving a Mercedes Benz; I'm driving a Mercedes Benz,"* all while you're really driving a beat-up shitbox. And that voice in your head screams, **"This is BULLSHIT!"**

Now, don't misunderstand. I'm a big believer in the *true* (**not** the prostituted) Law of Attraction. However, I also believe in the Quaker saying, *"As you pray, move your feet."* Your willpower can't override anything you don't REALLY *believe*.

The point is: The life you're living right now (the amount of money you have, where you live, the car you drive, the clothes you wear, what you do for work, etc.) is a sum total of all the defining moments you experienced **and what YOU'VE DECIDED they mean to you.**

This is good news if you're *already living* the life you want. However, what if that's NOT the case? If you're still struggling with your prosperity consciousness then that probably goes against the grain of your current experiences, right? Hard to hear (and even harder to buy into), yes?

If so, fear not, my friend. Relief awaits.

Are You A Newness Addict, Like Me?

New starts in business (and in life) are one of my biggest strengths.

Come to think of it, it's also a *weakness*.

See, I love new beginnings. The fresh, excited feeling of embarking on something new. The positive expectations of what's next. I admit it: **I'm addicted to it!** Luckily for me (and my lifestyle) I've learned to also become addicted to action and *completion*.

And, yet, it wasn't always that way. There was a long period of my life when I was *only* a "newness addict" (def: someone who's driven by fresh new desires and gets bored quickly once the excitement of the newness fades). My game, out of the starting gates, was stronger than anyone you'd find... but had no follow-through.

Sure, I always had a great story (excuse) about why I had to move on to the next project before finishing the current one in excellence. At the end of the day, I had zero results. All because I let fear of failing stop me from *really* going for it.

(That's partly why my first marriage failed: My ex-wife stopped believing in me because I "cried wolf" too many times. It was always the *next* deal that was going to make us rich; the *next* one would fix everything and put us on easy street. However, reality was different. Drowning deeper and deeper into delusions (and debt). It wasn't long before our favorite pastime became blaming each other and finger pointing.)

Whatever.

The point is, I'd never have been able to finally breakthrough and LIVE the life I always dreamed of living (family, millionaire, respect, freedom, private islands & jets, etc.), if I didn't also become addicted to consistently focusing on getting into action. Even when venturing into areas you know nothing about, I'm sure you already intuitively know, **success is more about finishing than starting.**

It's about taking one good (or even so-so) idea and making up your mind you won't allow yourself to get distracted by another one until you close the loop and put the current one to bed.

See, before breaking through, I'd open a new loop to distract myself from the truth: That I needed an excuse to avoid the risk that the great idea I bragged about might not work. That I might "fail." Or worse, be called a "failure." Subconsciously, I reasoned that if I never actually dared to raise the curtain and show the world my ideas, I'd stay safe and secure as a work in progress (or so I *thought*).

Today, however, "failure" doesn't scare me because I have a different relationship with it thanks to the information you'll discover here. Imagine having the power to take on the things you *don't* know with the same confidence as anything "old hat" to you. What if you could be excited about the constant challenge of stepping into *new* successes (ones beyond your past accomplishments)? It *keeps* you sharp; and *makes you even sharper*.

Sure it's scary. Because the first time you do anything, you don't know what you're going to encounter. And, yet, you'll learn how to tap into that unseen power that assures you get the answers you need, on demand, as you go. Keep focused on moving forward with the expectation that you'll eventually find the answers, and a funny thing happens:

You always seem to figure it out.

Look at life (and what you want to accomplish) the same way a baby looks at the world. Everything is new to them, right? Yet, they aren't scared by this new world. It's fun because all babies naturally love to explore. The process of discovering new things *excites* them because **"failure" is a learned concept!**

In fact, until we *teach* babies to fear failure (or to fear anything) they're just as pleased with what we call "failure" as they are with what we define as "success." No baby is born with fear. They have to learn what "failure" and "success" means before they can be conditioned to fear either. And, come to think of it, they also must to be taught to believe in fear in general before they can be fearful of anything.

I watched my daughter, Aimee, learning to walk and it didn't matter if she successfully pulled herself up or fell: She still had the same smile of joy and wonderment. She loved it all. It was all brand new discoveries. She was exploring new frontiers without any apprehension whatsoever. You saw her glee and excitement. Her power exploded with such force, I experienced it with her every time she flashed that look at me!

It's the secret to power. In fact, every time Aimee fell down it made her more determined to try again and again *until* she figured it out. And, I've come to discover, it's a Universal Power. It works the exact same way with all accomplishment.

If you are determined to figure it out and enjoy the process, you can overcome any obstacle standing in your way (any obstacle, like: lack of knowledge, money, experience, help, etc.). No, it's hardly ever instant because it often involves a learning curve of trial and error, but there's nothing you can't conquer with the positive expectation a baby naturally has towards life!

Feel the fear and go for it anyway.

Try it for just a month and see if that alone doesn't give you renewed sense of power and confidence that allows you to take your control back. I bet you'll begin to access a hidden side of you says, *"it doesn't matter what life throws at me because I can figure out the solution to this problem if I'm committed to finding it!"*

Onward...

CHAPTER 2:
The Yin And Yang Of Your Power, Control & Confidence

Why YANG without the YIN plays 'keep-away' with your success no matter what else you think, say, try or do!

Since I've already admitted I'm a newness addict, why not go for broke and confess: Sometimes I'm a *schizoid*!

But guess what? I'm not alone! Tell me one person you know who *doesn't* have several different voices in their minds tugging at 'em. Go ahead. I'll wait.

With the exception of a few thousand rare people (out of over 7 *billion* on this planet) who can turn off their minds anytime they want (for as long as they want), every single thought we think is another voice in your mind!

When it comes to success, I'm *constantly* playing referee between two very powerful parts of me. When these two sides <u>*agree*</u>, success is **unavoidable**! And when they're at <u>*odds*</u>, success is **impossible**!

See, I believe that you, me (and everyone) also constantly struggles with this inner battle. We **all** have two sides to our success (or lack thereof).

It takes both the Yin AND the Yang working together to travel the Profit Prophet path.

<u>Let me explain</u>: There's a part of me that is *very* <u>pragmatic</u>; *very* "reality" oriented; that's the hard-core, driven, bottom-line businessman who deals in facts. That part of me is results driven (some might even say *obsessed*). It's the part of me who's never satisfied with what is. It keeps my focus on "the numbers" because I'm always looking for ways to increase results and lower costs.

This side has a "Type A" personality and can be abrasive, impatient, and unrelenting. It cuts to the quick if time is being wasted. It believes *"how many, by when"* is all that matters. It's all about ruthless schedules, setting and meeting deadlines, productivity and checking everything off the never-ending "to-do" list, with extreme urgency (because, after all, time is the most valuable asset it believes we have). It lives its word as if life depends on it (and gets pissed if/when others don't honor their word to him).

When I'm in this mode, it's best not to get in my way because nothing sidetracks me. Those who get in the way are dealt with swiftly (and apologized to later) because this mental force seduces me with *"the ends justify the means"* LIE.

I call this my "Yang" side. It's the *"go-to-guy"* you depend on when the game is on the line because the Yang side always has a plan and will work 24/7 to execute it! In excellence! And on time! Yang is a massive doer, loves to take charge, and only measures success by crossing the finish line (and how fast).

My Yang side says *"ideas are great, but you've got to put them into action and see them through. You live in the real world. You've got to produce results. You can't operate your business as you WISH things would work, this is how things ARE so don't waste my time with all that positive thinking crap, I've got work to do!"*

As you've no doubt already figured out from the take-no-prisoners-tell-it-like-it-is tone, my Yang side takes lead in my business building, execution, and strategy planning sessions.

And, then, there's the other half: **The "Yin."**

Yin drives creativity. It filters intuition so you *see* the answers you need, when you need 'em. Yin is the path by which all the ideas, love, and inspiration we ever need comes to us. It's our direct connection to fulfillment, gives meaning and purpose to our lives, and is the doorway to our higher powers and spirituality.

Yin delivers, with spooky accuracy, the exact right inspirations, at the right time that Yang turns into millions. Yin is inspired and knows the answers but doesn't care about the outcomes. Yang sets goals, develops all sorts of plans, and gets to work. Yin (if not ignored by Yang) <u>makes sure Yang sets the *right* goals, strategy, and isn't just taking action for action's sake</u>.

Yes, Yin is the "out there" side of me that believes in the power of thought to control life, the Law of Attraction, and that prosperity is our birthright. It knows the universe is infinite, full of abundance and instantly delivers all requests without bias, judgment, or "worthiness" of the asker.

Yang rolls his eyes and makes fun of my Yin side all the time.

However, you need both Yin and Yang to experience the type of Profit Prophet success you've come here for. Yet, if you're anything like me, you sometimes get out of balance. There's been times when Yin run my life. And other times Yang's 100% in charge. But things never seem to work out the way I want unless both are in sync and working together.

If either get too far out of balance problems start. Too Yang and I get sick, run down and alienate the people closest to me. Too Yin and I get lazy, complacent and battle depression (justifying lack of results, procrastination, and confusion as not mattering or not caring).

It's all about having the right mix of both Yin and Yang. Keeping focused on constant, *balanced* momentum forward in *both* areas.

IMPORTANT: I believe any goal, desire or pursuit should *always* start with your YIN side, *first*. That's because if you just plunge ahead with lots of massive action you will very likely find that the actions you take won't have the results you anticipate. **You need alignment with your inner, creative, Yin side so you are inspired to take the RIGHT actions.**

Because, after all, what good does it do you to drive like a bat outta hell, at a million miles an hour, determined to get the gold, only to find out after you've been working your ass off for weeks (or months or years), that the race you've won isn't at all what you *really* want?!

What if Yang had you traveling on the WRONG road all that time?

But by taking the time to connect with your Yin side on a daily basis (also called self-development time), Yang's goals, plans, and actions will be focused right. That you run the race you really want. That'll be fulfilling. That your life will have meaning beyond just checking one more achievement off your list.

CHAPTER 3:
Bridging The Profit Prophet Gap

We have gaps to bridge.

One of the biggest is the one between learning and *living*. The difference between knowing *what* to do and successfully *applying it* in the real world (so you can <u>live</u> the results and the outcomes you want on demand).

In the last chapter we talked about the gap in between your Yin (inner personal development journey) and your Yang (outer action journey of implementation), right?

Here's the next one we need to bridge:

The gap between the outcome you WANT and the outcome you EXPECT.

See, you always (yes, *always*) get exactly what you EXPECT. But often what you expect to happen is *not* what you WANT. And, there lies a huge gap we're usually completely blind to! **Until you bridge this gap you'll attract what you fear instead of what you want into your experience.**

If you hope (or wish) for power but inside don't believe you can have it, you never will. We need to make what we want, **BE** what we expect to happen or else we'll hit one frustrating roadblock after another.

Success will always be just outside your grasp. But when what you want **IS** what you expect, you enter that zone where your desires swarm to you like bees to honey (*without* all the hard work and struggle most people think it takes).

Let's ease into this because if this is your first time being introduced to this concept it might feel like a smack in the head.

When I started to learn this subject it felt like bullshit to me. I thought it was nothing more than new-age positive thinking mumbo jumbo (but little did I know it was the secret – the REAL secret – of having everything; of making the impossible, possible).

It's counterintuitive, right? On the surface, this concept seemed completely *invalid, untrue* and *just plain wrong*. I used to think, *"no matter how hard I try or how hard I work, I just can't seem to get ahead so it can't be that I always get exactly what I expect to get because I really <u>want</u> to succeed."*

Can you see how the very mindset I held, actually proved the concept right? I believed that simply *because* I desperately wanted something (and was willing work really hard for it), that it was the *same* thing as *expecting* to be successful. Because, after all, why would I ever attempt something that I *expected* would NOT work?

First we need to dig into what a *want* really is. How do you know if you want something? When do you decide you want it? It's almost always after we're faced with a person, place or situation that we do NOT want.

Interesting, isn't it?

What we DO want is born from what we DON'T.

Why do you want more power, control, confidence, freedom, success, money, or better relationships in your life? How do you *know* you want any of those things?

You can only come to want something new AFTER you become aware that your current situation is NOT what you want. The core of any desire is the feeling that something is missing because, after all, **if you had it now you wouldn't want it because you'd already have it, right?**

Now, this means that *we learn to closely identify our wants with the problems that created them in the first place.*

Please read that again because that's the rub.

See, we all have a tendency to stay focused on the problem that gave birth to the desire instead of switching focus towards the solution. We are usually so dialed-in to the conditions that caused you to want something different, it's all we allow ourselves to see.

And continued observation of any problem INCREASES the gap because as you continue to focus on what birthed the desire (aka, the problem of the current circumstances), it intensifies your wanting to satisfy it **because it makes you even more aware that what you have now is not what you want!**

Can you see how, if you allow this to continue, it's not long before the gap becomes a canyon? Whereas, a small gap is simple to bridge, it is downright paralyzing when you are staring at a canyon and think you have to cross it in one jump, right?

Where and how does expectations fit in?

Glad you asked. ;-)

Expectations are powerful thoughts you *know* to be true (aka "Core Beliefs"). However, the process by which you come to "know" and believe in their "truth" is fascinating because it's 100% imaginary! WTF? Yup! It's only true for you because you believe it is.

Just like a baby must learn to be fearful before fear becomes "true" and infects them, what you believe is true is actually based on the repeated mental conversations you have with yourself. Your mental recordings form your beliefs and, therefore, expectations. **The life you are living is a reflection of the consistent inner thoughts and conversations you've gotten into the habit of having with yourself.**

Look inside the mind of any successful, self-made person who has abundance and you'll discover most of their self-talk focuses their energy towards unlimited *possibilities*. They don't just want things... they *expect* them!

They *expect* positive outcomes. They *expect* to win. They *expect* to figure out the answers even when they're confused. They *expect* to turn things around.

On the reverse, don't you know someone who's *always* broke? People who just can't seem to ever get ahead, right? If they get some unexpected money, somehow the car breaks down or something else "just happens" to go wrong and the extra money gets sucked up so they stay stuck, behind the eight ball, and never get ahead, right?

How about people who are lightening rods for abuse? Aren't there certain people who always seem to wind up on the shitty end of every deal? No matter what they do they always seem to wind up neck deep in one sort of drama or another? Constantly victimized, "wronged" and taken advantage of, right?

Sure they WANT things to be different, but if you eavesdropped in on their mental chatter, you'll find a VERY different kind of conversation. The thoughts, beliefs, and recordings they have to be habitually replaying on an endless loop go something like this:

"Why does this always happen to me? How could they do this to me? Why can't I ever get ahead? Why are they all out to get me?" and so on.

Do you see how these thoughts actually focus them towards expecting bad outcomes?

Look, your expectations are formed over time based on thoughts. Practice a new thought often enough <u>and you create a new habitual thought pattern</u>.

New thought habits create new expectations. New expectations produce new results because you always get exactly what you truly expect to get.

So how do you break the cycle and align what you want with what you expect to happen?

Turn the page and find out;-)

CHAPTER 4: Your Recipe For Personal Power

Let's fine-tune our prosperity consciousness, shall we?

By drilling down on exact process by which you've come to believe and expect the outcomes you do, you'll be able to reengineer any expectation at the speed of thought. It's how to see and access the abundance of opportunities you're swimming in right now!

Your belief system is the foundation. We can call this your subconscious. Your ego. Your inner-game. Your self-concept (or whatever else is the trendy lingo of the day).

How did your belief system come to be? It was formed by your parents, family, friends, teachers, religious upbringing, life experiences, the books you read, the news you watch, etc.

But more important than who, what, where, why, and how your beliefs formed is understanding that most of your deepest core beliefs happened _accidentally_! Most of us are not consciously aware of our self-concept. We aren't consciously aware of what's fully going on inside our minds. Sure, if you've done any personal development work at all, you _do_ have some awareness, but that's just the tip of the iceberg.

How do I know? Because if you are struggling with any subject… if you aren't _already_ living the results you want, it can only be because what you want lives in the 99% of your beliefs that are **unconscious**! That is, the self-talk & image you hold is now so automatic, it's goes undetected.

Look, we all have unconscious mental pictures driving us. This self-concept drives who you are and is your inner-game.

To help you visualize how important your self-concept or inner-game affects your life, draw a triangle where the base represents your self-concept. If you have a self-concept that says you're bad at handling money, your entire life will reflect this belief and your subconscious will do everything in its power to make you "right."

That's why you absolutely must consciously reprogram your self-concept to a new one that supports your beliefs and desires about wealth. To make it easy to visualize how your self-concept forms the foundation of your life, picture it as the base of a pyramid.

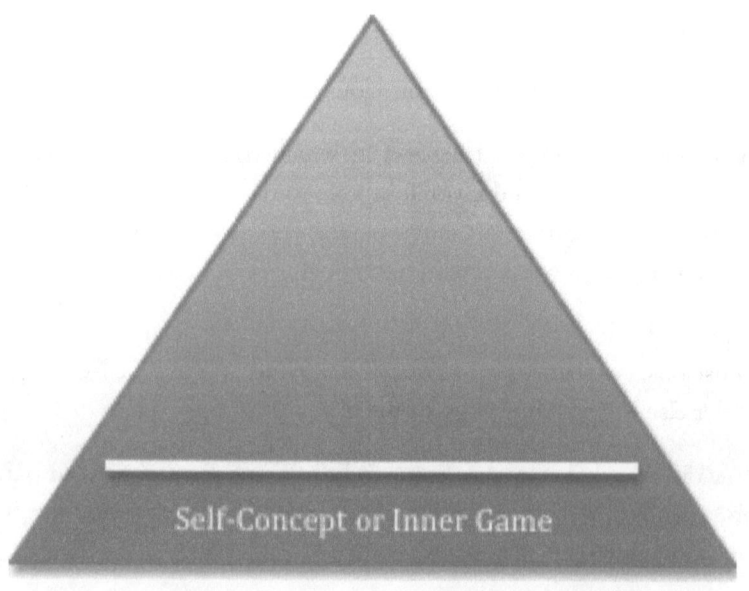

On top of that is the next, in the middle part of the pyramid, is your outer-game. Your outer-game is who you are in the world.

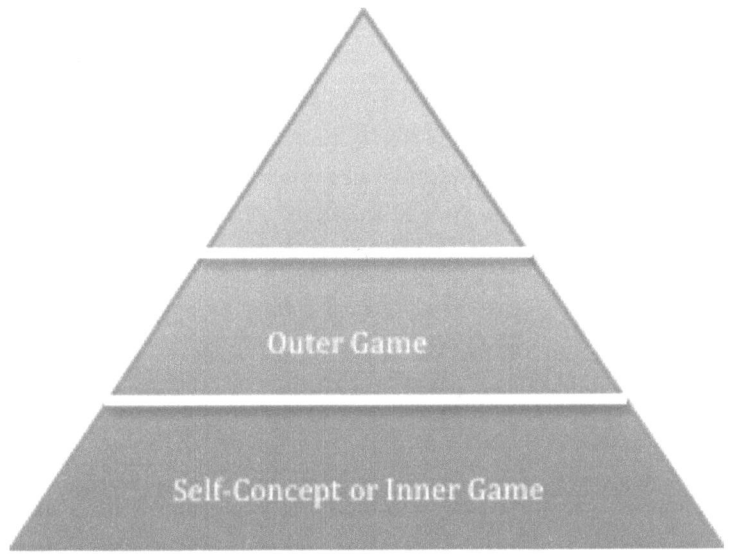

Based on your inner-game, your self-concept, and your vision of yourself, now you project a certain way of being out in the world. The world perceives you based on how you behave. What happens is your inner-picture and outer-picture of yourself shifts back and forth, and they reinforce one another.

You're looking for evidence that supports your point of view.

Did you catch that? Based on your self-concept and situations in world, you're always gathering evidence that fits in with what you already believe to be true! You do it. I do it. We all do it. Automatically!

See, if I've got a point of view that says I'm lousy at making money, the concept I put out there and demonstrate to the world is that I *can't* handle money (even though what I really WANT is to be good with money). The world is a mirror reflection of my inner way of being (my unconscious and subconscious "truth"). It unconsciously reinforces my true beliefs because that's what I've unknowingly programmed myself to look for.

The evidence I'm looking for (and allow myself to see) must support the self-image I hold as "real." Here's a little fun exercise you can try yourself to get a feel for this on a simple level: As you drive around today, be on the lookout for all the blue cars you can find. All of a sudden, you'll think, *"What happened? Did they run out of any other color paint? All I can see is blue cars, blue cars, blue cars."*

But wait, it gets better. Tomorrow, look for red cars. Because you're looking for them, that's what you'll start to see. It's not that no other colors are there. Just that's what you've tuned into. It's what you're focused on. Your filters, based on your self-concept, directs your focus in the outer world.

Everyone's self-concept defines their reality. It's a solid reality for them. However, that does NOT mean it's the *same* reality for you. If your self-concept says you're lousy at handling money, your reality HAS to reflect back to you a life where money is either hard to get and/or hard to keep. If I have a self-concept that making money is easy, can you see how my reality will cause me to act differently and therefore experience a life of abundance, **even if we both live in the <u>exact same conditions and circumstances</u>?**

Balanced on top of your outer game is your point of attraction, right at the top of the pyramid. Your point of attraction is what "The Secret" and the *'wooie-wooie'* stuff is all about. It's about whatever you put out in the world comes back—all your self-concept and all the different facets of your self-concept—is now reinforced by the outer game.

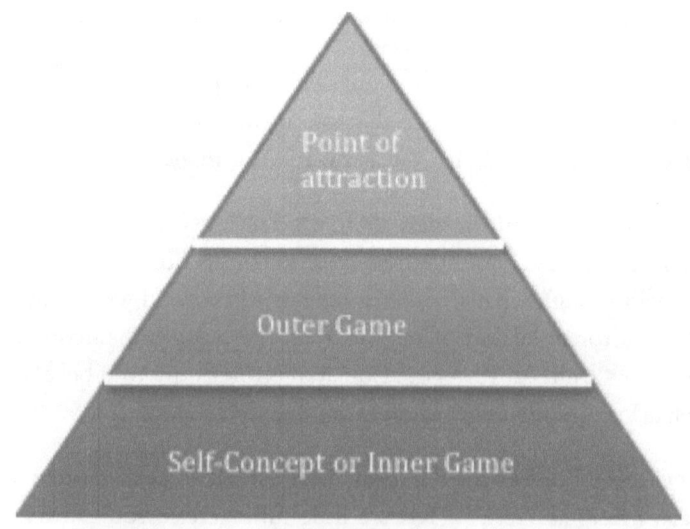

Another way to look at these three levels is this way:

1. Point of attraction = **<u>SEE</u>** (the results you wind up **HAVING** in your experience)

2. Outer game = **<u>LOOK</u>** (the actions, situations, conditions, reactions, etc. you look at to decide what you're going to **DO**)

3. Inner game = **<u>TUNE</u>** (who you **ARE** at your deep inner core that's 99% unconscious: Who you are "being" in any given moment)

Your inner game defines who you *are*, your outer game determines what you *do*, and your point of attraction determines what you *have*. **In order to HAVE a specific result, you must DO something, and you'll only do something if you ARE being the type of person who sees that result as congruent with the core belief held about yourself.**

What everybody wants to do is first focus on the 'Have' part, so they set goals. They do affirmations. But an affirmation you don't believe is BS (by the way, I don't think it's any accident that BS stands for bullshit and belief system because our beliefs are completely made up anyway). Over time, if you continue to say it and you say it in a way that you actually start to believe it, then you start to shift your point of attraction.

This 'Tune (Be) – Look (Do) - See (Have)' concept defines us all.

Even Donald Trump.

Remember when Trump filed for bankruptcy? Did he ever stop being a billionaire? Nope. Who he WAS in his self-concept and his 'Beingness' was a billionaire. So he naturally behaved like a billionaire. Reinforced by his outer-game, it didn't matter if he had the tangible outside evidence of a billion dollars to be a billionaire, **that's who he was <u>inside</u>.** And, very quickly the results that he ended up HAVING soon reflected who he was being; and he became even richer than before going bankrupt.

Conversely, this why 99% of all lotto winners usually wind up dead broke now or worse than they were before they hit the jackpot.

Jim Rohn once said…

"If somebody gives you a million dollars, best you become a millionaire so you get to keep the money."

That's the same thing with lottery winners, except they work it in reverse. If somebody just gives you a million dollars, your way of being may be a bankrupt mentality. Unless you shift into somebody who is worthy of a million dollars, you're going to screw it up because your 'Beingness', your self-concept, your outer-game and who you are in the world can only reflect back to you what you ask of it.

You always get what you want or expect to get. Here's where it becomes really fun and interesting. This pyramid model explains how you approach every aspect of your life.

Picture a seesaw teetering on top of your pyramid, which represents different life situations you face. On each side of the seesaw, picture the numbers 1 through 5 where 1 is closest to the middle of the seesaw and 5 is the furthest tip of either end.

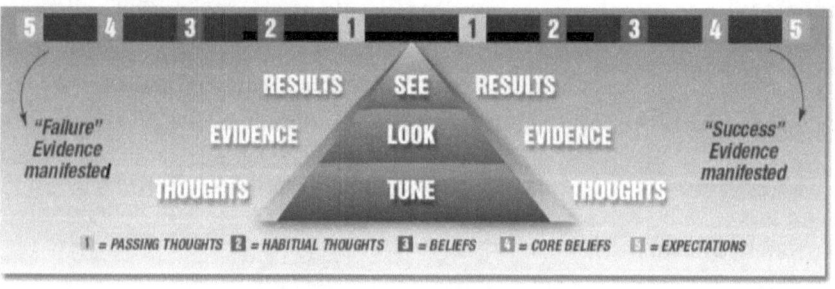

It's just like a regular seesaw that can tip up or down on either side. And each seesaw balanced on top of your TUNE, LOOK, SEE pyramid represents a different subject (life situation).

Wherever you are, there you are. It's true for you because you said so; for no other reason than because your belief system declares it to be and you truly have that expectation. Your point of attraction is the very point of the pyramid your subject seesaw is balanced on. Whatever you believe, that is your reality. Now, what if your absolute *knowing* is, **"I'm broke, and that's the way it is right now. I'm just too darn stupid to make money."**

If you keep telling yourself, "life sucks," that's your reality because your point of attraction reflects that back to you by tipping your seesaw over to the left. What if, however, you kept telling yourself, "I'm a millionaire, I'm a millionaire, I'm a millionaire," which is way on the other side?

For most people, making that quantum leap from "Life sucks" to "I'm a millionaire" is too great a distance. But what if you just inched up the seesaw a tiny bit closer to where you want to be?

That's not a quantum leap. Just a baby step.

Here's the exciting part to me. The entire fulcrum, the entire pyramid here, actually can shift along the subject line. It can move to the left or the right making it easier or harder to tip to one side over the other! How?

Based on: 'Your Beingness', 'Your Doing', and 'Your Having'. See, it's an emotional journey of aligning your inner energies. It has nothing to do with the outside world. It has everything to do with how you **FEEL** about the subject (the balanced seesaw).

That's because each one of these notches on the seesaw is a feeling, emotional journey that ONLY YOU can take.

What if your absolute knowing is that you're broke, you're a loser, and you might as well just hang it up now? If that's your frame of mind, and some idiot comes along and says, *"Just think positive,"* what happens? You wanna thunder punch 'em in the throat, right? Nobody in that frame of mind wants to hear that. When their absolute knowing is on the other side, they can't handle anything *that* drastically different from their current belief about the situation.

If, on the other hand, you didn't try to move all the way to other side of seesaw in one fell swoop, you can avoid the negative pushback. Perhaps, telling yourself, *"Maybe it's not as bad as I fear right now. Maybe there's some hope,"* allows you to start edging up the seesaw a little bit without being a blow to your belief system.

Even though it's still resting heavily on the 'I'm missing this' side, if you continue to make that journey, eventually it'll shift the seesaw ever so slightly off the ground. All of this can happen very rapidly by taking these small little baby steps. As soon as you make that little shift, you immediately have access to new things that you didn't have before.

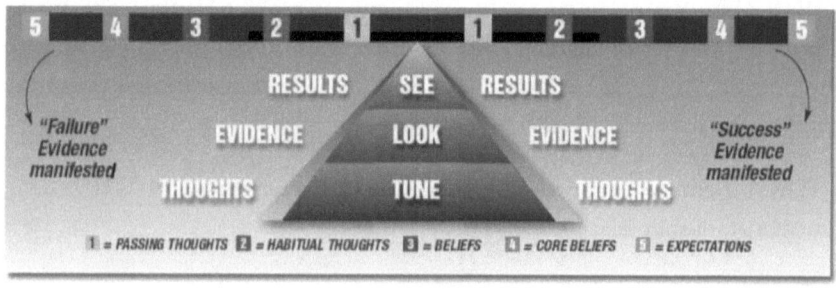

It actually works in the positive too. If you program your core belief that you're really good at making money, every time you take on something new, and a little self-doubt creeps in shifting your point of attraction a bit further down the seesaw… It won't be long before your self-concept eventually shifts your seesaw back towards prosperity and abundance again.

That's the cool thing: You can make little bite-size incremental shifts and it reengineers who you are. As soon as you reengineer who you are and how you're thinking, that passing thought becomes a habitual thought. That habitual thought, if reinforced, becomes a belief. That belief becomes a core belief. And core beliefs become your absolute knowing, your true expectations that activate your automatic filters accordingly.

In Donald Trump's world, his pyramid doesn't rest on the zero mark of making money. It's way on the five-point mark. When it comes to wealth in Donald Trump's world, there is no more teetering or doubt.

For most of us, there is teetering. To change, all you have to do is focus on putting one foot in front of the other and make a little bit of progress toward reengineering or reestablishing the core belief, a passing thought, or unwinding something on a certain subject.

Most people are pretty much somewhere between a belief and a core belief on most every subject. The problem is that we don't stop and question, *"Wait a minute! How did I get this belief? Where did it come from? Is it even reality?"*

At this point people have a tendency to say (or think), *"I've got to face reality, Josh. That's easy for you. You can make a million. You can do these things, but for me, I can't. That's not reality."* And what they're really saying is that their core beliefs tell them they're stuck, without any way out.

It's working for them. They're seeing *exactly* what they expect to get. They're arguing for their "stuck-ness," and, if I let 'em, they will give me their long list of "evidence" that "proves" they're right about their situation.

See, if you make just a little bit of progress, you inch up that seesaw on any subject. The question is, "How big is your desire?"

When I first started off in business for myself, I thought, *"If I could just get this done and create this book, I'd be a success. My goal is just to get this book done and then self-publish it if necessary."*

This thought allowed me to inch up the success seesaw. Then, once my first book was written and published, the next step was to play the what if game at the next level, *"What if I could just sell ONE copy, how good would that feel?"*

When I sold that first copy of that book, I started crying tears of joy because it turned me inside out. My self-concept about making money kept shifting.

Then I started to wonder, *"Do you think I could turn it into $1,000 a month consistently?"* And less than 30 days later I was there! Then I went from $1,000 a month to $3,000 a month within six-weeks. Then it sky-rocketed to almost a $5,000 a month!

Now, you need to know that when I started inching my way up the seesaw, $5,000 a month might as well have been $1 million a year! That amount was almost impossible because it was more money than I had ever earned in a month by myself. However, each time I reached a small milestone, it moved me closer to a larger reality WITHOUT shocking my previous self-image.

From a standing stop of about a two-year stretch from trying hopefully to making $1,000 a month to making $526,000 **in a single week**, my journey crept along in gradual steps. Do you think going back to, *"If only I could make $1,000 in a month,"* computes to me anymore?

No way!

I've shifted my way of being. Shifted my belief system. Shifted who I AM on that subject.

I believe it's possible **now**, but there's NO WAY I would've allowed myself to believe I was worthy of it back when my filters had me gathering evidence that supported $1,000 a month was a lot of money, right? If you told me that less than 2 years after making my first thousand bucks, I was going to generate over a half-a-million in just 7-days… I would have said, *"No way! No way! I don't believe it!"*

The journey was fast because of the small, incremental steps.

That's the big trap people fall into. When it comes to money, I found that you have to set your sights on a goal that's large enough to inspire you to take action, but not so big that it set your BS-meter off.

Really, it comes down to two things: Where are you right now? And where is it that YOU SAY you want to go?

It's about having a big vision and small goals. The big vision launches you towards a goal. And the small, incremental steps gets you there.

PERMISSION TO <u>FAIL</u>

Now, before I figured this seesaw thing out, I kept telling myself, *"I have to know one more thing,"* so I bought all these books and tapes. I was scared to move forward. I felt incomplete. And it was always just one more thing that was going to fix me. Then I could finally get rich because I'd know the exact path to take and not make any mistakes along the way.

However, it wasn't until I gave myself permission to fail, that I started making real progress towards living my dreams. As we've already briefly discussed, there is always a difference between learning and putting into profitable action, right?

So, here's how I overcame it for the first time. I sat myself down and said, *"Yes, I still want to be a millionaire one day, but I'm not going to put pressure on THIS project having to get me there. Regardless if this project is a success or not, I'm still gonna see it through to the end. It doesn't matter if I ever sell one copy. What I'm going to do right now is promise myself I won't sell out on myself again!"*

I went through this process everyday. The night before, I'd set a specific **progress** goal (<u>not</u> an outcome goal). A measurable goal about the specific things I was going to get done the next day, no matter what! I'd remind myself, it didn't matter if the overall success outcome I wanted for the *project* happened or not. **All that mattered was I pushed the ball down the field just like I promised myself I was going to do for that day.**

Of course, the first few days I bit off way more than I could chew. I set myself up to fail because there simply wasn't enough hours in the day to get it all done. However, I learned to set the kind of progress goals that set me up to win WITHOUT being too easy on myself.

So first, it was, *"I'm going to sit down in front of my computer and write for 8 hours today even if it's all shit and I trash it all."* Then whatever I committed to the night before got done. Each evening I looked at what I needed to do to progress forward what I decided to be an acceptable amount. Some days it was researching technical stuff. Sometimes it was web design. Sometimes it meant going through home study courses on direct response marketing and copywriting.

Whatever was the next logical step based on where I was and where I made up my mind I wanted to go that day is where the process took me. Even though I had no knowledge (or proof) I could even do what I wanted, I still moved forward because I took the pressure off by giving myself permission to fail. Unknowingly, I was working to reprogram my beliefs and expectations enough that my self-concept said, *"I can figure this out. Other's can do it… have done it… why not me? There has to be a way, I just have to find it!"*

And that inched me up what ever seesaw (subject) I needed to conquer so I met my daily progress goals. I promised myself that I was going to honor my word to myself. That was big for me. That I wasn't going to sleep the next day until I got done whatever I promised myself the previous day.

Sometimes, the next day I said, *"Wait a minute! I'm not going to get too ahead of myself. I'm going to set myself a smaller goal so I can design a winning feeling at the end of my day. I'm going to go to bed tomorrow feeling good about honoring the word to myself about what I was going to get done."*

If I'd promised myself I was going to get something done, it got done. I wanted to feel good about my progress. And, soon, that became the only reason for doing it: To honor my word to myself and to feel good so I could go to bed happy & fulfilled.

That's what Permission To Fail means: Not putting pressure on the overall outcome for each of the smaller incremental daily pieces. It didn't matter if the big picture worked or not. What *did* matter is that I honored myself by keeping my promise to myself.

That's how you set yourself up to win!

And, you know what? I started to gain momentum. Like working out, soon, I could do more, take on bigger things. I got more done.

There wasn't this pressure on me anymore. Now, I could move forward freely at my own pace based upon what I said I wanted to have happen in my life. I started living the **"I can accept failure, but I can't accept not trying"** philosophy.

This is what's missing. If you don't handle this stuff, it doesn't matter what self-improvement book you buy. It doesn't matter what business building resource course you invest in.

It's like painting over rust. It might look good for a second, but before you know it, it peels right off. You have to scrape down to the raw metal and then paint on it. You start with, *"What do I want?"* Then progress to, *"If I want that, what's my current level of belief? Where's my seesaw set on that subject?"*

Then it's just a matter of identifying the gaps between what you want and what you *truly* expect. In other words, what side is your seesaw tipping towards on the subject? Does it feel too big? Does it feel like you've got to go from a "negative" 5 on the left side all the way to a "positive" 5 on the other side?

If so, that's too big a jump. Ask yourself how can give yourself permission to fail and you ease your "negative" expectation just a bit?

What can you do to move from a "negative" 5 to a "negative" 4.9? You can make that mental move really easily. Then move from 4.9 to 4.5 or 4.0 if that doesn't feel too overwhelming. Then maybe your momentum will carry you to the negative 3. Before you know it (like within minutes if you don't try to bite off more than you can chew), you can be to the neutrality of "0" where you're not attracting or expecting anything on the subject. Your seesaw is perfectly balanced.

Now you can start the mental tipping process towards what you want.

Here again, though, you don't want to try to go all the way from neutral to a level 5 expectation of what you want, skipping all the steps in between. Instead, just pick up one small thought that you can believe might just be possible given where you are right now.

And, the second you believe that thought, you'll have access to a new possibility you didn't have before you made that small mental shift.

In this way, you can tip your seesaw to a level 5 self-concept of positive results on any subject, no matter where you start!

Inch by inch, it's a cinch!

CHAPTER 5:
The Zero Factor (Vision Vs Circumstances)

LIVING FROM VISION:

Listen up. This is vitally important stuff...

It might just be THE most important part of creating your Profit Prophet success story.

What happens if you multiply any number by zero? The answer always falls to zero, right? Even if multiply a zillion by zero you still get zero results, yes? Well this is one of those zero factors that makes your success either _unavoidable_ or _unattainable_! Until and unless you learn and master this, you'll find reaching meaningful, sustained success impossible.

So let's get to it.

You have two choices as to how you can live your life. You can live it from your VISION for it. Or by allowing your CIRCUMSTANCES to dictate your life and determine its direction.

One makes the impossible, possible. The other will have you throw your hands in the air with frustration and disgust at the world for serving you a "raw deal."

One gives <u>you</u> (and *only* YOU) absolute control over your life. The other places you at the effect of the whim of the world.

One is empowering and inspiring. The other is depressing and will have you declare, *"I guess this Profit Prophet thing just doesn't work for ME."*

We'll talk about circumstances first.

Circumstances are your *perceived* problems standing in between where your are in the current moment and the bigger future you want. Your life's situation is what it is. All of us have numerous reasons, conditions, and/or circumstances that *can* prevent us from living the life we want (if we let them limit us).

Here's some typical circumstances that might be limiting your life right now:

- **...I don't have the energy and/or enough time to _____ (I'm too busy).**

- ...I don't know _____.

- **...I don't have enough support, help, relationships, etc. (no one will help me and I can't do it alone)**

- ...I don't have enough proof it will work; all my experience proves it will be too difficult (it's too big and nobody's done it before because my circumstances is different).

- **...I'm surrounded by liars, thieves, and cheats so I can't win against them because I refuse to sink to their level.**

- ...I don't have enough skills, education, experience, etc. (I'm not strong enough).

- **...What I want is too risky to pursue.**

- ...All the family drama I have to put up with every time I want to do something for myself is too painful.

- **...I don't deserve it (I'm not worthy enough yet).**

- ...My personality won't allow me to go for it (I'm not motivated, driven, outgoing, etc.).

- **...I don't have enough money, resources, knowledge, etc.**

- ...I don't have enough savings to follow my heart.

- **...I tried it before and it didn't work for me.**

- ...I'm not smart enough to make this work.

- **...This stuff won't work for me because my life and personal situation is different.**

- ...I'm not clear, I don't understand, I need more clarity to figure this life puzzle out.

- **...I'm totally alone and my kids depend on me so I can't do it now even though I really want to.**

- ...I just lost my job, so right now I can't (I can't afford it).

- **...My spouse, partner, family doesn't support me and I can't continue when I'm being beat down by the world at every turn.**

- ...I'm facing unfair "rules" that makes what I want impossible.

- **...I'm too old (or too young); I don't have enough credibility, experience, respect, etc. to pull it off.**

- ...I'm scared (I still haven't overcome my fear of success and failure).

...and on; and on; and OOONNNN!....

Get the idea?

These are all circumstances; *real* conditions of *real* life situations, right? Yes, our current circumstances are they *are* "real" in the sense that they *do* exist (we ain't making them up or imaging the conditions).

HOWEVER, our life situations, circumstances, and conditions can only limit us if we let them. Therefore any effect they have on your future IS completely made up and only exists in your minds! Circumstances are not limiting unless we believe them to be.

Otherwise how can the exact *same* situation stop one person, yet be the driving force behind success for another?

See, there are as many reasons why someone CAN'T succeed at living the life they want, as there are grains of sand on South Beach Miami.

I'm sorry to have to break the news to you, but the question is not **IF** you're going to hit roadblocks in your journey to success... because unforeseen circumstances, conditions, and situations **WILL** **happen.**

Fact!

The real question is how will you choose to react when an unfortunate situation does take you by surprise? Will it stop or spur you on?

Will you choose and make decisions concerning your life based on your VISION of the bigger future you want… or based on all the circumstantial crap that life serves up?

When we make decisions because of our on current conditions, you focus all your creative powers on why it's impossible to live your dreams. It makes us argue FOR why we can't have what we really want. We end up actually justifying our limitations.

Forget about searching for a solution. In fact, we do the opposite. Remember, we look for, collect, and store all the *evidence* we can find that "proves" why these circumstances are insurmountable.

We have an unconscious need to justify to the world why we're stuck in the situation we don't like. This process *automatically* rejects any idea, possibility, or prospective contrary to our long list of justifications. It filters out anything that doesn't jive with our unconscious beliefs so we can continue to **be right** about why we're trapped. Why it's beyond our control to change things.

Albeit 100% unconscious, we wear all this so called evidence as a badge of honor because it supposedly proves why we're limited. See, if we suddenly became aware our freedom isn't controlled by conditions, we loose our built in scapegoat for the powerlessness we feel over our lives.

It's craziness.

Until we break this unconscious cycle, we'd *rather* gather all the evidence we can to prove we are right to blame our circumstances than to take power and control back over it!

But here's the good news: Decide to live life from your vision of a bigger future and you set the polar opposite power to work for you! It'll have you living in terms of possibilities (your "what-if" vision for what you want). Because it activates a completely different set of unconscious filters.

Now you'll look for, collect, and store all the *evidence* you can find that "proves" why your current circumstances are the stepping-stones to what you want!

Living from your vision actually blinds you to failure because it reprograms your mind to filter out anything that moves you away from that bigger future. Switch to this prospective and you'll find yourself automatically arguing for possibilities of "there's a way" instead of "I'm stuck, it's hopeless."

See, a person who lives from vision collects evidence that proves she can make it happen and is blind to anything of the contrary. Who she is being (remember the last chapter on self concept?), what she tunes into, are all things that support her vision of what she wants to experience (no matter how long it takes to see the results).

Whatever we tune into controls what we look for.

And what we look for, we *will* see!

Which end of the seesaw you wind up on is a matter of choice (and perspective): Vision or Circumstances. It's the flip side of the same coin.

Vision says...

"I will have this happen REGARDLESS of the outside circumstances. The world will either see me victoriously pounding my chest from the summit of the mountain or find me dead along the way because I refuse to give up. I will not be denied!"

What if you decided to have that type of committed vision towards your life? Nothing would be impossible! Do you *really* think any of so-called roadblocks listed above stands a chance against a mindset like that? If you had that kind of commitment exuding from you, is there anything you could think of (or would ever encounter) that could possibly keep you from your eventual success?

Of course not!

Because, in the light of the grand vision you have for your life, any situation, condition, or circumstance is only *temporary*, right?

Think about some of the greatest visionary leaders of our times (or the leaders and top money earners in the world for that matter). People like JFK, Henry Ford, Martin Luther King, Jr., Helen Keller, Thomas Edison, Mother Teresa, Nelson Mandela, Jeff Bezos, Steve Jobs, Ellen DeGeneres, Bill Gates, Mark Zuckerberg, Warren Buffet, Oprah, Jay-Z, and, of course, the Google boys; **these brave souls shifted the entire world because of their guts to stand for their vision of a much bigger future!**

But do you really think it was clear sailing for them or do you think they had to conquer some major league negative circumstances along the way?

I mean, what do you think JFK encountered when he declared he would *"... put a man on the moon by the end of the decade?"* Talk about a man of vision. All he had to work with *was* his vision. After all, at the time he made that decision, human space travel wasn't even a possibility yet... he had not one single role model to follow.

And, yet that's **not** the case for you.

After all, you *know* it's POSSIBLE because you're holding the roadmap to doing it in your hands right now. Tons of people have already walked the Profit Prophet path. And this book is your step-by-step proven blueprint to creating that bigger future you deserve.

But *not* JFK. Nope. No role models blazed the trail before him; definitely no blueprint; no one ever walked on the moon until JFK's "crazy" vision was made manifest in the world. I'm quite sure JFK got sick and tired of all the criticism and "nay-sayers" he faced along the way to realize his vision. But he didn't let them stop him, did he?

What about Henry Ford? When Ford decided to produce his now famous V8 engine, all of the engineers that worked for him, stuck in their present circumstances, said it was impossible to cast an 8-cylinder engine block in one piece. But Ford, standing in his vision (and I'm told stubbornness... which can be very positive if channeled correctly) made all his decisions from that vision (not the circumstances) and told his engineers *"I want it, I shall have it so go make it happen, produce it anyway."*

I'm sure his engineers tried to convince him that he was crazy. That he had to stop clinging to an engineering "impossibility" because they were "smarter" than him. Because if Ford understood everything they did about engineering, he'd see they were right and he was wrong.

However, as we now know, Ford's vision (and resolve to have it) was stronger than their circumstances and beliefs about the situation. He told them to *"stay on the job until you succeed, no matter how much time is required."* They tried everything. Worked day and night for over a year without success.

Still they were convinced it was "impossible!" But it wasn't impossible for Henry. His vision was so real he saw it as if it was already a reality. Ford was clear that nothing else mattered. It was clear, in no uncertain terms, that he wanted it. That he would have it. And that he was unwilling to accept anything less.

Then, one day, as if by *magic* (by the way, a committed vision really is magic - it produces amazing miracles) Ford's vision won out over the engineers' circumstances... and they "stumbled upon" the solution. Thus, the solid block V-8 engine *was* created!

How about what Nelson Mandela encountered on his *'Long Walk To Freedom'*? He was thrown in jail and falsely imprisoned for **27 YEARS** because of his vision! Yet, his vision (and therefore his freedom and power) eventually won out over the conditions.

What JFK, Ford, and Mandela faced kinda makes any conditions or circumstances you face seem like child's play, doesn't it? After all, there were a whole lot more "limitations" standing between JFK, Ford, & Mandela than I'm guessing exists for any of us, right?

Get "it"?

If so, you have just discovered how to guarantee your success! If you missed it (even if you didn't miss it for that matter) I suggest you go back and read it again. In fact, I suggest you read it every day until you "own" it as a part of who you are.

How do you know when you "own" it? *When* you're unwilling to settle for anything less than the bigger future you want: your life's mission, dreams and desires. *When* you have the attitude of *"I will not be denied. Period."*

Before we get to the "how," let's take a brief look at the "why" - WHY your life vision is the strongest Profit Prophet power you've got. It holds the secret that makes people stand in line and beg you to guide them to live a bigger future themselves. It's how you'll flip the tables and enjoy success chasing you!

Think about someone you respect. Someone you have ultimate confidence in. A man or woman you'd follow (maybe even take a bullet for). The kind of person who inspires others to action. A real leader who you (and everyone else) can't ever to get enough of being around. You know, they have that twinkle in their eyes, a certain something that sparks a desire in you to join their ranks and be a part of whatever they're up to, right?

It just feels great to hang out with them. Because somehow they bring out the best in you. You feel better, fully empowered when you're with them.

Got that person in mind?

I'd bet dollars to donuts that whoever you just thought of has a very clear and powerful vision for their life and knows exactly where they are heading next. Think about it. Are they a "lost soul" wandering around looking for a place to plug their umbilical cord in? Waiting to be granted permission to succeed?

Or are they a passionate, inspired, self-directed leader who knows because they say so is all the permission to win they need?

I'm betting that it's the later of the two... that nothing short of death would deter them from their passions and intentions, right?

Let's return for a moment to JFK. His vision changed the world. He inspired everyone. Millions upon millions of people would have followed him to the end of the earth. They were drawn to him, almost by magic. Excited by, and enrolled in, the picture he painted of bold possibilities. **People are hungry to be a part of something bigger than them.**

Have you ever looked at someone and knew instantly that they had the "Fire in the Belly"? That you just KNEW they were either already successful or on the fast track to success?

When someone has a powerful vision and direction for their life they communicate it *without* speaking a word! It's this non-verbal power that people pick up on (which, by the way, is much stronger than anything you can ever say, act, or fake). It's what attracts people to us. It's what makes people jump through hoops to qualify to belong. After all, everyone wants to be part of a winning team.

YOU can be that kind of person.

In fact, **you ARE that person right now,** this very moment... if you choose to be. The instant you **start consciously choosing your actions based on possibilities** (instead of limitations) **you transform yourself into that kind of person.**

Now, the "how" part is not hard. Actually, it is very simple. Anyone can do it. But it does take consistent effort (and so, very few people stick with it – **see, the trap here is that because it's easy TO do, it's also easy NOT to do).**

For the majority of the world, when faced with a decision (however small or big) it's rare to find someone who will actually stop and <u>consciously</u> take a beat to ask themselves, *"Am I making this decision out of my vision or out of my circumstances?"*

Yet, it is EXACTLY this type of conscious decision-making that kicks your life into high gear. This type of self-monitoring takes effort in the beginning until it becomes a habit.

So, do you *really* want power and freedom that comes when you take your life back? Do you *really* want to attract success, people, and prosperity to you the Profit Prophet way? If so, the first step is to consciously stop and notice your "come-from" (are you operating from your vision or circumstances). Are your decisions possibility driven (based on your life vision) or are they controlled by the limitations of your current circumstances? Which side are you choosing from?

The second step is easy to say, even easier to understand, *but* takes discipline and consistent effort to apply:

Make sure that *every* time you catch yourself making a decision because of conditions, that you stop, think again and make a new decision out of your passionate vision for the bigger future you see for everyone who engages with you on any level.

So, the next time you feel anything like...

- **...I don't have the energy and/or enough time to _____ (I'm too busy).**
- ...I don't know _____.
- **...I don't have enough support, help, relationships, etc. (no one will help me and I can't do it alone).**

- ...I don't have enough proof it will work; all my experience proves it will be too difficult (it's too big and nobody's done it before because my circumstances is different).
- **...I'm surrounded by liars, thieves, and cheats so I can't win against them because I refuse to sink to their level.**
- ...I don't have enough skills, education, experience, etc. (I'm not strong enough).
- **...What I want is too risky to pursue.**
- ...All the family drama I have to put up with every time I want to do something for myself is too painful.
- **...I don't deserve it (I'm not worthy enough yet).**
- ...My personality won't allow me to go for it (I'm not motivated, driven, outgoing, etc.).
- **...I don't have enough money, resources, knowledge, etc.**
- ...I don't have enough savings to follow my heart.
- **...I tried it before and it didn't work for me.**
- ...I'm not smart enough to make this work.
- **...This stuff won't work for me because my life and personal situation is different.**
- ...I'm not clear, I don't understand, I need more clarity to figure this life puzzle out.
- **...I'm totally alone and my kids depend on me so I can't do it now even though I really want to.**
- ...I just lost my job, so right now I can't (I can't afford it).
- **...My spouse, partner, family doesn't support me and I can't continue when I'm being beat down by the world at every turn.**
- ...I'm facing unfair "rules" that makes what I want impossible.
- **...I'm too old (or too young); I don't have enough credibility, experience, respect, etc. to pull it off.**
- ...I'm scared (I still haven't overcome my fear of success and failure).

...or any of the other myriads of conditions, circumstances, or life situations that you previously allowed to control, limit, and zap your freedoms...

Make up your mind that from here on out, from this moment forward you'll look at those circumstances as **gifts**. As the opportunities they are for you to strengthen your visionary muscles.

I invite you to draw a line in the sand, this very second, and make the conscious decision to be:

A passionate, inspired, self-directed leader who knows because YOU 'say so' is all the permission needed to live a bigger future starting now!

When you choose to be this type of person, you exude confidence.

You're filled with power because you *know* that although you might not see the answer right now, there IS a way you WILL overcome any circumstances standing between you and that bigger future! The world will succumb and bend to your will and you truly become unstoppable.

This type of a person is unwilling to settle for anything less than their desired outcome, *not* because they have to force it: but because they don't fear it. They *know* the current situation is temporary and ask themselves empowering questions to focus (not force) the solution.

Here's a few questions you can use to redirect to a vision prospective:

1. If JFK overcame all the obstacles to putting a man on the moon, what can I do to overcome this?
2. Who do I know who has faced similar problems and what did they do?
3. Who can help?
4. What can I read to help me find the answer?
5. What would I do if my life depended on solving this?
6. How can I solve this and have fun at the same time?

7. Will what I'm choosing right now bring me closer to my bigger future or further away?
8. Is this decision about what I want for myself... or is it about my fears?
9. Five years from now, which will be more important?
10. If not now -- then when?"

If you adopt this discipline, you'll find you will attract higher, better and bigger possibilities (and therefore opportunities) than you ever dreamed possible.

You will attract situations and people in bigger leagues, up to playing much bigger games.

Remember it's rooted in personal leadership. And, in order for you to lead yourself and your life to freedom, **you first have to <u>BE</u> someone worthy of following.** You become such a man or woman the instant you begin thinking and believing in your vision and the unlimited possibilities it holds for you.

Got the vision? I knew you would.

CHAPTER 6:
Knowledge In Action

Have you ever come across someone that had *everything* going for them?

You know, someone who has everything it takes: All the natural talents, skills and abilities to make a super success of life? They can run circles around 99% of everyone else?

YET...

Yet there must be something missing because their results are flat. You know the type of person I'm describing, right? It leaves you scratching your head because you can't figure out what's stopping them (<u>*they're*</u> probably puzzled too, for that matter), right?

They should be sitting on top of the world, but they never seem to get it together! *Ever.*

What do you think stops them from accessing their power? Is it their ambition lacking? I don't think that's the issue, do you? I bet they are full of ambition (in fact, it might be keeping them stuck because the bigger the ambition we have without fulfillment leads to frustration, anger, and procrastination).

After all, what does ambition mean? It means you have an eager *yearning* for something more than your current situation, right?

Tell me one person you know who that *doesn't* describe. I don't know one person who doesn't want more than what they have right now (they might not admit it to you or even themselves, but we all want more).

Why is it that less than 2% of the American population has a six-figure income? *How come?*

Have you ever bought a millionaire lunch so you could pick her brain? If not, you *should*. I did that before I had my big breakthrough and I can tell you it changed me in profound ways.

But not because he let me in on some big secret that the world conspired to keep from me!

In fact, exactly the opposite. See, if you hang out and talk to enough successful people you'll discover the difference between breakthrough power and those who just can't seem to get their shit together is tiny! It's actually surprisingly small.

I'm sure you've heard a version of this cliché, *successful people do what the failures won't*, right? It's not that winners necessarily LIKE to do those things either but "somehow" they can discipline themselves to do it anyway.

So is "discipline" the answer?

Getting warmer – maybe even hot – but still not quite all the way there. Maybe if we talk about the opposite it will bring it home for you. What's the opposite of discipline?

Here's my list of antonyms: Fear, Indifference, and Inactivity.

They're *all* success killers (and offshoots of the same exact thing). Destroy dreams in a blink of an eye. Or keeps a dream from ever hatching, right? When any of them are present in you, anything else you attempt is thwarted at every turn (no matter what else you try or do).

Talent can't make up for fear, indifference, or inactivity. Neither will anything else because without consistent action – then you won't see results and you won't make a dime!

Common sense right?

If you don't take action – even with all those things in your favor – you ain't got nuttin! Oops! The cat is out of the bag now.

Did you catch it? You did? I knew you would!

Yes, **the missing ingredient is INITIATIVE!** But not hot and cold initiative. Because super intense bursts of initiative often compounds problems because it breeds self sabotage (and it's not long before old habitual and unconscious patterns of procrastination take over again).

It takes *consistent* action. *Consistent* initiative.

"*Oh, Look A Kitty!*" *(and other bright shiny object distractions)*

Many people talk a big game. They even believe it themselves. They want to take the world on. And some DO it right away. But others – the majority – have many of (if not *all*) the raw ingredients necessary to set the world on fire, but the only thing that gets burnt is *them*!

And what happens if they make a big push but don't get the results they hoped? Reality hits. *"Hey this ain't gonna be as easy as I thought it was going to be."* So they give up trying after a week or two and get distracted by the next bright shiny object that comes along, right?

This is where good old-fashioned *grit* comes in. A Profit Prophet finds the guts to say: *"Shoot that didn't work. There's got to be another way. No way will I let that stop me from reaching my dreams."*

You <u>choose success</u>, <u>know it comes at a price</u>, and <u>are willing to pay it</u>. You take full responsibility for your success. Even though it may be uncomfortable to do some of the things necessary to achieve success you take the initiative to do them anyway. We do the things we fear and master them instead of the other way around. Every day, week in and week out, we take action and refine, improve, and tweak our approaches based on results <u>*until*</u> **we get to that bigger compelling future**.

Keep going *until*. *Until* we form new habits of consistent initiative. Until we gain mastery of our success seesaw (see the last chapter).

(And when that vision is realized, we grow even bigger. Focus our pack on an even bigger, more powerful future. Constant and never-ending expansion is the natural order of the Universe.)

Normally, all my reading centers around sales, business, spirituality, marketing, copywriting, and personal-development subjects. Practical, non-fiction 'mind-feed' type stuff that helps me become a more accomplished Profit Prophet, right?

Which is why it's really odd that I decided to buy a novel by <u>Richard Armstrong</u> called *"God Doesn't Shoot Craps"* because I'm not a gambler and I almost never read fiction.

But, I bought it anyway because I listened to that little voice inside me that urged me to do it (and I've learned the hard way to never ignore my gut). So, I justified it as a good weekend diversion, and dug in.

Boy, am I glad I did because not only did it suck me in (I found myself half-way through it in a few hours), but it really got me thinking deeply on profound subjects. When I got to page 158, I read a few paragraphs that struck a cord so deep with me that I retyped it and kept it in my office for the last 4+ years.

It fits perfectly here. Check it out:

*****

"We live in a society nowadays where very little emphasis is placed on the concept of mastery. People want to get rich quick. Lose weight fast. Learn how to play golf overnight. And there is never any shortage of books, systems, programs, formulas, and self-help courses designed to help you do just that.

"But it can't be done. The road to mastery, mastery of <u>anything</u> from playing chess to flying an airplane, is a long and arduous one. It is a road with many hills and valleys. Many twists and turns. Perhaps most frustrating of all, it is a road with many plateaus – long stretches of featureless terrain where it seems like you're going nowhere fast.

"The road to mastery is littered with many people who have simply given up because the journey was too long, too difficult, too unrewarding. But the master stays on that road. Not because he is focused on getting to his destination, but because he finds satisfaction and fulfillment in the road itself. He likes the hills and the valleys. He enjoys the hard work that is sometimes required of him, and he learns from the many disappointments he suffers along the way. Most of all, he likes those long, empty stretches when he doesn't seem to be making any progress. Why? Because they are peaceful.

"The master understands that he may never become the best chess player in the world or the best golfer in the world. And it bothers him not in the least. Because the joy of mastery is not in the attainment of your goal, but in the pursuit of it..."

*****

Can you get a sense of the power that type of "come-from" gives you?

Initiative means not waiting for permission. It means you don't need excuses because you're tuned into your power. It means it's no longer a question of "if" you can realize that bigger future because you ARE the second you decide to live from your vision. It changes your relationship with "failure" because you can only fail if you stop the tick-tack pursuit of your mission. It gives you the confidence to discover (or create) the path.

Hey, take this little initiative power quiz:

Who will gather more gravity, momentum, and get what they want faster: Someone who puts 60 hours a week in for a week or two; OR someone who puts a solid 2 hours a day of solid focus time, consistently every day until they get where they're going?

Smart money says the sharp person with the disciplined initiative will achieve excellence in whatever they do. The person who slams out the 60 hours immediately while still working full time tends to burn out fast (plus, it's a clear sign their "come-from" is one of desperation because that mindset indicates the need to find a magic pill to instantly fix things).

You've got to remember the biggest obstacle to your Profit Prophet success is your unconscious habitual belief patterns. So, in the beginning it probably will feel odd, weird, and different because living this way is a brand new experience. It takes getting use to. Any time you replace an unconscious habit with a conscious one, it can drain your energy because you've never focused your attention so sharply before.

It does get easier and easier. Yet, until you gain a little momentum consciously overcoming the inertia of unconsciousness pulling you back towards the familiar, it takes consistent effort for a period of time long enough for your new intention to take root.

You're got to prime your Profit Prophet pump before it'll flow whenever you need it to. And, it's the priming that takes the most time and energy; and, believe it or not, **it's also when your *greatest progress* is made**.

However, because you don't see anything flowing for our efforts until the pump is primed, it's also the hardest. That's because those *old circumstance-focused pumps are already primed and spewing distractions like a MoFo!* When attention strays from vision, the current situation will capture your focus again because it has the strongest gravity field.

So I must fairly warn you: If you're one of those people who has to have results BEFORE you've primed the pump to *believe* the process is working, you'll almost always quit long before you can reap the rewards of your behind the scenes priming.

The priming process takes consistency.

Stop priming for too long and you throw away all the hard work you've already done and start all over again.

And it gives your old unconscious habits even more power and control over you. That's because it'll use your current lack of results as "evidence" you're not making *enough* progress, fast enough because it tricks you into ignoring that 90+% of your success has to happen mentally BEFORE you'll see it in the physical world.

True dat…

CHAPTER 7:
Risking ~~Your~~ *FOR* Life!

So if *consistent* initiative (knowledge in action) is the key to leading yourself (and your audience) to experience a bigger future, what's the silent killer that keeps us from it?

Our old friend, FEAR, of course!

But what **IS** fear? I mean, *really*, what is it?

Ever *really* pondered it? I *don't* mean someone else's idea, like the *"False Evidence Appearing Real"* cliché.

What are **YOUR** feelings, thoughts, and beliefs about fear? Where do *you* feel it comes from? Why do *you* think some people react fearfully to some things and not to others? And, more importantly, why is it that SAME things other people are fearful of, hold no fear whatsoever for you and visa versa? Why is that?

Have you ever pondered it?

Here are some of my insights on fear after lots of deep, personal reflection:

We feel fear when we anticipate our future to be smaller (worse) than our present. See, fear *can't* exist without *comparison!* We *can't* feel fear *until* and *unless* we compare two different points in time against one another.

One specific experience, situation, or circumstance if taken in isolation has no meaning because if "cold," for example, is all you've ever known, you have no frame of reference to know what "hot" means. Actually, without getting a taste of anything other than "cold," do you even have a frame of reference to *experience* "cold" beyond just an intellectual exercise?

Hmmm...

Now, here's where things get interesting.

Where does this comparison HAVE to take place? <u>It can *only* take place in our minds</u>! We can't be in two places at the same time, can we? It's only possible in our imaginations or minds.

So, if we experience "hot" after only knowing "cold" we have to call up our past memory of what we believe "cold" felt like in order to make the comparison. If we decide we like our memory of cold (notice it's the memory and *not* the direct experience of cold) over our present experience of hot, we may prefer cold. If our memory of cold in comparison to hot doesn't please us, maybe we decide hot is "good" and cold is "bad," right?

Fear, then is really a memory of a *memory.*

Let that soak in for a second. **It's <u>deep</u>!**

You *can't* label something as "good" or "bad" without at least one side of the comparison being a memory (and, more often than not, the comparison is two memories). But to feel fear we have to make another comparison. We have to compare our memory of "bad" and project that memory into a future experience in order to fear it!

Since, the process of comparing, defining, and assigning meaning took place unconsciously, fear seems "real" (notice "real" is *another label* like "fear" that requires a memory comparison for you to know and define it's meaning;-).

We don't realize we can dissolve all fear by **simply becoming aware** of the mental conversations we have all the time to compare our memories and *decide* what we fear!

These conversations go on all the time.

You know what I'm talking about. Take the last few paragraphs you just read. You HAD to have several different mental conversations with yourself. It's the only way you can decide what all this means to you. It's the only way you can decide if I'm brilliant or a crackpot; if you agree or disagree; if you like or dislike what we're discussing here or not.

Most of the time we're totally unaware of these internal dialogues. However, a little awareness goes a long way because every time you shine the light of awareness on the shadow of fear, what has to happen? It transforms every fear into power, which adds to your momentum towards the bigger future you want. All you have to do is start the process and you'll be shocked how fast your limitations melt away.

Now, because your unconscious conversations have been deeply conditioned in you, the first step is to become aware of what you're telling yourself.

Just simply observe and notice what mental conversations are automatically taking place. Don't judge them. Just note them.

By observing without judgment (or trying to change them), usually the memory dissolves itself! It only sticks around if you are hanging on to it by judging, justifying, or defending what you're feeling. So you just want to eavesdrop in on the conversation. But don't take sides (because taking sides is adding more comparisons and therefore reinforces your fears instead of dissolving them).

The key is to let the conversation run it's course without giving a rip about it's substance. You don't have to understand where the conversation came from to observe it, do you?

Now, if you find you can't observe without taking sides (try it first before you assume you can't), don't sweat it. I gotcha covered...

Shake It. You <u>Won't</u> Break It.

The secret of overcoming your fears when you are so wrapped up in them that you can't observe them without experiencing them is to: Set up a stretch situation for yourself. See, the only other choice is to dissolve your fears by facing them <u>*consciously*</u> and directly.

Because when you <u>*consciously*</u> experience fear and allow yourself to move past it anyway, you get 3 gifts that instantly gives you so much power it's almost <u>*spooky*</u>. You know those people who make it look so easy? Everything they touch turns to gold? *That's* the "magic" powers waiting for you to command with these 3 gifts:

1. Choosing action over fear *instantly makes the unconscious <u>conscious</u>!* Fear can only stop you if you fight against it (which is an automatic, unconscious reaction). Fighting with fear makes it stronger! The only way you can feel fear and do it anyway is to let any fear be present. The moment fear is consciously observed without resistance, it begins to dissolve because you're no longer feeding it.

2. Consciously choosing to act on your vision over conditions of fear *instantly plugs the hidden leaks in your personal power!* You'll see how you've been unconsciously giving your power away. If you *knew* fear needed your consent to control you, would you ever grant such permission? No way, right?

3. *You'll go way beyond understanding to a gut level <u>knowing</u>, at warp-speed!* Direct experience transforms conceptual learning into an inner power and confidence that quickly becomes who you ARE! **<u>Experience</u> is not only the fastest way to mastery but it's also the only way to avoid falling back into old habitual, unconscious patterns.**

You get *true <u>lasting</u> power* that can't ever be taken away because <u>it comes from *within* you</u>! Until we *experience* what it's like to observe unconsciousness and make it conscious for ourselves, the level of personal power you have access to will always be limited by outside people, places, things, conditions and/or situations.

Are you starting to see the fallacy of "fighting through your fears?" It's a funny thing about fear: **It never stands still**.

It's either growing or shrinking!

You're either intensifying them or dissolving them. No other choice.

Every time you resist fear by mentally yelling "NO!" at them, anticipate a negative outcome, or try to beat it into submission to prove whose boss, **fear gains strength.**

You can only win a battle or two over fear, **but *never* the war.** It takes so much sheer willpower to fight fear, it's not long before fear sabotages your future success because it mutates into a new and improved super versions of itself.

Fear is a mental cancer that can only survive by mutating and feeding on itself. It's implanted in our minds under the guise of an ally there to protect and keep us safe from harm. Then the mutating begins. At first it's content to follow our lead because it's a baby mutation. Soon, however, it takes over because the bigger fear grows, the more energy it must leech from our minds to feed itself.

The only way to shrink a fear tumor is to stop feeding it. So, if you want to reclaim your power, **you've got to let fear burn itself out**.

How?

Simple. Fear does all the work *for* you if you **stay out of its way.**

Fear will instantly surrender control to you if its final mind game doesn't trap you: The *"You're Risking Your Life Without Me"* LIE.

See, when all else fails, fear tries to trick you into believing that *feeling* fear is dangerous. That *feeling* fear is painful. But, actually, the pain and suffering we feel *isn't* from fear itself; it comes from *anticipation* of (and *resistance* to) the fear!

The TRUTH is **consciously allowing fear to be present is the**

greatest relief you will ever feel! Because here's the thing: Anything you fear is *already* present.

If you consciously *welcome* your fears, instead of fighting them, they'll float up and out of you just like letting go of helium balloon. Up, up, and away it goes. Don't fight to keep your fear balloon and you'll experience a cathartic release of energy and power within you that feels so good it might just move you to tears!

And, oh, by the way, fearing the pain you *think* feeling fear will bring IS resisting.

When you are *feeling* resistant, like taking something on is a risk, it's because you're moving outside your comfort zone. But this is a good thing because you don't want to learn to be comfortable with pain. <u>Daring to release your fear balloon *feels risky only because you've grown accustomed to hanging on to it*</u>.

We all have areas that we're comfortable and uncomfortable with. If you don't have the success you seek yet (or you feel something's missing) it is because what you want is *outside* your comfort-zone. See, if it was inside your current comfort-zone, you would see, live and experience it right now this very moment!

You'd HAVE the bigger future instead of SEEKING it.

So, if you're not experiencing what you want right now, all it means is that it's just outside of what you're comfortable with. The bigger the risk "feels" to you is just an indication of how *far* outside your comfort zone it is.

If it feels like a little risk, then what you want is very close by.

If it feels like a big risk, it's just an indication that you *anticipate* your bigger future as being WAY outside what you're comfortable with (notice the role that word anticipate plays in fear and riskiness).

Can you see now why it's **<u>not</u>** risking your life, but risking **FOR** life?

CHAPTER 8: WARNING! Skipping Book One Is Hazardous To Your Wealth

A QUICK CHECK-IN

Before we move to BOOK TWO (which, for many, is where the fun really begins), let's take a minute to take an inventory of where we are in creating your Profit Prophet story so business comes to you automatically.

For many of us Type-A personality types, it's tempting to skip over BOOK ONE because we want to get straight to the hard-core, bottomline moneymaking secrets from the front lines of business. We often ignore the personal leadership side of the equation.

This is a mistake. A BIG one.

That's because your business (and your profits) can only grow as much as you grow personally. Working to build yourself MORE than you work on your business is *vital* to your success. In fact, it's a zero-factor in your Profit Prophet Journey. Meaning: Without growing personally, every other business building strategy or tactic will eventually stop working because it's faked instead of genuine leadership.

At it's core, being a Profit Prophet is about *being* an attractive leader to the core of your being. Showing people bigger possibilities than they can see without your vision. Which means it's about standing for something. Having a mission. A vision that once embraced will positively impact your follower's lives! *Real* **value.** Not bullshit you think people want to hear so you can talk them into giving you their money.

Embrace this truth, and (with the help of the breakthrough strategies revealed in the next two books), you'll find people will WANT you to lead them. Not only that, because you create real value for them, they will feel the pain of loss if they STOP doing business with you.

And, that translates into HUGE bottom-line results for you! Immediate profits, as well as business equity and longevity *far* into the future!

Enough said?

Good.

Now it's time to roll up our sleeves for BOOK TWO…

BOOK TWO:

PACK LEADERSHIP AND VISION

(Audience Attraction & Ascension Processes To 10X Your Profit Prophet Influence)

CHAPTER 1: Charmed!

Being a Profit Prophet is a rock-star life!

Or at least it *could* be once you know the 7-step process revealed here.

What if, in other peoples' *minds*, you became a rock-star *without* changing a thing about you? What if you commanded Oprah-like influence?

How would life change if a little "voodoo" allowed you to, systematically, mentally "reprogram" people to automatically trust, respect, and even *idolize* you?

Because, let's face it, making money is easy when a long line of people *beg* you to lead them, yes? When people flock to you and feel honored you'd even give them the time of day, success is a piece 'o cake (plus, it's *really* **fun** when YOU'RE the one picking who gets your time, attention, and love)!

I've been on both sides of the fence. And, *being* begged is MUCH better than doing the begging. ;-)

That's because, by nature, I'm *not* someone who can sell ice to Eskimos. Far from it. In fact, I HATE selling. Cajoling, convincing, and begging people to buy, just plain SUCKS!

You'd never know it from my business success, however, I *am* (and always have been) a recluse. I often have a tough time in groups. Never liked small talk or "smoozing" people into liking me. I'm that stiff guy who can't loosen up to have fun at parties, clubs, or any new situation where I have to meet people for the first time.

Yet, I discovered the hard way that **you <u>can't</u> build a profitable business (big or small) WITHOUT people.** There's no way around it (believe me, I tried to find one).

If you want to make money (even a minimum wage job) you need to interact with people. Because, as the saying goes, *"you can't get rich in a vacuum."*

So, if you can't enroll others in your vision for *their* bigger future (i.e., being an effective pack leader by powerfully communicating your ideas), you can have the best solutions since sliced bread, but the world will *never* listen because your message is a fart in a windstorm.

Sorry.

Now, it wasn't until I stumbled on to some "voodoo" that **changed my financial life completely.** And, changed it so fast it was almost *spooky*.

You're about to discover a powerful 7-step process. It's my Profit Prophet recipe for cooking up the kind of rock-star influence that makes people idolize and hang on your every word.

It's a crash-course in the psychological triggers we all have implanted deep in our subconscious minds. Once you know this process you can use it to create automatic trust, respect, and Oprah-like influence on demand.

For real: Because...

YOU TOO CAN BE A "<u>VOODOO</u>'er"

Before we get into the meat of the matter, let's talk about elephant in the room: Her name is *"Voodoo."*

Right away, it conjures up feelings of magic and mystery, right? Good. That's exactly why I'm using it. See, some try to explain my knack for influence as "magic." And, yet, it's really *not* mystical at all.

In fact, <u>it's completely systemized and predictable</u>!

Now, there **IS** an "X" factor. An unknown piece that even *seasoned* business people miss (that's why a client once paid me $25,000.00 to teach them how I **DO** the "Voodoo" I do, so well ;-)).

Oh, and by the way, they paid me the $25K AFTER paying me more than a million dollars for simply adding my systemized marketing voodoo to help grow their business.

Why did they gladly pay me well over a million to implement my voodoo in their business? Because it helped them grow from a $2 Million to a $19+ Million dollar business in about 18 months!

Anyway, in this book, I'm going to take you back stage and show you HOW the magic is done. You're about to come inside; you're about to discover what this "Voodoo" is that gets your ideal audience all 'n bothered. And, more importantly, I'm gonna show ya HOW IT'S DONE!

Once you're done with this book you will be able to lead your ideal tribe of prospects, clients, customers, students, distributors, franchisees, independent reps, etc. to *their* promised land (and live a rock-star life at the same time)!

No bull.

So, turn the page and let's get started...

CHAPTER 2:
The "Oprah Effect"

Ever hear (or use) the term *"Oprah Money?"*

How did Oprah Winfrey become a billionaire? What voodoo does she leverage when a passing *"Oh, by the way"* mention of something she likes, triggers a stampede of millions? How can a single, black woman, who refuses to "sell," simply give her nod of approval and unleash a sales frenzy, virtually guaranteeing a best seller overnight?

How could a daytime talk show host grow to command so much power and influence that many credit her with getting President Obama elected?

How? *How* indeed. I'll tell ya how:

Oprah knows her audience better than they consciously know themselves. She's a master of *their* mental conversations. And she knows how to enter those conversations without conflict and how to redirect them in positive ways. People THANK her because they can't help but feel empowered when Oprah is in their head!

She gives people love, hope and belief that tomorrow will be better than today. (Sound familiar? It *should* because it's from the deep dive we just finished in BOOK ONE, right?)

And, let's face it, can you ever get enough of feeling *that* good? Who doesn't want feelings of powerlessness and hopelessness reprogrammed to courageousness, faith and even confidence?

See, for 25 years Oprah Winfrey created a level of trust, connection, and powerful relationship with millions of people through her TV show. She created a bond so strong that 7.4 MILLION "besties" (*raving* fans) never missed their *daily* "chats" and "visits" with her! And 49 MILLION "friends" (*regular* fans) who couldn't go without at least 1 Oprah fix every week!

Talk about leading a tribe!

Millions consider Oprah their *best* friend. They *never* met her. Oprah doesn't hang out with them and certainly doesn't know them individually. **Yet she understands, respects, and loves them.**

They willingly gave her full access to their most valued possession: They let Oprah inside and allowed her *unchallenged* influence over their thoughts, beliefs, and behaviors!

For an hour every day for 25 years Oprah let everyone inside. She shared herself in a way that everyone FELT as if THEY were Gale King (Oprah's real life best friend).

Creating Your Own "Oprah Effect"

Here's two things might not know:

FIRST: Did you know, you don't have to *be* Oprah to command the same power over *your* audience that she has over hers?

You may never have 49 million fans, but you can still have incredible influence. And, when you command that kind of power, you don't need millions; a thousand is more than enough to give you rock-star, Profit

Prophet status.

SECOND: Did you know you can model the exact same process and establish irresistible Oprah-like influence for yourself? There are only 7 steps to it.

And, guess what? Those 7 steps are **hard-coded** directly in the mind of your ideal audience right this very second! Which means these 7 mental programs are triggered to "run" without any *conscious* awareness. Powerful shit, girlfriend!

Now, I bet you didn't know these programs only run one at a time and control exactly what people think, feel, and believe to be true about YOU, didja? Did you know creating your own Oprah Effect only requires you to activate each of these 7 mental programs in the proper order, at the right time? Tip over the first domino and it triggers a chain reaction.

Did you know your "pack" *unconsciously wants* an Oprah-like **confidante** to trust, believe and follow? In fact, your target audience is suffering in unconscious silence because they haven't found someone who can lovingly lead, help, and inspire them to live a bigger future! Did you know, right this very second, they're begging for someone to relieve the stress, pain, and pressure caused by their limiting mental programs?

In a sense, your tribe *wants* to be *ethically* brainwashed!

They *want* freedom from the way these mental programs control and limit them. They *want* the relief that comes every time you clear away another mental barrier for them. They *crave* the kind of human connection that only comes from a having a trusted confidante to guide them!

You didn't know all that? Don't feel bad. You're *not* alone! That's because as universal, simple, and powerful as all this "voodoo" is, it's a huge blind spot for almost everyone.

See, we have almost no conscious awareness that these 7 mental programs have been hard-coded into us without our permission. Unless you've studied it, you don't know how each interrelates. And, the chances are slim to none that you're aware that the very pain, fear, and stress we struggle with (and want relief from) are actually only present *because* we unconsciously run these mental programs.

Because when we can't see the *true* **source** the problem we look for the solution in all the wrong places (and can't find relief without outside help).

However, because we don't want to be manipulated, tricked, or controlled we think "mind control" or "brainwashing" is evil because we fear it being used to cause more pain instead of bringing relief. Ironically (or paradoxically), it's the fear of being controlled that actually "writes", "installs" and drives these programs deep into our unconsciousness!

Anyway, we tend to rebel against or resist any perceived threat to our freedom (which, by the way, **IS** a form of mind-control because any knee-jerk automatic reaction brings more pain, reinforces our fears, and drives it even deeper unconscious).

Personally, I choose to see brainwashing as washing out these negative mental programs. It's not about control at all. It's about helping people find the freedom they desperately want.

Yes, it has the added benefit of attracting wealth, power, and people to you like steel to an electro magnet; but it's very power comes from *helping* people live the bigger life they want (*not* manipulating them into more pain to make a quick buck).

Anyway, you're about to discover a form of positive and ethical brainwashing that trumps all other forms of mind-control because it gives THEM complete control. You might facilitate the process at times, but it's always THEIR choice to follow. Which gives the relief they feel soar beyond anything they've ever experienced before! And, because you engineered that relief, their *love* for you also far exceeds logical explanation!

Very few entrepreneurs and businesses (even the successful ones) *truly* understand the art and the science of what follows here. Some accidentally stumble on the process but, unfortunately, can't seem to duplicate their results *intentionally*, on demand.

Perception Really IS Everything!

Becoming that Oprah-like confidante, the Profit Prophet your audience desperately wants in their life comes down to relationship, right?

Actually, more accurately, **it's all about the PERCEIVED relationship that your customers (and <u>potential</u> customers) feel THEY have with you.**

Now, of course, there are different levels of relationship. Oprah's influence is so powerful because she's established the ultimate level of trust with her followers: She's MORE than a friend; she's MORE than an authority figure; she's MORE than a leader.

The secret to Oprah's influence is 49 million people looked to her as their *trusted <u>advisor</u>*! If YOU want to flip the tables and make people stand in line and *beg* for the chance to be guided by you, *they MUST be mentally conditioned to think of you as their most treasured and trusted confidante!*

Why do you think this is?

Well, if people want your counsel, advice, and guidance before making a decision, what **has** to take place in their minds?

You can't be someone's confidante until <u>they</u> mentally elevate you to that position. THEY put you there. With this high honor, effectively they're admitting to you, them, and the rest of the world **they value your thinking over THEIR OWN <u>and above all others</u>!**

It must be earned, *never* demanded.

How many major shifts in someone's mental conversations has to happen before they give you enough authority, trust, credibility, and respect that **your word is LAW** in their mind? Before they willing surrender their judgment to yours? Before they stop questioning and simply *comply*?

At a minimum, there's 7 conversations people have with themselves about you *before* they've conditioned themselves to perceive enough of a relationship with you so your council triggers instant compliance (this just so happens to be what this book is all about. ;-)

But that's the best news of all! Because that's what ensures you can deliberately establish your own "Oprah Effect" (instead of leaving it to chance like almost every other entrepreneur does).

It's only a matter of consistency, repetition, and committed reinforcement to mentally program your pack with your own Oprah-like influence.

Here's why: You become a trusted advisor through mental conditioning. Because, if they tell themselves the same story enough times, soon it becomes a belief. And, as they continue to tell that story with belief, mentally it becomes *truer* and *truer*. Soon that repetition reinforces their "truth" into absolute conviction.

And, our convictions are the invisible filters that *automatically* sift, sort, & screen out anything incongruent with storyteller's self-concept (remember from BOOK ONE?). Whatever they allow through their conviction filters becomes *reality*!

Did you notice every part is *conditioned*?

It's a trained response in THEM. And, that, my friend, means *anyone* who knows the training process can eventually condition the deep trust and respect that psychologically triggers the automatic influence of a confidante!

No special magic, wishing, begging, or selling required;-)

You're only 7 main mental conversations away from the type of advisor influence that makes profits come to you! Think you're ready to learn how?

Then you know what to do...

CHAPTER 3:
Mind Reading Voodoo (Marketing Telepathy)

What if you had the power to read minds?

Or if you had marketing telepathy? The gift of clairvoyance where you know what someone was going to think, say, or do before they even knew?

Like a grandmaster of chess who sees checkmate 30 moves before winning, how much confidence would you have if you knew beyond a shadow of a doubt, <u>it's not *if* you will establish your Profit Prophet influence, but *when*</u>?

Chess is great metaphor for this process and strategy. In chess, the winning strategy is the one that anticipates your opponent's moves and leads them to make moves you want. However, even a grandmaster can't go from opening move to checkmate in a couple moves (even if she's playing against a novice).

It's a *process*.

A winning strategy is a series of moves and counter moves all stacked on top of one another that creates the eventual outcome you envisioned from the opening move, right? See, even with telepathy, you still have to lead people through the process because **you <u>can't</u> make your next move <u>*until* they make theirs</u>.**

You *can't* force, push, or rush them because implementing your winning strategy depends on their willingness to engage and continue to play the game all the way to the end. You *can* create a game "environment" that makes them enjoy and eagerly anticipate playing with you. They control the speed by which they follow your lead.

Before you get too lost in this game metaphor, let me make it absolutely clear that **you <u>never</u> want to think in terms of winning and losing.**

Even though they'll be working against you at early stages of the process, they're *never* your opposition to be beat into submission. No. When they decide to make you their trusted advisor, <u>you *both* win</u>!

And they're the *bigger* winner because they'll only trust and respect you that deeply <u>when you help them *experience a bigger future* with you in it (and if you've *never betrayed them*)</u>.

THEIR Mental Journey To YOUR Oprah-Like Powers

Influence is 100% mental. It's THEIR mental journey, NOT yours!

Think of your Profit Prophet influence as the penthouse of 7-story building without an elevator. <u>You</u> already live in the penthouse. The only reason your followers aren't living in the lap of luxury with you is because they're trapped outside.

Your first job is to show them inside and entice them in out of the cold to check out your lobby.

Your second job is to invite them to climb the secret staircase to the second floor.

Your third job is to ease their fears enough so they'll make it successfully to the second floor without running back outside.

You can't lead and encourage them to climb to the third floor until and unless they make it to the second, right? And so it goes with all 7 sets of staircases that lead them to the penthouse.

Rinse. Lather. Repeat.

You can't throw your penthouse keys out the window in a sock to a complete stranger and expect them to figure out how to (or even want to) climb all the way up and move in with you!

At each point in the process, **<u>they always have 3 choices:</u>**

1. **They can run away** from the scary unknown future they don't trust or believe in yet; or

2. **They can stay put,** paralyzed by fear, like a deer in the headlights; or

3. **They can follow you to what they hope will be a bigger future** even though the mental story they've been telling themselves is *"This is a big risk because it could backfire and cause me even more pain and suffering."*

The mental conversations they are having with themselves unconsciously *will* trigger 1 of those 3 possible *automatic* reactions.

Each of the 7 levels shifts their mind to a *new* conversation (and therefore a different mental program runs their show at each level). So, if you want to lead them to the upper levels of influence you have to know what those conversations are, right? It's the only way to trigger them to unconsciously follow you forward. Otherwise your process stops 'em dead or makes 'em run and hide!

If you make them feel "wrong" for the feelings they have, they won't let you lead them anywhere. **You've got to meet their fears (no matter how crazy, unwarranted, or irrational) with loving understanding because it's always 100% real to them.** Almost everyone is scared to death to trust (even though they desperately want the kind of love and connection that comes from it).

Therefore, you need to know as your process moves people through each of the 7 levels, **you WILL AUTOMATICALLY stir up their fears!** That's a guaranteed part of the trust building process.

However, even though they will direct their fears at you, it's *not* personal (their fears are the mental stories they've conditioned themselves to believe are true). So, instead of taking it personally and reacting to them with frustration, anger, or impatience **treat them like your 5 year old daughter who had a bad dream and needs the safety and security of mom and dad's bed.**

Moving From Asshole To Advisor

Here are the 7 major mental shifts a stranger goes through (and *what* they'll unconsciously be thinking about trusting you at each stage):

1. The *"You're An Asshole"* Mindset

2. The *"You're A Pest"* Mindset

3. The *"You're On Probation"* Mindset

4. The *"You're Like Me"* Mindset

5. The *"You're An Authority"* Mindset

6. The *"You're A Leader"* Mindset

7. The *"You're MY Advisor"* Mindset

Before we start drilling down on each of these, let me ask you a question: What instant reaction did you have when you read *"You're An Asshole"* above?

Did it offend you? Did you take it personally?

Well, I'm not trying to offend you, but you *do* need to understand that's often how your ideal lifetime fans will start out thinking about you! They won't tell you, but that's the recording they have running in their minds.

It's just a mental defense mechanism.

So, look at the 7 stages. It's really how a deep relationship unfolds. As they move up each level, their resistance dissolves a bit more.

A level 1 program makes their fears about you, your solutions, and business processes **run at an all time high.** Fear dissolves a bit when they shift into level 2, which creates just a little openness. At levels 2 & 3, fear is still the primary driver, but less and less as they ascend up your Profit Prophet influence ladder.

As fear dissolves more and more, trust has the opportunity to show its face. When they shift into a level 4 conversation the fear-trust scale in their minds finally tips slightly in your favor for the first time. It hasn't tipped far enough to the trust side to influence their actions, but it is the foundation you need to continue building.

It's not till they shift into a level 5 mindset that the trust scales tip far enough into the respect mindset that triggers the belief they need in order for them to dare to do business with you for the *first* time.

Please read that last sentence *several* times.

Notice you have to lead them all the way to level 5 on the Profit Prophet influence ladder *before* **they'll ever do business with you for the** *first* **time!** This is where most people screw up and why they'll NEVER discover the secret of making success chase them.

See, almost everyone assumes their would-be ideal lifetime fan is *already having* a level 5 or 6 mental conversation with themselves. So they attempt to communicate with them for the first time from that place. It's total mismatch! When you ignore the first 4 levels (or try to skip any step in the process), and try to influence action immediately, you trigger their fight or flight unconscious reactions.

It's because their level 1 (or at best 2-3) recordings, blocks out everything that's too far ahead of their *current* mental conversations (beliefs).

Now, interestingly enough, they can hear any of the lower level conversations from their current position, but *never* the upper level ones. This means THEY can shortcut, sidestep, or rush up your influence ladder, but *you* can't. Depending on their personality type, they may be more open and therefore habitually comfortable at, say, level 3 on the influence ladder in every new situation.

But you can't *assume* it.

If you want the kind of Profit Prophet Influence that makes business chase you, you MUST assume everyone starts at the lowest level *"You're An Asshole"* mental conversation and lead them up the ladder, systematically, *from* there.

This covers all bases.

You'll meet most of the world where they already are: in their distrust of the unknown; *and* it still allows those rare open-minded folks to skip themselves several rungs up your influence ladder.

Okay, now, let's dig deeper into each level…

CHAPTER 4: LEVEL 1 – The Fear Based, *"You're An Asshole"* Mental Conversation

Level 1 is the bottom rung on your Profit Prophet ladder. You might be wondering if there's any influence down here at all.

Tons!

With the "You're An Asshole" mindset, you wield major amounts of influence. It just so happens to repel instead of attract! At this stage of the process, you definitely influence them: **Their mindset triggers automatic actions to avoid you like the plague.**

See, it's always easier (and *feels* safer) to say "no" rather than to give someone (or something) you don't know the benefit of the doubt. **Fear runs this mental conversation 100%.** And, fear is what triggers our unconscious "fight or flight" reactions.

As a result, at this first stage of entry, the pack you want to lead will be at the highest state of alertness. With mental alarms blasting, *"Warning! Asshole on the horizon. Pain approaching! Look out! You've been warned! Avoid! Avoid! Avoid!"*

They're scared of you. They will blow up all their past fears, worries, and "boogiemen" nightmares bigger than life and attach it *all* to you.

Their walls of resistance (though will shatter easily with the right approach) will never be stronger than at this moment. Because their automatic mental conversations filters out anything that doesn't support their current mindset. They simply *can't* hear anything other than their imagined fears.

Ever watch the TV show, *"The Dog Whisperer?"* Cesar has 3 rules a pack-leader must follow when introducing yourself to a dog for the first time:

1. No touch;

2. No talk; and

3. No eye contact.

Because if you try to pet, praise, or look at them before passing their sniff test, they assume that you are challenging them.

You trigger their curiosity instincts, instead of defenses, by entering their space and going about business *without* acknowledging them at all. This simultaneously lowers their defenses and raises their curiosity.

You've passed the first test: They ain't running or attacking, **YET**.

See, at this first level, your *only* goal is to enter their environment without friction. For people the "space" isn't physical proximity like it is for dogs. You're introducing yourself into their conscious awareness.

Their mind-space.

At this point, your goal is NOT even to trigger their curiosity (that happens at level 2, when they come to you, cautiously). Your job is to *slightly soothe* the irrational fears automatically triggered by entering their mind-space.

Notice my *"slightly soothe"* choice of language. If you try to completely solve or eliminate their fears before they acclimate to your presence, it's the equivalent of lunging to love on a dog before she welcomes you (you're more likely to get bit than sniffed if she hasn't yet come to her own decision to check you out).

But this is great news because it's much, much easier to <u>slightly soothe</u> than it is to <u>solve</u>. In fact, it's just a matter of entering their mind-space for a few seconds without adding any fuel to their fears. **Because their** *"You're An Asshole"* **mental conversation quickly burns itself out IF you DON'T <u>pour gasoline on it</u>.**

Do you get the power this gives you?

Fear controls the momentum and direction of the conversation. So, you simply trigger the conversation; don't add any more to the fear side of it; and **<u>it dissolves itself!</u>**

Once the *"You're An Asshole"* conversation dissolves, they instantly replace it with the *"You're A Pest"* mindset. They automatically MOVE THEMSELVES UP to the second level without you having to do anything else!

That's why it's said that a good approach gets you 90%+ of the way to the finish line; and also why it's almost impossible to recover from a bad approach no matter what else you do.

See, the first 3 levels are more about what you DON'T do, rather than what you *do*, do! (Yeah, I heard it. I said, "do-do" — Hahahahaha!)

Whatever.

The point is the conditioning starts with teeny-tiny baby steps and grows exponentially with each level up the ladder.

And, because you now know what to expect with this process, you can meet your audience with love and understanding, right?

CHAPTER 5: LEVEL 2 – The Fear Based, *"You're A Pest"* Mental Conversation

Since only a few thousand people, out of the 7 billion of us sharing this planet, have the ability to turn off our minds, even though it's *unconscious*, <u>we are *never* without a mental conversation</u>.

It's a chain reaction. When one thought, story, or conversation ends, it's *always* replaced with a new one that's in close proximity to the last one.

The next conversation will either be *slightly* more negative or positive towards you. But its tone NEVER ventures more than a bit from the benchmark of the previous conversation. That's why people can't move from asshole to advisor without having all the mental conversations in between.

They can move through each conversation very fast. Or excruciatingly slow. However, make no mistake about it: They ARE having them with themselves to *some* degree.

So once you successfully insert yourself into someone's mind-space at level one, and let the first conversation burn itself out, *they* will replace it immediately with the "You're A Pest" mindset. Obviously, thinking you're a pest is a slight improvement over an asshole, but it's still a fear-based conversation.

And, remember, *all* fear driven mindsets trigger our "fight or flight" instincts because they are automatic, unconscious defenses.

As a pest, you've created a little more openness but it's *far* from trusting. You've helped them dissolve the fear they had at level 1. Now you want to keep that momentum going and help them feel even better by allowing them to burn out the fears behind their replacement *"You're A Pest"* mentality.

A pest is an unwanted distraction, right? Something to be swatted, yes? Unwelcomed and aggravating. Yuck!

You have their attention, but it's a _negative_ attention at this stage.

As you help them burn out the fear that's fueling it, their attention towards you turns more and more positive (even though they're still defensive). This is the highest level of outright defensiveness that you will encounter from them. That's because now they are aware that they've let down their guard enough to let you in a bit.

Like a little kid who fights sleep because they don't want to miss anything, when people run this mental recording, they are resistant.

The primary thought process people have at this level is, *"You're annoying because you're interrupting me. Hurry up and say something stupid so I can validate my first impression and go back to thinking of you as an asshole."* This mindset tunes their filters so that they can gather the right evidence about you because they're **trying to prove that their irrational fears are right**.

NOTE: They are probably ticked at themselves for upgrading you to "pest status." So they're looking for any excuse to shut down the interaction with you fast.

Here your only goal is to set the stage so they can "hear" you at the next level. The only way they will replace the pest conversation with the next one up the ladder, is if they mentally flip from negative to *positive* attention.

Remember to keep your cool. None of *their* fear-based mindsets are about YOU.

It's just how they've been programmed (and conditioned) to react based on their past life experiences. Basically your job is to let them vent until they get it out of their system.

Because <u>until they drain themselves</u> of their past negativity, <u>nothing</u> you communicate (regardless of it's revolutionary power) <u>gets through</u>!

Just like all fear-based conversations, you pass the pest test by allowing it to run its course without introducing *more* fear into the situation. Once it burns itself out, they will automatically replace it with the next level.

CHAPTER 6: LEVEL 3 – The Fear Based, *"You're On Probation"* Mental Conversation

Even though this is still a fear based mindset, this level is the beginning of a greased shoot they're about to have a blast sliding down.

Meaning, if you successfully lead them to and through this conversation a Profit Prophet momentum builds. And it increases at increasing rate through the remaining levels of your influence process that only stops if you throw barriers in the way.

See, when someone puts you on probation it means <u>they're giving you a chance</u>. You've got the tiny mental opening that creates interest in checking you out deeper. This mindset naturally ignites a _curiosity_ that pulls them deeper into you and your story.

Curiosity marks the beginning of it being THEIR idea to pursue you!

Even though it's usually only a matter of a few minutes to get to this mindset, a lot has taken place mentally with them.

Let's return to our Dog Whisperer example for a second. Dogs (and people) instinctually get a "feel" for outsiders based on who we ARE (*not* who you try or pretend to be in that moment). They read and immediately mirror your inner mood and mindset towards them back to you. If you're uptight, nervous, or unsure they *know* it. They only feel at ease with us when we really are calm, confident, and relaxed with them.

(Don't you know someone who can change the entire mood of everyone in a room without saying a word?)

Anyway, a person (or dog) comes to you only if they're allowed to get comfortable enough to lower their guard. Their reaction to you will either be fear-based or curiosity-based, depending on their comfort with you. A dog accepts you into its space without friction only after you pass its sniff test; and that sniff test only happens if they're interested enough to investigate you.

A dog's probationary period is the sense they get from you during that initial once over investigation. That's how they decide if they're going to welcome you, challenge you, or run away in fear of you.

Let them satisfy their natural curiosity without triggering fear and your probation ends quickly. They aren't ready to be your best friend and they certainly won't respect or submit to your leadership yet; but they they'll let you join the pack without incident.

But jump the gun and try to pet, play, or love on 'em before they're interested enough let you make a first impression and they'll feel threatened (which is why a dog growls, snarls, shows its teeth or snaps if rushed).

It's exactly the same for humans when we replace a level 2 mindset with this *"You're On Probation"* mental conversation.

Without sensing any immediate danger, their curiosity gets the better of them and makes 'em come to you. Probation is still a fear driven mentality so your primary job is to make sure you don't throw up any red flags that adds fuel to their fear fires.

The difference at this level is that because you're on probation, <u>they'll let you help</u> them to dissolve their fear conversations.

See, for the first time their mental filters let tiny bits of your message in. They want to satisfy their curiosity enough to decide if they're truly interested or not.

Yes, it's a ways away from trust. But they'll start to explore the potential opportunities and threats they associate with letting you deeper into their minds. Now they finally start to "hear" you, whereas at levels 1 & 2 when they couldn't hear anything but their own inner chatter.

Still extremely guarded and iffy about you, they'll be thinking, *"Okay, you've got one foot in the door, and the other's on a banana peel. You've got my attention and are starting to capture my curiosity, which I don't like at all because if you break through my walls I might start to trust you. I've got to cover my ass because I can't risk being hurt again. The first sign of trouble and it's back to jail you go!"*

The most powerful (and influential) part of this mental conversation from your point of view is that it always includes a *"What-If?"* element to it. This is where they start to dream a bit. As their interest grows they wonder what would it be like if whatever you're sharing with them *will* actually help them.

You need to remember, they will be mentally wrestling with things like, *"I know it probably won't be as good as it's starting to look, but <u>what if this time</u> it really is true? I don't want to risk missing out on something that could really, really help me."*

It becomes a fear of loss conversation for them.

And you can use that knowledge in leading them through the rest of the process. It's a very powerful motivation tool! People will often act more because they fear being left behind. They don't want to miss out on the good stuff.

At this third level, this mentality takes root automatically (and takes very little from you to kick it into high gear).

Since they're automatically starting this fear of loss conversation here, you might as well use it to help them reap the value waiting for them when they ascend to the upper levels of your Profit Prophet scale (see, it's an influence scale from *your* prospective, but it's a *value* scale from *theirs*. And **they reward you with more and more influence in direct proportion to the VALUE you give them** at each stage).

Besides being aware of, and sparking new "what-if" aspects to their mentality, you can help people dissolve this conversation (and automatically replace it with level 4) by not being emotionally involved. In other words, if you can remove yourself from caring one way or the other if they see the light or not (or how fast), they won't feel pressure.

When you aren't attached to the outcome it fuels their fear of loss even more because they sense your confidence. Which builds even greater interest and curiosity because people want what they *can't* have.

Your attitude, without being arrogant or stating it directly, should come across to them like, *"hey, I know I got the goods; I don't have to over-hype things and make bold promises because what I do works; by the time we're done here you'll know beyond a shadow of a doubt why and how it works;*

"I'm happy to show you the facts so you can make a sound decision if this is right for you or not; because the last thing I want is a dissatisfied client; I only want to work with people who are a good match for me. If the ideas I have to share with you make sense, and you see the value in them then I'm happy to explore deeper possibilities with you. If not, that's okay too."

See, the tone? Just get a feel for the confidence that comes from standing there. **A strong but calm silent confidence is very attractive!**

Just one more thing before we move on to the next level: The more emotionally charged any fear is, the fiercer the fire burns. So while the fear-based conversations of the first 3 levels can sometimes provoke strong reactions in people, remember the more intensely they react, the faster it burns itself out.

That's why, although it might seem like a lot of work (or you might think it takes forever) to reach the trust based conversations, you can move at lightening speeds through them if you don't add any more fears to their fires. It's a fast burn that you can direct and control.

And, don't forget one of **the biggest value-building things you can do for your audience is to give them <u>relief</u>; <u>free them from their fears</u>**.

After all, who likes the feeling of being controlled by fear?

CHAPTER 7:
LEVEL 4 – The Trust Based, *"You're Like Me"* Mental Conversation

Congrats! As your audience transitions into this mindset, they've tipped their mental scales slightly into the trust zone.

Although fear will still be there, for the first time, trust is *more* influential.

Now, you not only have their *full* attention, but they've turned their passing curiosity into a full blown interest in you, your story, and/or your solutions.

This level is about painting a mental picture *where they become the star* and see themselves getting the outcomes you show them is possible. This is the secret of turning their interest into a desire for your solutions.

This mental conversation makes them look for similarities with you (the star of this Profit Prophet story). The degree they personally identify with the star and story determines your success at this level.

And, oh, by the way, the star doesn't have to be *you* (even if you're telling the story in your voice). They just need to be able to identify with the plight of the star (so you can tell third party stories about *other* people).

The star doesn't even have to be *human*. One of my best voodoo marketing processes stared "Fred, the flat-headed FLEA" (yes, an *insect* I brought to life, named, and built a story around that my audience really resonated with)!

Anyway, the key is getting them to connect *emotionally* with the star's highs & lows. You want them to <u>*relive*</u> the star's pain as you tell the story. If they actually <u>*feel*</u> the challenges it becomes "real" to them. When they connect to the pain on a gut level, not only will they automatically want it to stop, but it also makes "their" victory taste so much sweeter!

It makes them understand, appreciate, and truly value your solutions. Plus, now it's THEIR idea to want the solutions that relieves the pressure valve on their suffering.

Ever shared a tough, challenging, or traumatic experience with someone? A special bond gets created at the same time, right? Don't you feel a special connection with them because of that commonality?

See, when they *share an <u>emotional</u> experience* with you (even if you're not the star and it's not your story specifically), a bond is created between them, the star, the story, AND the *storyteller*!

Now they start to feel a level of comfort and familiarity with you. It's the beginning of trust because we trust people we think are like us. We feel like we "know" someone if their story rings true to us (interestingly enough, they don't *really* know you at all, but because it feels like THEY know you, they assume you know them).

We like people who we *believe* are like us.

At the beginning of this mental conversation they have qualified themselves as being a good _candidate_ to _potentially_ do business with you.

However, even if you successfully direct this conversation so they feel like they know and like you, they still aren't ready to do business with you until they get to level 5 of this process.

At the end of this mental conversation you will only have the "know you" and "like you" parts established with them. But there are 4 big pieces to the puzzle required before someone will risk doing business with you for the first time:

1. *Know* you;

2. *Like* you;

3. *Trust* you; and

4. *RESPECT* you.

People won't like you until they feel like they know you. And, while, yes, if someone gets to know and like you, it means they also trust you, it's not yet a *buying* trust. If they stay stuck in this level 4 mindset, they'll *never* trust you enough to give you money to lead them to the promised land.

Think about all the people you know and like enough to call them an acquaintance, friend, close friend, or even a "besties." How many of them do you feel are qualified to lead you?

How many of them do you trust enough to guide you because their results and life are clearly far superior yours?

You might have a couple people you trust and respect to that level, but it's nowhere near the total number of people you know and like, right? Just because you know and like someone does that automatically mean you trust and respect them enough to give them money and follow their advice?

No way!

So don't jump the gun and expect people to do business with you for the first time if they are still smack in the middle of this level 4 conversation.

This is your time to build enough of a bond and connection so they recognize all the ways you're like them; so they feel like they know and like you; where they say, *"As much as I hate to admit it, this guy/gal is actually kinda cool. They ain't the evil, bloodsucking leech I thought. I'm still very, very skeptical because they need to show me proof, but damned if I'm not enjoying getting to know them."*

Besides connecting and getting them identifying with you, **the key to getting them to replace this mental conversation with the next one is working proof into your story.** Because they need to be able to easily justify to themselves that your solution(s) is better than everything else available to them.

They need you to give them supporting *proof* for what makes you unique.

So start brainstorming about the missing ingredient(s) *you* bring to the table that they can't get from anyone (or anything) but you? How have others benefited? Why is it exclusive? Special? Powerful? Limited?

Don't make a statement or assertion without backing it up with all the reasons why!

Why? Why? Why?

They need justification that what you're sharing is not only *true*, but also **why it will work for THEM.**

After the emotional connection is made (or, better yet, at the *same* time), it's all about piling on all the reasons why.

Hit 'em with everything you've got so there's no reason (or excuse) remaining and they'll go from only being interested to actually <u>*desiring*</u> your solutions!

And *desire* just happens to be the doorway to...

abused or misused)?

What if, now, *they* had to pass **YOUR** sniff test **and QUALIFY to work with YOU?**

Flip the switch on them like that, and without you doing anything else, it triggers two HUGE mental shifts in them automatically:

1. Suddenly, **their headache hurts much more!** Because, now, they're aware they might not be able to get your relief. And, also simply because it gets them to focus 100% of their attention squarely on their headache (the next time you get a headache focus on how bad it hurts and watch what happens); and

2. Suddenly, **their perception of the value (and uniqueness) of your relief soars!** That's because, when they see how protective you are, only allowing access to people who can handle your brand of powerful relief responsibly, their imagination starts to run wild because only something *really* special would be this hard to get, right?

Because all this takes place mentally, **the value they see (or** *don't* **see) is subjective.** In fact, ALL value is actually 100% perceived value (like beauty, value is in the eye of the beholder).

Why do people camp out and stand in line to be first to buy the new iPhone? What happens to our desire when we *think* supply is limited? We want it even more, right?

It's economics 101: Supply and demand.

Demand (the *intensity* of our *desires*) increase in direct proportion to how limited we *believe* the **supply** is. That's why someone with a low to moderate desire for something all of a sudden HAS TO HAVE IT if there's even a *hint* of a chance they *can't* have it.

It can be a limited supply of anything (not just a product) that triggers this increase in mental value (desire). Bragging rights of being first; being on the "VIP List"; exclusive clubs; love, praise, or **recognition** from others with stature; trying out and getting accepted onto a winning team; and many, many, many more!

In fact, those examples are MUCH more motivating for people than the common limited time offer or special discounted price!

Anyway, the point is, the deciding factor if someone will do business with you for the first time or not *all hinges on the <u>intensity</u> of their <u>desire</u>*.

Please read that sentence again. It's vital at this level 5 mental program.

Successfully addressing this 5th level mindset is all about cranking their desire up until they can't stand it anymore and mentally decide they gotta have it NOW!

But Be Warned:

Most people royally screw the pooch when it comes to cranking up desire intensity. They'll misuse the power of supply and demand (or introduce it at the wrong point in the process).

Want people to lust after you with the intensity of their first crush?

Then never, ever, ever dare to turn up the desire volume before they enter this respect-based *"You're An Authority"* stage of this process!

Otherwise it's worse than throwing a bucket of ice water on them just as they finally settle into their steaming hot tub. It's a complete shock to the system that's sure to piss 'em off! You MUST have enough credibility, trust, and respect banked up in their minds before they'll welcome a good game of *"tease me, please me."*

Even *with* enough banked authority, if supply & demand is misused to manipulate (instead of truly help) people, you'll eventually crash and burn no matter what!

Manipulation <u>always</u> bites you in the ass.

Although people might be tricked into doing business with you once (or maybe twice) before they see the truth, **they're a ticking time bomb.** Because besides disputing the charge with their credit card and smearing your reputation on google, twitter, facebook, etc., something MUCH *worse* happens:

They'll NEVER do business with you again!

You'll miss out the most profitable part of any business: The ongoing stream of *future* sales. Then it's just a matter of time before it all caves in on you. You can't outrun it for long because **it's impossible to build a business that depends on the first transaction for profitability.**

Even if you manage to squeeze a small profit in the beginning by manipulating, within about 90 days there'll be so much carnage in your wake, say bye-bye to profits (and hello to legal woes)!

Know the real tragedy here? It's *easier* to build a loyal following with tons of fans *eager* for the next time they can *gladly* give you money! If people knew the legacy of obscene cash-flow, goodwill, and wealth they're throwing away, they'd commit *Seppuku*.

(Seppuku is a Japanese ritual suicide in front of spectators, where they stab themselves in the abdomen with a short blade and proceed to disembowel themselves with multiple left to right motions, repenting for their sins and shame before dying. Lovely, eh?)

Look at all the effort it takes to reach the point where someone decides they know, like, trust, and respect you enough to risk doing business with you the first time. No matter what, you must *always* work your way through the first 5 of these mental conversations. It's the *only* path to that first money transaction.

There's simply no way around it. *Ever.*

So, even if you look at things from a purely selfish standpoint, why would you *ever* throw away all the "brain surgery" it took for them to finally know, like, trust, and respect you on the *smallest* transaction they'll *ever* do with you?

Because get this: Laws of Physics states a body in motion *stays* in motion; and a body at rest *stays* at rest. The transition between rest and motion (or drastically changing direction of a body already in motion) is the hard part. And, yet, maintaining and even *increasing* speed is a piece of cake

when motion is already present.

So if you honor your word and deliver a little unexpected "wow," you'll find the momentum of that first sale can carry you on it's back to so many future sales it will blow your mind! It'll do 99% of the remaining "work" *for* you if you harness, direct, and ride it all the way home.

You just keep the train from derailing.

How? Your 1% involvement now comes down to one simple thing: **Never betray their trust and respect.**

It's really *that* simple.

CHAPTER 9:
LEVEL 6 – The Influence Based, *"You're A Leader"* Mental Conversation

What's better than having people think of you as authority? **Having them trust and respect you as a great <u>LEADER</u>!**

After you consummate the first transaction you have to get it to <u>*stick*</u>.

Every sale is <u>*fragile*</u>! But none are as fragile as your <u>first</u>. The *instant* someone mentally decides to do business with you, your job switches from desire building to *fulfillment*.

And, by fulfillment I don't just mean delivery of your product or service. **You need to make sure <u>they</u> are fulfilled <u>personally</u>.** If you want a stream of future sales and tons of referrals, you've got to fulfill their expectations of value.

It's vital they come away from the first buying experience with you feeling so positive, they'll mentally pat themselves on the back for their wise decision.

How?

The same way we just discussed at the end of level 5. They will elevate you to great leader status if you _consistently_ refuse to ever do anything that betrays the trust and respect they have for you.

More "WOW!" And Less "YUCK!" With Expectations Management

Now, it's becomes all about how you create and manage their expectations.

See, if your audiences expects you to give them the proverbial, "goose that lays golden eggs," and, instead, you only give them 10 gold eggs, what happens? They feel tricked, get angry and are disappointed in you (even if you only charged them $100 for the 10 gold eggs worth $10,000.00)! On the other hand, if you promised 1 gold egg but give them 10 for the same $100 bucks, now **you wow 'em beyond their wildest expectations.**

Notice, either way they still wind up with the same 10 gold eggs at the same price. Nothing changes for _you_, but EVERYTHING changes for **them**!

One way confirms their worst fears and makes 'em feel like they just got doinked with their pants on. Unfulfilled expectations almost always feel like outright lies (no matter your intent). Even if they keep the eggs, they relive the perceived betrayal on a never-ending loop in their minds. Every time the mental recording plays they feel like a bigger and bigger sucker. Soon they hate you because the goose they expected, makes the 10 gold eggs look like a booger!

The other way, you become their hero. Surprise them with 10 x more than they expected, and what happens? They love you long time! That's what! Because a completely different mental recording plays under these conditions, right?

Each time they relive *that* buying experience in their mind they love you a bit more. Because each playback reinforces how smart, shrewd, and wise they were for discovering and doing business with you!

Plus, it creates a <u>mental debt of gratitude</u> that <u>obligates them to reciprocate to you with loyalty</u>!

Obvious, right?

Apparently *not*! Because too many people destroy their credibility (and kill all their success momentum) right here!

So, don't over promise and/or under deliver. Try to always daze and amaze your first time customers with 5-10 times the value they're *expecting*. This means you have to care more about the value THEY get, than what *you* get.

The extra love and respect *you give them*, they will come back to you 10 fold (or much more if you handle the two remaining levels of their mental conversations properly)! You can't out-give them because the more unexpected value you give, the bigger is the obligation to pay you back with loyalty, future sales, and referrals.

Build a legacy of integrity with your followers by living your word as if your life depends on it (because your business success *does*)!

Using Unpredictability To YOUR Advantage (Or It Uses YOU)

Life is unpredictable. So is business.

The point is, as awesome as your intentions are, mistakes are *inevitable*. You *will* screw up. Things *will* happen beyond your control. You *will* have to clean up other people's messes because otherwise it *will* affect your relationship with your followers if you don't. That's just the reality of the day in the life of a Profit Prophet!

Never run away from a sticky situation. You can spin every mistake, problem, and mishap into a major bonding opportunity. It allows you to demonstrate *with action* (not lip service) your love, respect, and caring for your tribe.

Leaders know <u>every sticky situation is a *gift*</u>. It carries the opportunity to increase the trust, respect, and influence far beyond what it ever was before!

How to turn the tables on sticky situations:

1. <u>***Acknowledge it***</u>. Don't harp on it. However, you *do* need to acknowledge it happened or else resentment builds and starts a brand new mental conversation about you.

   Amateurs mistakenly think if they ignore the situation it will go away faster (or that it's weak to admit the situation happened). And, yet, the reality is, it **DID** happen. You know it. They know it. Ignoring it makes you look, at *best*, out of touch and unfit to lead (and, at worst, you look like a manipulative asshole who tells bold face lies and doesn't give a shit about people depending on them).

   Yeah, I know, that's *not* the really the case, but the point is, those are the kind of stories people automatically make up about you if you don't give them another story to tell. In the immortal words of Mark Twain, *"A lie can travel halfway around the world while the truth is putting on its shoes."*

   All of us want to feel appreciated, valued, and a VIP. Your acknowledgement is vital because it makes them feel like they matter.

   It's how they validate their importance to you. It's a show of respect. How many people do you know who *like* being disrespected? It's the signal they need from you that lets them know you *really* do understand how the situation made them feel (and impacted 'em).

   Refusing to acknowledge compounds the problem because people don't consciously separate the situation from how they *feel* about it. It makes them *feel* you are intentionally making them wrong. But feelings are *never* wrong because what or <u>how we feel, **IS** how</u>

<u>we feel</u>.

Want a 100% guarantee that someone will dig their heals in, become irrational, and fight you with everything they got? Then "tell" 'em what they're feeling is wrong (and, by the way, that's exactly what you're telling 'em by *not* acknowledging the situation). This forces them to prove to themselves (and the world) that they're justified for feeling the way they do!

So really it's *not* the situation itself you're acknowledging, <u>it's their *feelings about* the situation</u>. Often times, acknowledgement is all it takes to remove the sting and *resolve the situation instantly*. Because if people feel heard without being made wrong for their feelings, there's nothing left for them to fight against.

2. ***Address it***. You don't necessarily have to apologize for it (although, I would, because that's the fastest way to help them dissolve any lingering negative feelings).

   Explain what created the sticky situation without defending or justifying it. Just give 'em the facts without your personal feelings about it (except any feelings and concerns you have about letting them down). Let them know the truth and set the record straight without getting caught up in the blame game.

   Be calm. Be like bamboo that bends in the wind instead of the oak that gets uprooted. Meet criticism with understanding. You don't have to agree with how they feel but you must allow them the freedom to feel as they do without making them wrong for it.

3. ***Right it***. If there's something you can do to make up for it, do it! And do it *swiftly*. If there's nothing you can do, show them the steps you have (or are or will) take to ensure it won't happen again.

   Accept responsibility, not blame. Blame is about pointing fingers but it doesn't solve anything because it fixates everyone on the problem. Responsibility is about how you respond and therefore focuses on the solution (our response to the problem not who's at fault for creating it in the first place).

   Remember, any kind of blame (even if you feel it's "your fault") is counterproductive because you can't see the solutions when your attention is on the problem. You can't run forward while you're looking behind!

Want to see an awesome case study of just how powerful these 3 simple steps can be? Check out this 4-part youtube.com video (https://youtu.be/fR5Z2wfEPf8). It's killer and demonstrates, from a master of Influence, (the late great Steve Jobs), how to turn a VERY sticky situation into BILLIONS!

I suggest you watch all 4 parts right now and model it (even if you aren't facing any sticky situations). Because with the understanding you now have from reading this far here, this press conference will be a goldmine for you!

Helping THEM Win THEIR Mental Tug Of War

When people replace a level 5 mental program with this one, the mental tug of war they *were* struggling with *begins* to dissolve.

Every positive experience you engineer that makes them feel fulfilled creates more value in their minds. Frequency of these experiences makes a bigger impact than their sizes.

Several seemingly tiny experiences in a row does more to wash out the nasty taste of their old experiences. One grand gesture *temporarily covers up* the nastiness but is *quickly* forgotten. Whereas, a *series* of small experiences that *slightly* exceeds expectations eventually *replaces* the bad taste of their negative memories.

See, at this stage not only do they desperately *want* **the relief that comes from powerful leadership, but also now they're** *starting to believe* **you're qualified to give it to them!**

When they *first enter* this mental conversation with themselves, their belief in you as a leader is weak. The past negative experiences are still winning their mental tug of war. If you want *them* to win, it's your job at this stage to weaken the old memories by giving them a *consistently consistent* stream of "wows!" to focus on.

No, "consistently consistent" isn't a typo.

Consistent repetition of positive experiences (i.e., mental conditioning) grows _their_ _belief_ in **your** leadership stronger and stronger.

Consistently consistent conditioning (that's a mouthful;-) takes the wire strands of trust, respect, and authority they credit you with and forms a steel cable of leadership strong enough to tow a super tanker through rough seas.

It's all that's needed to lay the foundation for the kind of unchallenged and unquestioned belief in you, your ideas, and your Profit Prophet guidance!

Creating & Molding Your Profit Prophet Influence

Level 6 is the first time you'll taste of <u>the power _automatic compliance_ holds</u>.

Once people start to trust and respect your leadership, with repeated conditioning (and no betrayals _without_ the applying the rules for spinning sticky situations we just discussed), you lay the foundation for a fan-type relationship to develop. At this stage, your followers are starting to _look_ to you for solid guidance because they trust your leadership.

When they replace a level 5 mental program with this one, the mental tug of war they _were_ struggling with begins to dissolve.

With every positively managed (and fulfilling) experience you lead them through (no matter how small), their negative memories of the things that didn't turn out the way they wanted, looses more and more of its mental pulling power.

At this stage, not only do they desperately <u>_want_</u> **the relief that comes from powerful leadership, but also <u>now they're _starting to believe_ you're qualified to give it to them</u>!**

When they first enter this mental conversation with themselves, their belief in you as a leader is weak. But all it takes is constant repetition of positive experiences (i.e., mental conditioning) to grow _their_ _belief_ in your leadership stronger and stronger.

See, as we've covered several times, a belief is just a thought we think over and over again, until we *believe* it to be true. Remember, a passing thought becomes a habitual pattern of thought by simply thinking it again and again. And, when you reinforce that habitual thought by thinking it enough times, it forms into a belief. Beliefs become core beliefs the exact same way.

That's the way ALL core beliefs are formed!

Yours, mine, and everyone's!

This *is* the mental "voodoo" that creates the kind of automatic compliance where people *immediately* believe everything you say is the gospel truth. Because when something (or someone) aligns with our core beliefs, we don't question or challenge it, **we simply comply with it because we "know" it to be true.**

If we *believe* something to be true, then it **IS**. If we *believe* something to be a lie, then it **IS**. That's why the *same thing* is a rock-solid "fact" to one person and demonic to another. Both are "true" only because the person thinking them believe they are!

The thing to recognize is, the *process by which EVERYONE forms their core beliefs is ENTIRELY based on mental conditioning*. And, the conditioning almost never takes place *consciously*! We know we believe the "truths" we do, but almost nobody knows *why* (or *how*).

Familiarity based on repetition. That's how!

Careful Or You'll Unknowingly Cook Your Own Goose!

It's all too common for people to really screw themselves over at this stage by changing the tone, direction, and transparency of the "voice" that created the bonded relationship with their audience.

See, not only do you have to stay consistent with your messages, but also the *context* (the Profit Prophet's "voice") by which you communicate can't change.

You've created a persona in your audiences' minds. That's how they've come to know and trust you. If you all of sudden show up or sound completely different than what they're use to, they will start to assume you are trying to manipulate them (even if it's unintentional).

If they are going to trust your leadership, they need you to look, sound, taste, smell, and feel the same consistent "come-from" that they've come to know. They have a mental picture of who they've decided you are. You must continue to talk to them in that voice, as the same person they "know" you to be. So, Managing expectations extends to your voice as well as the consistency of your message.

Ongoing reinforcement of both gives you the first taste of the power *automatic compliance* holds. Careful, it's <u>addictive</u> (for you <u>and</u> *them*;-)

You've found the doorway to the 7th level mental conversations (the luxury penthouse of influence): Where people show you the kind of loyalty, awe, and reverence that makes them *want* to take a bullet for you!

Rock Stars Only Hang With Other Rock Stars!

As they start to mentally elevate you to rock star status, they also start to reinforce just how special and cool it is to be a member of your Profit Prophet entourage.

The higher they mentally regard you, the more exclusive, elite, and treasured their VIP status is to them. They talk themselves into valuing the association with you personally more and more (why do you think celebrities are paid a fortune for their endorsements or to even just appear without saying a word?).

And, as soon as they place a high value on being a part of your inner circle, they also don't want to be kicked out. There's an unspoken (and often completely unconscious) feeling that now starts to control their mindset here, *"I don't want to lose my VIP status. I like being on 'the list.' I need to stay in good standing."*

See, NOW they <u>*know*</u> how special you *really* are because they've *experienced* it first hand.

Now they _know_ how exclusive your club is.

Now they _know_ you don't hang out with just anyone.

Now they _know_ how important your time is.

They "_know_" all this only because of the mental journey you've led them through.

Keep this knowing rolling and you eventually graduate to the highest mental "My God & Savior" level of...

CHAPTER 10:
LEVEL 7 – The Influence Based, *"You're My Advisor"* Mental Conversation

You're a rock star!

You've worked so hard to get here so don't pull a Charlie Sheen! Don't forget where you came from.

Treat your audience with the same love and reverence they hold for you, and they will continue to deepen the Messiah-like feelings they have for you. So long as you don't abuse the influence you now wield, you will know what Oprah feels like because your word is gold in their mind.

Now you have that special, coveted spot of honor inside their heart, mind, and some might even say, soul. **This new mindset they hold for you is what creates automatic compliance without questioning or conscious thought.**

Because YOU say it, it "has" to be true because that's the new mental story they now believe to be true about you. Just like the *"You're An Asshole"* mindset triggers them to want to instantly run away based on instinct, the *"You're My Advisor"* conversation triggers instant, unquestioned knowing that what you say goes. They truly believe that you know what's best for them better than anyone else. You've reached the Profit Prophet zone where they have so much admiration, respect, and trust for you, that they will actually second guess and doubt themselves until you validate them.

Sound extreme? It *is*! That's why...

With Great Power, Comes Great Responsibility

Just like Oprah takes great care to protect her *brand*, you must make sure you don't abuse or take your new place of influence for granted. Like all power, it can be used to help *or* hurt people. And, *this is too powerful to misuse.*

I hope you'll treat this with the utmost respect and **NEVER manipulate people into a decision that isn't in their best interest!**

The only reason to love people through the 6 previous mental programs is because you *know* in your heart-of-hearts that your influence will help them breakthrough the limitations caused by those old mental programs. That before they met you, they were stuck and because of the level of faith they've given you, you're truly leading them to live a much bigger future.

A fulfilling and better life of freedom for deciding to join your pack.

Protect your tribe as if they're your newborn babies. It's your job to keep them safe, help them grow and *empower them to live an even better life than you have!* You want them to live the dream. Achieve *more* and greater levels of success than you have. You want more for them than you do for yourself.

Truly.

All of us crave love. We want to feel important and valued. We feel under-appreciated.

By always putting your tribe first (make it 100% about _their_ wants, _their_ interests, _their_ desires, _their_ needs, _their_ success, _their_ life, etc.), you give them the greatest gift anyone has EVER given them.

If you've been beat down, feel forced to live a life of quiet desperation, and don't feel valued (like you, your opinions or life doesn't matter), you'll take a bullet for the Profit Prophet who relieves your suffering! Because, let's face it, who ever feels they have too much love, inspiration and empowerment in their lives? Who says _"stop making me feel powerful; stop appreciating my contributions and value"_?

No one! That's who!

I've never met a soul who feels appreciated _enough_; who feels valued _enough_; who feels validated _enough_; who feels good _enough_; who feels recognized _enough_.

And know what? I bet you don't know anyone 100% fulfilled on those deep levels either!

It's <u>insatiable</u>.

Be the one who ALWAYS makes them feel _that_ good (not as some calculated manipulative technique, but as your genuine sense of duty) and they'll reward you with undying loyalty!

The secret to success is growing with your tribe _because_ they grow! You help them succeed. From their success, they give back to you because:

All of <u>your</u> success lives in <u>their</u> FUTURE!

The better job you do making their future bigger than it was ever going to be without your empowerment, and the more influence they'll gladly give you!

Plus, you'll sleep soundly because there's no better feeling than getting what you want by "out-giving" your pack the "love" they want!

Remember, it's all about helping the people you serve to assimilate your vision to improve THEIR life. What you get is only a byproduct of the process you've led them through. It's what you conditioned them to expect from you.

Get it? Got it. Good! ;-)

Welcome To The Inner Sanctum

When someone enters into this ultimate level 7 mindset about you, you're welcoming him or her into your inner circle.

And, <u>THEY'RE</u> welcoming you into <u>THEIRS</u>!

Don't forget it's a two way street. They've earned the place in your heart and you've got a place in theirs. And we protect our hearts with everything we've got because no one wants to be hurt, right?

Now, they feel a very close, deep and *personal* connection with you. They've *experienced* the positive results from your guidance, mentoring and leadership that got them here. They know your council works wonders because they've lived it several times by the time they elevate you to this mental position.

The relationship has grown to the point where they join your personal mission. It's no longer about buying a product or service. It's no longer about should they trust you or not. It's no longer about do they believe and respect you.

<u>Now it becomes about *their* commitment to *your* vision</u>. They like what you stand for so much that they want to support you to achieve it; **they want to be a part of your "movement" and mission that you're taking to the world.**

You give their lives *meaning*!

It's HUGE for them because now they're a part of a cause. They belong to something that takes them out of the quiet desperation we feel when we don't have anything bigger than ourselves to believe in (and be a part of)!

Think about that for a second. Let it *really* seep into your consciousness.

That's the transformation that builds the most powerful and loyal volunteer army you can imagine. They go from "customer," "client," or "student" to mentally deputizing themselves. It becomes their _duty_ to follow orders and fight to the death to protect the mission at all costs!

It's _personal_ now!

They've found a place to call home. It becomes a lifestyle that fills them with pride, acceptance and even love. They hope to prove themselves worthy of being a top Lieutenant and dream of the day you publicly recognize and praise them for their contribution, help, and support.

Sound far-fetched? It's _not_, I assure you!

> *"I have made the most wonderful discovery, I have discovered men will risk their lives, even die, for ribbons!"*
>
> ~ Napoleon Bonaparte

When you get to this level, your followers will take it personally if anyone outside of the inner sanctum says anything negative about you, your ideas or your work in the world. It's the birth of that special kind of rock star admiration for you where you can do no wrong.

It's where Oprah's power comes from.

It's why and how buying Apple products has become a battle of "good" verses "evil" to their believers. Want to have a little fun sometime? Sit down with an Apple zealot and question a product or Jobs' thinking on something and watch the fireworks ensue!

Remember that 4-part YouTube video I shared with you in the last chapter? You know, the press conference where Steve Jobs handled a potential shit-storm of negative publicity and spun it into a huge opportunity?

I suggest you watch at least the first 2 minutes and 25 seconds again right now, because you'll see some brilliant influence voodoo in action (https://youtu.be/fR5Z2wfEPf8).

How'd he kickoff this supposed "antenna-gate" cover-up press conference? With a very funny music video that a fan of Apple wrote, produced, sang and posted on YouTube, right?

The guy who did it *wasn't* hired, paid or even asked to do it. It was his <u>duty</u>.

And, what did Steve do by opening his press conference with it? He set the tone, publicly recognized the guy who rushed to Apple's defense AND **he signaled to all the other Apple zealots to step their game up another level if they want that kind of praise, right?**

Brilliance in motion!

See, this final mental program takes people way beyond products, services, and solutions into a higher calling. Are you familiar with Maslow's hierarchy of needs?

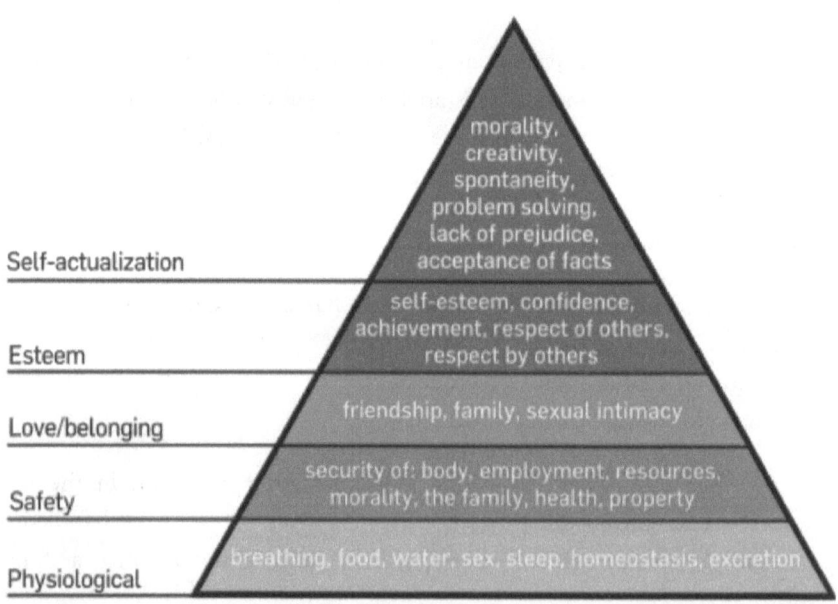

You know, how our lowest level needs must be met first? And to the degree they're satisfied new needs and motivations emerge? With the ultimate driving force being self-fulfillment, where it's human nature to strive for more and to be the best we can be?

Can you see how this seventh level mental program of influence actually carries with it the power to feed our connection, ego, AND self-actualization needs?

Do you see why this mental conversation is actually something people WANT to have with themselves because it feeds their deepest core needs?

Are starting to see why the trusted advisor position is so damn powerful and influential?

CHAPTER 11: Confessions Of <u>This</u> Profit Prophet

It's confession time.

As you probably already figured out, this book is a key part of moving you through my personal conditioning process, isn't it? It's your full access, back-stage pass to see this process in action. I suggest you *really* study and model what I'm doing here so you can adopt, adapt, and apply it to your business.

Specifically, now that you know the exact 7 levels of this process, how much of what you just learned do you see at work here?

How many things can you spot throughout this *entire* resource (The Profit Prophet) that fits? How has it been strategically designed? How have I been *practicing* the very things I've been preaching?

Doesn't it start at ground zero? Assumes nothing about your past knowledge of me, my work and/or previous track record, right?

Why did I painstakingly break down your consumption of this body of work into 3 different books? Why, for that matter, did I create a "mini-book" as the introduction to the main event? And, why did I position that intro as *"Curing Success Blindness"*? Can you see how I addressed *all* of the first five of those mental conversations up front *before* digging into the "meat" you came for?

Even though, technically, since you're reading this, you're already a first time customer, why do you think I started with the very first mental conversation anyway? Why not *start* with a level 5 or a level 6 conversation since you already made your initial decision to buy this book?

Why indeed?

The answer is simple: Because I didn't want to leave anything to chance in our relationship building process. See, I assume the first time anyone buys one of my books it's only because of the trust, credibility, and respect they feel for *Amazon.com*, *Barnes & Nobel*, or whichever trusted outlet you purchased it from.

However, it says *nothing* about how they feel, think, or believe to be true about *me* personally, right?

See, if I want to build a loyal following of fans… Who LOVE what I stand for… Who will consume everything I produce… Who want to belong to a tribe on a worthwhile mission (because of the sense of meaning they get from joining the Profit Prophet vision)… If those are my *real* reasons for writing this book, then I had to figure out a way to transfer those feelings of trust, respect, and authority felt for Amazon to *me* personally.

Maybe this is the first time we've ever "met."

Or maybe you've gotten so much value from my other books, products and services (which are all full of the same conditioning process, btw) that *this* book isn't the beginning of our relationship. Maybe you've already elevated me to a level 6 conversation. Or maybe, just maybe, you're *already* a lifetime fan.

However, since I have no way of knowing for sure *which* mental conversation you happen to be having about me, the only safe bet is to *assume* we're strangers meeting for the very first time. That's why I started at the very beginning and did everything in my power to address the "You're An Asshole" program that you may be running.

It's the only way I can make sure that everyone gets exposed to the proper relationship building process. The first few sections of the introduction quickly transitions people into the *"You're Like Me"* mental conversation that's necessary for people to get value from the rest of everything in my audience ascension process that follows.

Then, we can systematically transition through the first 5 levels together because that's the only way to be sure I'm doing everything in my power to meet you in the mental conversations you're already having.

It's the absolute best shot I have of getting to know you. It's how we move from an accidental friendship to a deliberate ongoing relationship. It's how you come to know right down to the core of your very being, of the admiration I hold for you because by daring to reach for a bigger life, you're helping reinforce the entrepreneurial spirit in us all... It's how our mutual respect shines through strong enough to build bigger futures for both us!

(Because remember, all *my* success lives in the bigger future I'm helping you create through the breakthroughs and value provided here. Just like all YOUR success lives in the bigger future you'll lead your pack to have.)

Now, realize this: Because you are reading these words which I've strategically hidden in the middle of the book, I know the lowest level of influence and relationship we've established with each other is at a level 5 mental conversation (or higher)! Because otherwise there's no way you would've invested so much of your life to make it this deep into the content, right?

Think about it for a second.

I mean, the stats clearly show that 90+% of non-fiction book buyers never make it past the first chapter. That means only 1 in every 10 gets here (which, by the way, is exactly why I have *other* supporting systems that guides my tribe to ascend up the ladder).

Anyway, it's a safe bet that because you've read this far, you've reaped value. If not, you would have stopped reading LONG ago.

Here's a key point: All my resources are carefully designed to provide incredible value, BUT ONLY TO THE AUDIENCE I CAN BEST SERVE. And, everything strategically produced to give my pack the full Joshua Experience, value and culture. In fact, *"The Profit Prophet"* book is a living, breathing model of the conditioning that automatically (and systematically) walks people solidly into the respect-based *"You're An Authority"* mental conversation.

You may have even decided to move into the influence-based *"You're A Leader"* or possibly even the *"You're MY Advisor"* mental programs (but only *you* know that for sure).

Can you see how this is a bigger vision and mission for people to become involved in? Haven't you gotten to know me in the process of learning all about this influence? Maybe we've grown even "closer" because my transparent confessions in this chapter (you picked up on that, right?) ;-)

Doesn't all that position this in your mind as much more than just a *book*? You ARE a part of a bigger movement, aren't you? You see *more* possibilities than before you started, don't you? That's because you're hooked into a bigger vision than before we started. And that anticipation is inspiring, isn't it?

Before we put a bow on this chapter, you should know that it took me over a week just to get clear on what needed to be conditioned for maximum results and success for you. It took another 5 weeks of full time writing to figure out how best to clearly communicate my Profit Prophet vision in a way that helps people overcome the first 4 mental conversations so knee-jerk reactions won't rob them of the value waiting.

All said and told, it took me well over 360 hours of intense focus to think through, plan and institute the process that *introduces* you to The Profit Prophet (and that was *before* I added the 3 books that make up this full resource).

So, if you're serious about living a rock star life, I suggest you drink in the introduction like it's the fountain of youth! Really study it. Grab a pad of paper and make notes (here's a few questions to guide you towards gold nuggets to look for):

1. What do you see now that you missed before?

2. What were you blind to that you had no idea was *strategically* built in to it?

3. At what point did you find yourself feeling or thinking, *"hey this guy really knows me?"*

4. Why am I spending so much time building value in reading the introduction many different times?

5. How many different mental conversations can you hear me speaking to? Which conversation(s) did I address, when?

6. How, specifically, did I help people drain their fear so they can easily transition into the next mental program in their hierarchy?

7. How did I gently nudge a new awareness without being too "in your face," too soon?

8. Can you see how it meets people where they are and how it *gradually* widens the scope of so much more being possible?

9. How did I set up an environment of future leadership and trusted advisor relationship status where consuming each book triggers the desire to consume more value from me?

10. How does it culture, condition, and reframe the new mindsets necessary to take a first time customer and systematically transform them into a lifetime fan?

11. How long did it take for you to transition from a level 1 mindset into a level 4 one? Did the speed by which you progress through the mental process surprise you?

12. How many examples of expectations management and value building can you find?

13. How much of my personal time does this process take from me now that I designed it and put it in place? Yes, I know it's a silly question, but so many people miss the kind of leverage that comes from having an automatic, systematized audience ascension process. Make sure you note the power it gives. The process does all the work FOR me; it works 24 hours a day, 7 days a week; never takes a day off; and it is _incapable_ of every giving less than 100% full on effort! Talk about power, right?

Seriously you should really digest the entire positioning and thought process behind the strategy that built this series. Also, notice how I didn't leave the conclusions you'll draw to chance (why do you think I primed your mind with those 13 questions above)?

Study it.

How many "real life" applications of these breakthroughs can you spot? It's probably the single best conditioning system I've ever designed for any client or myself. You'll start to see the true power behind what my business strategy is. Because the truth is, beyond creating value in each book, I'm doing something MUCH bigger and more powerful.

Can you see how *The Profit Prophet* is a MISSION for me? Can you see how it stands for something? It's WAY more than just about selling a few books for me, isn't it?

It's about creating my own Oprah Effect, yes?

It's about making a *real* difference.

About truly helping people find the success that's been eluding them (and making a permanent breakthrough without backsliding into self-sabotage).

It's about taking a stand for others. It's about leaving a legacy. It's about giving people an outlet to be a part of that legacy.

And, of course, every part of my business process reinforces that vision and conditions an even deeper relationship with you because each delivers ever increasing value to you.

Yet it's a chance to reach new first time readers AND encourage them to ascend up the value ladder at their own pace. It builds a community of momentum far greater than any standalone book that isn't strategically designed to guide people to very specific outcomes!

It even goes beyond other typical book series, doesn't it? I don't know of many authors (except for maybe J.K. Rowling with her Harry Potter series) where the author gives serious strategic planning to the business side of publishing, like this (or takes such great care to focus on *consumption* like this so each reader reaps the maximum value in minimum time).

It stands out clear as day as being completely different, right?

Can you see how some strategic planning in the beginning makes it easy to eat any so-called competition for lunch?

See how it's easy to stand head and shoulders above the crowds if you take time and think through how the 7 mental conversations will play out with the tribe you lead (or are planning to lead)?

How can you model my Profit Prophet strategy and adapt it for your business process? Remember, it's not about copying my words or exact process.

You <u>don't</u> want to be me.

You want to be YOU.

It's about understanding the strategy behind what, how, and why I've built what I have. If you can see the underlying principles, you can build your own Profit Prophet culturing model.

Even if, no scratch that: ESPECIALLY if selling books isn't a part of your business process at all.

See, my biggest business breakthroughs have come from looking at completely different business models and figuring out how to adapt and adopt their success for my needs.

Just like my business has nothing to do with computers, mobile phones, or the music business like Apple, they've still inspired me and shown me ideas to apply to my vision and mission. Yet, I'm building my own culture, not Apple's.

I *can't* be Oprah or Steve Jobs **(nor do I want to be).** And, you know what? They can't be *me*!

You have unique gifts, skills and abilities that can't come from anyone else except from you. We all do.

I CAN follow their *example* as a teaching model to focus me on how to create a similar loyalty for my business model!

Same goes for *you* and *your* business.

THE "HOW-TO's" OF YOUR AUDIENCE ASCENSION PROCESS

The next 2 chapters sparked a debate with myself.

You see, I was on the fence. Include them here? Or save them for BOOK THREE? That's because they're vital parts of *both* subjects. They're key to *implementing* your Audience Attraction & Ascension strategies AND also *critical* to your Business Model Preeminence.

Ultimately, I decided to include them here because both of the following chapters are about the "how-to's" of pack leadership, in the trenches. However, you'll definitely want to refer back here as you implement Business Preeminence plan.

Cool? Great! Then, here we go…

CHAPTER 12:
Your Magnetic Factor

This is called the magnetic factor because it draws people to your Profit Prophet communications and relationship-building marketing systems.

Now, there are *two* levels to attracting your audience: First, you've got to **get their <u>attention</u>.** You've got to give 'em a reason to stop long enough to listen to you for a few seconds in the midst of everything else competing for their attention.

Secondly, once you have their attention, now you have to communicate the value you have for them... and do it in such a way, that it becomes *their* idea to want to know more about your offer.

So it's two levels of Profit Prophet Attraction.

It's got to be *their* idea to join your parade. It's NOT about convincing, justifying, or talking them into anything. Everyone HATES being strong-armed. But they love to buy when it's their idea!

After you get attention, if you give a prospect something they want, they'll naturally trust you more and want to explore more ideas you have to share with them. That's the secret of turning the tables where it becomes THEIR idea: Value first!

It all comes down to **knowing your tribe. Being able to <u>speak your audience's language</u> to get their attention long enough to present them your irresistible offer.** This requires crafting a powerful offer that's so attractive… and… **communicating it in <u>the way THEY'RE most comfortable with</u>…** so they *want* to listen. And, after they're listening, it compels them to drop everything else to get more of you and/or your solution(s).

Picture your typical pack-member in their normal life. What does their daily routine look like? Now, think about *your* life. Aren't we all busy? Running around. Going here, there, and everywhere? There are millions of things always biding for your attention, right?

Well, you can't attract your audience and get them to ascend your value ladder if they tune you out, can you? Your communication methods MUST cut through their distractions long enough so you have a chance to help them see the benefits to spending a little time with you.

This means you need a *compelling* **offer** (in other words, what they'll get in return for giving you some of their precious attention AND for raising their hands to join your prospect and/or buyer's lists).

Here are some great magnetic offer structures and ideas (these are proven, profitable magnetic tools based on *measured* results):

- Insider Information
- Premiums (fast response extras)
- Association/exclusivity
- Connection
- Coupons
- How-to course
- Unique product
- Free Subscription

- Football phone
- Magic charm
- Stuffed animal
- Ancient Chinese Diet Secret
- Newsletter
- Unique info/ideas
- Critiques
- Phone Consultation
- Online Workshops (Webinars)
- Google Hangouts
- TeleSeminars
- Seminar
- Audio tape
- Video tape
- Swimsuit edition
- 30 days free
- Sweepstakes
- Product & Bonuses
- Price & Terms
- Guarantee & Risk-Reversal
- FREE Sample (Membership sites)
- FREE Trial ("Good faith deposit")
- Credit 1st purchase against future purchases (sets up the back-end sale and starts the upsell process from the first step)
- Offer complete product line, catalog, etc.
- Offer support with main product (fax-in, call-in consulting, critiques, etc.)
- Buy 1 – Get 1 Free
- Buy the deluxe version get some great benefit that they gotta have, but can't get any other way other than buying the deluxe.

Key Question: "How can I spice this up and make it so irresistible they'd be crazy to turn it down?"

Your OFFER is how you get your audience to take action. It differentiates you from your competition. Turns mild interest into burning desire. Guides them to the solutions that makes their pain stop. Asks for immediately action when their emotions peaks so they *don't* delay solving their problems.

Great offers (regardless if "free" to generate qualified leads or paid to generate profits) often use the "pile-on effect" to stack value on top of value… until your target audience <u>feels an *urgency* to take the action required or *risk missing out*</u>.

When you speak directly to a member of your pack, in their language, stoke their tribal desires by piling on value, they won't be able to rest until they've taken the required action to satisfy that deep seeded triggered want. **It almost hurts inside if they miss out on your offer.**

Get the idea?

There's no limit to what an offer can consist of. Over the next week just pay attention to the different advertisements you see online, look at the ads in Google, click on all the ads in your Facebook newsfeed, watch a few direct response TV commercials and infomercials, listen to different radio offers, read USA Today, The Star, and The National Enquirer and you'll get more compelling offer ideas than you can handle.

But let's dive deeper into a few of the more powerful ideas from the list I just gave you. This'll give you a better idea of what to look for and how to adapt them for your purposes…

Insider information -- The promise of some specialized bit of info that can't be found anywhere else. It's only available from you. This has tremendous magnetic pulling power.

Premiums -- Premiums are giveaways. If you've ever gotten a pen in the mail, that has your name on it already, that's a premium. They're giving it away. The, *"if you buy this, you get this for free,"* is also a premium.

Association/Exclusivity – People want to *belong*. To be on the inside (and how to stop being an outsider, forced to look in on the *"chosen-ones"*). It's the promise of being an *insider*. Run with the "big dogs" pack. Joining a winning team who has your back (it's why people pledge fraternities and sororities). To be a part of *special, elite* group, where only a *select* group gets to play (like a private invitation for lunch with Warren Buffet).

Connection -- We've already covered this in depth in almost all of the previous chapters. However, because it's *so* important, I'm listing here again to make sure you don't leave it out. This can be one of the most attractive force you can tap. Give people the opportunity to be a part of something bigger than just themselves. They desperately want a cause to fight for. A feeling that they matter. That they're important, worthy and making a difference.

Coupons are self-explanatory, yes? Simple, yet VERY compelling to incite deadline driven actions.

A How To Course -- So many ways to use "how to" courses/classes. Give away a special, specifically targeted free email training series. Free & Paid email coaching courses, videos, audio podcasts, etc. Some specific useful "how to" training on a key area your audience desperately wants. **People are starving for solutions that cut through the B.S. and fluff. Somebody that knows what they're doing, that has a track record, that delivers the straight scoop, from the real world... will always clean up online (and off, too)!**

Something so unique that they can't find it anywhere else. **Like the information in this book: You can't get my experiences, prospective, training, anywhere else. It's unique. I have no competition because I created it.** Yeah, there are millions of books on business and personal success, but nobody does it The Profit Prophet way because no one has lived my life, but me! ;-)

And the same thing applies if your offer is for a "hard" or "soft" product. Soft products are things like eBooks, games, apps, software, email, youtube videos, membership websites, blogs, facebook, twitter, LinkedIn, any "digital" products, info products (webinars, workshops, teleseminars, newsletters, home study courses, etc.) and so many more fits into the "soft" category.

"Hard" products are tangible products like vacuums, diet pills, skin-care, solar equipment, acne treatments, vitamins, fruit of the month clubs, coffee makers, houses, hamburgers, hiking equipment, etc.

But here's something most people miss: **You can use soft products to sell hard products.**

Say you're selling bowling balls, to choose an obscure example. A bowling ball is basically a bowling ball, right? I mean, there's nothing *too* different or unique from one bowling ball to the next. And every store that sells 'em probably sells the exact same ones, right? They're basically a commodity, right? So why would someone buy a bowling ball from your store instead of another?

How do you differentiate yourself? How do you create that Magnetic Factor? How do you get people to buy *your* bowling balls (instead of any of the countless other options available to them)?

Well, you can differentiate yourself by giving people something they can't get anywhere else. Something extra, like *information* (a soft product). How different and unique (not to mention irresistibly attractive) would your offer be if everyone of your bowling balls also came with a special report (or training DVD) like: *"The 10 Deadly Sins That Most Beginning Bowlers Never Overcome."* Or something like that?

Now you just combined a "soft" aspect to the commodity and it became completely unique! Now there's a very compelling reason to buy a bowling ball from you instead of your competition.

Making sense?

A Free Subscription -- A free subscription to a blog, podcast, newsletter, or some sort of episodic series that offers solutions to problems your prospects have (more on this in a bit).

Selling the Bonus -- Borrowing from Sports Illustrated: They spend the *whole* ad <u>**selling**</u> the Free football phone and/or the Free swimsuit edition. That's a premium or bonus offer, right? The whole commercial is dedicated to selling the football phone, isn't it? And, oh, by the way, how do you get the "free" football phone? Subscribe to Sports Illustrated. It's real simple. You can do the same thing with your business model.

Here's some bonuses you can build your offer around (like the football phone): A special mug, a "magic charm" of some sort (maybe there's a good story about it having some *special mystical powers* that were revealed by the Dali's in India… or its healing agents were buried deep in the *secrets of the lost scrolls*).

Follow? It's all about the *story*. The *mystique*. The *intrigue* attached to some *new breakthrough discovery*. The journey you had struggle through to find the solution. The adventure. The "fool" mistake you stumbled upon. How about the "Ancient Chinese (beauty, diet, youth) Secret" – that's an oldie, but goodie. People love stories. We buy the story first, *then* the product/service.

Critiques are powerful soft products add-ons. Revisiting our bowling ball example: What if you offered a free critique with every purchase? Maybe you could show them a special technique or coach them on their present technique if they come into your shop to buy the bowling ball?

Now you've just "plussed" the offer and gave them another reason to buy from you, as opposed to anywhere else. Plus, that free critique (when used properly) will automatically upsell to private lessons!

Online Workshops, Webinars & Tele-seminars – People love the convenience. Instead of having to go to an hotel seminar we can stay home, in our underwear, and get the same (or even MORE) value and training without travel hassles.

You can use Tele-Seminars to deliver your sales presentation. Or it can also be straight content and value that delivers info to end-user. Or a combo of both. You can do all sorts of things with that. You can record it and offer it to everybody that just for attending the event. Or only if they purchase. Or whatever the next step up in your value ladder is. See where I'm going?

Again, this is just designed to jumpstart your brain. The offshoots and possibilities are endless (plus, more get innovated daily).

Anyway, **your offer is the compelling reason WHY** someone stops long enough to explore your solutions and either signs up as a qualified lead in your prospect database or makes the first buying decision and add themselves to your in-house customer list.

Different Offer Structures:

The base product plus "pile-ons." — This is where you keep piling on the "stuff" so it becomes crazy if you *don't* buy.

You know TV infomercials and commercials were the announcer asks suddenly, *"How much do you think you would have to pay for this?"* And then they interrupt themselves again and say, *"Wait, don't answer yet... because you also get, this, this, and that... Now, how much would pay?"* And then they do the same thing with the price drops after they add so much value and make you anticipate a huge price tag; like, *"you'd probably expect to have to pay $700 for all this, but today only, you won't have to pay $700; you won't even pay $600; not $500, $400, or even $300! If you order right now, it's only 3 easy payments of only $49.95!"*

By the time they get done piling on all the extras and do the price drops, **you almost HAVE to buy** if it solves a headache you have.

Some offers let you keep the bonuses even if you return the product. Sometimes *everything* must be returned. It just depends on the structure you set up. You can get as creative as you want with your offers because you make the rules for *your* business model. It's YOUR game.

(Personally, I like to set my offers up so my audience *always* wins. That way, even if they decide to return it, they come out ahead for at least giving it/me a try. It leaves the door open for future business.)

Pricing and payment terms are other parts of your offer structure that will influence your peeps to take advantage of it or not. Can you can offer something on a free trial basis? Let them try it before they buy it. You know, the "puppy dog close" (where you let them take the puppy home, let their kids fall in love with her, and then *can't* give it up).

You can structure your offer where you send them the product now and bill them in 30 days.

"If you don't like it send it back to me before that and I won't bill you. If you do like it, keep it, and I'll bill you in 5 easy payments."

Or, *"three easy payments, five easy payments,"* or whatever can all change how successful your offer is...

Because often people really *want* your offer but they can't afford it in one chunk. So if you offer to bill them in smaller monthly installments, it lets them start enjoying your solutions right away. And sometimes that's the only thing holding them back from doing business with you.

Risk Reversal:

Risk Reversal is another key aspect of your irresistible offers.

Look, you already know about money back guarantees, right? Risk reversal, however, goes way beyond. You've got to recognize the way your customer views the first transaction they make with you. Doing business with someone you've never done business with before is always thought of **as being risky.**

Therefore, to the degree that you figure out how to structure your offers to **take 100% of the risk on your back,** your offer will be much more successful. The better the job you do here, the more business you will get for the exact same effort and expense.

So, some examples of risk reversal, versus a simple guarantee are:

"If you don't make at least 10 times your money back, I'll double your money back." There are people who have used that very effectively. Now, I can almost hear what you are thinking.... *"Who would do that? I'd go broke!"*

Well, actually, often times you end up making much more with these types of bold offer structures! Yes, your returns will go up, but generally, your sales double or triple so your overall profitability shoots straight through the roof. Of course, you have to test the offer, track the results, and calculate the differences, but usually you can tweak these offers into major lucrative homeruns even with the extra returns!

Yes, some people will take advantage of you on an offer like this, but who cares if you wind up making double or triple the profit you would have made for the exact time, energy and expense without it?

Remember, it's all about the *math*: How much more do you get to put (and *keep*) in your pocket as a result?

Look at some simple example numbers. Say, your old standard offer does $1,000 in sales, with a 5% return rate ($50 in returns). So it's netting you $950, right?

Now let's say you try a bold risk reversal of offering double your money back. And let's assume it doubles your returns and triples your sales. Look at the math: So your returns are now 10%, however, with the new offer you generate $3,000 in sales (instead of only $1K).

The 10% refund rate is $300 in returns plus another $300 for the double your money back portion of the offer. So that's $600 against $3,000 in sales. Or $2,400 in your pocket!

Do you see how this makes your net 2.53 times bigger? Here's a tough question: For exact same time, effort and expense which would you rather make, $950 (with 5% refunds) or $2,400 (with the double your money back and 10% refunds)?

Take your time with that one...

So just sit down with a calculator and work it out. If the math works, ramp that sucker up as strong as you can! As fast as you can!

Another form of risk reversal is an unconditional, no questions asked money back guarantee for, say, 90 days; and then you PLUS your guarantee with a second guarantee that might be conditional upon them doing something with the product; like, *"Plus on top of that, I'm going to give you another guarantee that I'll double your money back if you can just show me one technique that you've used from this, and you haven't made at least 10 times your money"* (or whatever your offer is) I will give you all your money back... plus an extra $1,000 for your efforts (or whatever).

Get the idea how it works?

You can always stack guarantees on top of one another to enhance your offer and remove the risk of the transaction from your prospect's shoulders at the same time.

Here's a term you will want to become familiar with. It's called *"Till Forbid."* Till Forbid was pioneered by the book and record clubs. It's where you buy in on some low/no cost deal (like 8 records for a penny… I know, I'm dating myself with that reference ;-)) and then they send you other products monthly, and it's up to you to say "stop." Until you *forbid* it, they keep sending you product(s) and bill you.

This is a very powerful concept that actually has a lot of value to the customer (if used correctly and *not* abused) because it keeps them connected with a continuous stream of what they want more of.

At this point you should just know what the different possibilities are so you can start to think about all the ways you can "spice up" your offers because if you start it right from the beginning you'll find that it goes a long way towards creating Profit Prophet business preeminence (which we cover in depth in the third book here).

So start asking yourself: *How can I spice this up? How can I pile it on? How can I make it so irresistible, so risk free that people would be crazy not to do it?*

The point is that creating sales becomes very easy with an irresistible offer, right?

Check it: A friend lets you in on a little known secret restaurant. It's got great ambiance. Not to mention the best dry-aged New York Strip steak you'll ever put in your mouth! Oh, and the seafood, never frozen, is flown in fresh 3 times a day. This restaurant even sends a limo to your door and picks you up (at no extra charge) because they have the single largest collection of fine wine, vodkas and tequilas (and they want to make sure everyone drinks as much as they want without safety worries).

Now, as you wipe the drool off your chin, you wonder if you'd have to second mortgage your house to afford the appetizers, your friend tells you the restaurant owner is a philanthropic billionaire who was once homeless, forced to eat out of dumpsters for 5 years and now he gives back by only charging a flat rate of $10 per person…

At what point in that story, would you be running to your computer or phone to get your name on that LONG waiting list?

That's what irresistible offers, risk-reversal and value-stacking are all about. After a while, your mental scales tip to *"buy it right now"* with all that keeps getting piled on. At the tipping point, you stop whatever you're doing and do whatever it takes to get it, right?

When your offer is structured the right way, **they sell** *themselves*.

It's not anything that you *do* to them. *They* make the decision to buy. They don't have to be convinced or sold because it becomes their idea to want it. They do it to themselves. **Your irresistible offer does the work.**

That's why, if you want to become the Profit Prophet and lead your audience to their bigger futures, you'll build several irresistible offers that make people drool at the mere thought.

Communicating Your Offer Powerfully

Now, how about some practical, step-by-step action strategies?

Here's my 9-step formula to make sure you communicate your marketing message and offer in its most powerful light. Use this as your checklist, they are:

1. What's your amazing **Angle (Positioning)** that drives all else?

2. What's your bold benefit driven **Headline**?

3. What's your intriguing **Story** Opener?

4. What's your **Benefit** List (bullet points)?

5. What's the **Third Party Voice** you will use as testimonials to conquer the 2 levels of belief (1. believing that you are telling the truth; and 2. believing that it will work for *them*, and not just you)?

6. What's your **Close (CTA: Call To Action)** that gets them to act now?

7. What's your **P.S.** that pulls them back into the message?

8. Who's the **Voice** for the message going to be (is it to come from you personally or someone else… ties back to the first step, angle/positioning)?

9. How have you used **Curiosity** throughout the whole process?

So, let's talk about a plan for developing your **killer** marketing message.

First, understand your marketing message is actually a tool to FILTER OUT the people who *are* interested and well suited to join your pack from those who are **NOT**. Your marketing should turn away *more* people than it attracts if it's doing its job properly!

Please read that last paragraph at least 5 more times out loud before continuing. It's key!

That's because you *don't* want *everyone* to join your tribe. Only people who are *interested* and **QUALIFIED** to work with you. You'll NEVER get rich wasting time trying to sell everyone. Try to be all things, to all people just insures you end up being nothing, to nobody!

See, spending your time with the wrong audience is a rookie mistake. That's because even if you work your ass off and *convince* them to buy, the chances are good it won't be a happy experience for you or them. They won't appreciate your brilliant solutions because they're not ready to reap the value. Plus, you never want to put yourself in the position where you have to defend, justify, or convince people to do business with you.

Your marketing needs to automatically sift, sort, and screen your ideal audience from the others who would be better served elsewhere. Only TRUE prospects for your offer(s) should make through. You want a big list of raving fans who can't wait to give you more money for new solutions you provide them with. **You DON'T want a huge list of prospects who are active and opinionated, but will <u>never</u> do business with you.**

In other words, people who DESERVE your time. Don't get caught in the trap so many people fall into where they want everyone to join their pack (as you'll discover when we get to the X-Factor in the next chapter, I'm gonna show you how to get *major* results from relatively small tribes… but you won't be able to do this if you've got tons of unqualified, non-responsive people clogging up your process).

This does something else very important for you. Know what it is?

It builds posture into your marketing process. And this posture is the foundation of what makes people stand in line and beg to do business with you.

That's because when you have the right posture power built into your marketing messages and processes, people feel lucky to be "let in on it." And, when you know that you are trying to filter people *out*, it gives you posture, control and confidence. You're in charge, in control because *they* **want you and your offer *more* than you want or need them.** Again, as we already discussed in previous chapters, you don't do it in a mean or arrogant way.

You get to set the rules under which they have to play if they want your solutions! That's the attitude. It's almost magical in its power. Plus, who wants to beg for business?

When you know people want what you have – it gives you your power back. It's the right posture. Because it puts your prospects in the right, predisposed mindset to act in the manner you can truly serve them the best.

And, of course, it goes without saying that when you have a huge pack interested, engaged and predisposed to think the way you want them to regarding your offer, business building is a much, much easier game (not to mention fun and exciting).

How to make sure your marketing message does <u>NOT</u> work…

Before we talk about what works let's discuss briefly what does *not* work so you don't fall victim to "marketing suicide." The fastest way to make absolutely sure your marketing message will NOT work is to talk about what you (as the "star") wants - instead of what's important to, and your audience wants.

How do you craft a message that appeals to your prospect's selfish interests? Glad you asked. Here's how:

STEP 1: It's about THEM, not you

Sit down and really think about who your IDEAL audience is. Pick one single person in your pack to focus on. Who *is* that person? What does their life look like?

You've got to think about life from THEIR perspective and what THEY want - NOT your perspective and what *you* want! You need to know what makes them say, *"Oh Yuck!"* and what makes 'em say, *"Hell Yes! Gimme some more of THAT!"*

See, most marketing misses the mark entirely! It talks about them, their company, how great the founder is, and generally how much they love their own products. But the cold, harsh reality is that your prospect doesn't give a rat's ass about you, your company, its products, services, or that your company made a Gazillion dollar last year.

No!

Your prospects are selfish. They only care about themselves. As world famous sales trainer, Brian Tracy says, *"All prospects listen to radio station WIIFM."* Which, of course, means *"What's In It For Me?"*

So, it stands to reason that if you want to communicate effectively to your prospect, you've got to speak their language. And if WIIFM is their primary language, then YOU had better learn to speak it. Otherwise you may get them to pay attention to you for a second or two… but the likelihood they will ever ascend beyond a level 1 or 2 mental conversation about you is slim to none!

Do *you* like to hang out with someone who drones on and on, bragging about how great they are… how important they are… and never misses the opportunity to name drop and give you the detailed resume of all their past accomplishments every time see them?

Of course not!

But we all know people like that, don't we? And what happens when we see them coming? We roll our eyes and run the other way as fast as we can, right?

That's the *"Oh Yuck!"* **reaction.** And, it happens in our marketing communications all the time!

But you'd listen forever to the exact same person if they talked to *you*, about *you*. All of a sudden that person becomes the smartest, most interesting person in the world in your eyes. Funny, huh? That same person who was arrogant, self-centered, and cocky is now one of your best friends (that's the power of guiding your audience to ascend to Level 4 on your value ladder).

Well, it's the same for your audience. You've got to talk to your audience, about THEM. Do this effectively and they will tell you how smart YOU are. They will feel they've known you their entire lives. It's a powerful rapport-building tool. Everything begins and ends with your pack in mind. IT'S ABOUT THEM.

This is true for building *any* business. However, it's especially true online because our defenses run high to protect ourselves. We are all guarded and skeptical. Plus, you don't have the luxury of altering your message on the fly to suit each prospect. Because it's not a true two-way conversation. You can't ask questions to customize your presentation in a way that lands best with your prospect.

You get one shot to gain their attention in a way that engages them and makes them want more. So make it count by *"listening"* to what your prospect wants *before* you write your marketing message. And, this listening takes place when you think about the typical prospect's life looks like.

What other tribes do they belong to besides yours? What does his/her life look like? What are their concerns? What do they long for more of in their lives? What do they want?

What do they want less of in their lives? What are they frustrated with? What are their problems? What pains do they face? Are they looking for more money? Are they dealing with a messy divorce? Married? Single? Wish they had a life partner? Gay? Straight?

Do they feel trapped and want freedom? Are they earning a good living but feel life lacks meaning because it's not their own? Are they business owners controlled by the limitations of how they've built their business model? Are they HUNGRY? Satisfied or even COMPLACENT?

Get the idea?

STEP 2: Keep 'em curious and wanting more

You've got to meet your audience where they *are* (identify with them). That's because *before* they'll let you guide them, *first* they need to feel you understand them. And, as you now know from the 7 levels of their value ladder, it's *incremental* process.

Said differently: You need to feed them in smaller, bite-sized pieces because otherwise they will "throw-up" all over you!

That's why people have the tendency to say "NO" immediately. It's a defense mechanism, right? However, pull them through your marketing process with a *series* of mini-cliffhangers, and they'll anticipate the next step! Your message has got to give 'em just enough so they want more.

It's like dating. Play hard to get. Get 'em excited. Hot 'n bothered. And you become that insatiable yearning they just can't seem to shake. An itch they can't fully scratch without moving forward.

CURIOSITY is one of the most motivating human emotions. Some mystery that people don't understand, but want to figure out. That's why if you speak in your audience's WIIFM language, tease them the benefits they want… but *don't* quench their thirst to know *"the rest of the story,"* **then they almost *can't* stop.**

Actually, because our minds hate open-loops, if it's something your pack cares about, **they will feel <u>uncomfortable</u> until they can close the loop!** Done right, they jump in your lap. It drives them "crazy" with desire to know more (yet, they LOVE it because anticipation is life giving). Now they WANT more. And, it's *their* idea. It turns the tables because instead of you pushing and them resisting (or automatically pushing back harder), now it's a fun game of tag... and, **you just tagged them, "IT!"**

Wanna see a practical application of this concept?

Are you sure?

The only reason I ask is because not everyone can handle *this* kind of magnetic influence. Plus, honestly, sometimes I struggle with revealing this stuff to people I don't know personally. Because in the wrong hands, it's almost *too* powerful.

What's that, you say?

You promise to use these secrets responsibly? Well, I guess you wouldn't have made it this far if your character isn't up to the Profit Prophet standards.

Alright, you talked me into it. I'll give you the practical application in part two. ;-)

Want a hint of what's to come?

Alright, alright... You're *so* impatient. You're about to discover:

- The exact 4 stages you must move your prospect through for any marketing presentation to be successful

- **How to make your prospect think they are having a REAL conversation with you even when they're NOT! (Master this and your audience will feel like they've known you forever... It'll be love at first sight)**

- What the most important part of your message IS (and how if you *don't* do this right, your message has a snowball's chance in Hell of working… in fact, get this wrong, and even if you do everything else perfectly, you will most assuredly <u>FAIL</u>! And most don't have a clue this is working *against* their success)

- A simple secret that makes people feel *lucky* if you **LET them** do business with you

- And much, *much* more!…

So, turn the page **(if you dare)** and see how to use curiosity to compel your audience to take the actions you (and they) want.

The rest of the story awaits…

> (By the way, even though you might be shocked by what's revealed next, I think you'll also be amazed because it is as **incredibly powerful** as it is <u>elegantly *simple*</u>. Seriously.)

See how I did that? Clever, right?

Apply the same principles in your marketing messages and you'll leave people craving more.

Now, let's continue with the lesson. Where was I? Do you remember where we left off? You <u>do</u> remember, right? After all, it was only a page back.

So, what's going on here? Why did I split up the topic into two sections? Am I some kind of a nut or something?

Maybe so.

Come to think of it, I've yet to be accused of being sane (or conventional for that matter)! However, there's *always* a method to my madness.

You already figured it out, right? That WAS your practical application. I did it so you could *actively experience* (rather than just passively read about) the power of CURIOSITY. And now, my friend, I'm going to show you how to harvest what you just experienced and apply it yourself.

First of all, if you've been paying attention, you've already learned several lessons that will dramatically increase your bottom-line. Did you miss them? I bet *not*.

What I'm talking about, of course, is <u>the way I *teased* you</u>. How I gave you a glimmer of the promise of what was to come on the previous page. How about the way I positioned the practical application as being almost *too* powerful? See how that created mental tension? It was a mini-cliffhanger to keep you in mystery and wanting more: An inner circle that you might never get to see, right?

Did you notice how the 4 bullet points were written with the promise of very specific (and compelling) benefits, while designed in a way to create maximum curiosity and wonder?

Remember? Remember those dramatic (and, incidentally, very *sincere*) bullet points? Let's take a second look:

- The exact 4 stages you must move your prospect through for any marketing presentation to be successful

- **How to make your prospect think they are having a REAL conversation with you even when they're NOT! (Master this and your audience will feel like they've known you forever… It'll be love at first sight)**

- What the most important part of your message IS (and how if you *don't* do this right, your message has a snowball's chance in Hell of working… in fact, get this wrong, and even if you do everything else perfectly, you will most assuredly FAIL! And most don't have a clue this is working *against* their success)

- A simple secret that makes people feel *lucky* if you **LET them** do business with you

- And much, *much* more!…

Notice how each point offers a *specific* benefit that (if I've done my homework properly) you want. Each, also, opens a curiosity loop, right? Makes you eager to learn their secrets? Well, your marketing needs to do the same.

Use this as an idea generator… a template to follow.

What's that, you say? You noticed something else from the tone and style of this book that you can directly apply to your marketing and Profit Prophet journey?

Did you notice that I'm talking directly to you here? This ain't some boring (yawn), dry lecture to a thousand people, is it? Nope.

It's *personal* just for YOU (and for the tens of thousands of people in my pack who feel the same connection with my guidance here). Doesn't it almost feel like you know me… like we're buds?

You did catch all that, right? Fantastic. I knew you would. After all, you *not* only bought this book, but you are doing what 90+% of the other book buyers *won't*. You're reading and applying it! You're one of the sharpest, entrepreneurial-minded people in the world because <u>you are investing (and *invested*) in 10X'ing your life, influence and business success!</u> *Fact.*

STEP 3: Give 'em a headache

What if leading your pack was as easy as selling aspirin to people with headaches?

What if you created an atmosphere with everyone you came across where they felt lucky to "hangout" with you? Where they jumped for joy if you selected them to join your tribe? How fun, exciting and simple would business building be then?

Well, if banks can do it, why can't you? Think about it. Banks make money by "renting out" money, don't they? Yet, how do we feel when we get "approved for the loan"? We jump for joy and feel lucky, yes? And, yet, how crazy is that? That's like going into a supermarket and kissing the manager's feet because he LET you buy a loaf of bread!

Ridiculous. Or is it?

The secret of applying this to your Profit Prophet building activities is to make your audience raise their hands and want what you have *before* you offer it to them. See, there's only two reasons why someone will join your tribe: **Either to *gain pleasure* or *avoid pain.***

Here's a little known fact: *More* people will join you because they want to stop their pain. Gaining pleasure is NOT half as powerful. Yet, what do most people do? They push aside the most powerful persuader they've got and overwhelm their prospects with why their deal is the greatest and why they've "got to get in on it now!"

You can easily triple your results if you *demonstrate* all the pain that your prospect is currently living with… make them FEEL it on some level… then show them how it all ends by simply by becoming a part of your pack.

Now, don't misunderstand, I'm NOT saying you shouldn't present the benefits of your business, but your marketing results will go up dramatically if you use the carrot AND the stick! And, unfortunately, the stick is better at capturing attention. So your job becomes giving people headaches and then show them cure their pain.

Actually, you never really "give them" the headache.

You're just calling attention to the headache they <u>already</u> have. And, when they focus on it, **the pain appears to <u>intensify</u>.** Once your prospect knows (or finally admits to herself) what they are missing and, more importantly, that there is a quick and easy solution to stop their pain... well, then... they *want* it immediately!

Almost everyone desperately wants strong leadership at different times in their lives. We want people to help make life easier. Give us clear direction and instructions on how to effectively change the things we struggle with.

We want a coach. An expert to shadow. Someone capable of showing us the way through the mine-fields. A trustworthy, qualified mentor who leads by example (and has *our* best interests at heart).

<u>That someone can (and *should*) be YOU.</u>

STEP 4: Crafting Your Best Audience Attraction and Ascension Process

There are four parts to this process:

1. ATTENTION
2. INTEREST
3. DESIRE
4. ACTION

As we already covered, this process starts with getting your prospect's ATTENTION. Then it progresses in order through the 3 remaining stages.

Once you gain attention, you have the opening necessary for them to become INTERESTED and *engaged* with your *story*. Once engaged, DESIRE can be cultivated because part of your "nightmare story" will be about how you came to solve the problems you did. This extends directly into your dream story (which becomes <u>the reasons why you put the offer together and structured it the way you did</u>: The story-*behind*-the-story).

Through your story, they start focusing on their own pain. It stirs up their deep DESIRE for a solution. You simply transfer their desire to end their struggles over to your offer. Then getting them to take ACTION is a snap! It's simply a matter of telling them what they need to do next to if they want the pain to stop.

Ain't no thang, but a chicken wang!

Now, let's back up and look at the 9 components I listed earlier in this chapter. Look how each of the 9 parts are designed specifically to take care of the attention, interest, desire, and action steps for you. Remember the 9 components? They are:

1. What's your amazing **<u>Angle (Positioning)</u>** that drives all else?

2. What's your bold, benefit driven **<u>Headline</u>**?

3. What's your intriguing **<u>Story</u>** Opener?

4. What's your **<u>Benefit</u>** List (<u>bullet points</u>)?

5. What's the **<u>Third Party Voice</u>** you will use as testimonials to conquer the 2 levels of belief (1. believing that you are telling the truth; and 2. believing that it will work for *them*, and not just you)?

6. What's your **<u>CTA (Call To Action)</u>** that gets them to act now?

7. What's your **<u>P.S.</u>** that pulls them back into the message?

8. Who's the **<u>Voice</u>** for the message (will it be you, personally or someone else)?

9. How have you used **<u>Curiosity</u>** throughout the whole process?

Since the "angle" drives the remaining 8 components, here's a few examples of different positioning angles I've used very successfully (each project creates its own unique angle, but can be quickly adapted for your specific situation)…

=====

Bloated Bride To-Be Calls Off Wedding:

"That's it! I'm not going through with this! We're both too fat!" - she sobbed as we tried on our wedding clothes 5 weeks before the big day. The rest of story may SHOCK you... _____ saved our marriage," says Jon. "I lost 22 pounds and my wife, Mary, safely took off 34 pounds so fast, we got married right on schedule ! Thank you."

=====

"Little Known Marketing Secrets Cause Hoards of Prospects to Beg (even plead) to Join Your Network!"

Is it immoral to enroll people into your Network Marketing business this easily? The answer below may shock you.

=====

Your FREE Program Analysis

So, here's the deal: I have selected you and a small percentage of my other clients to receive this FREE personal and business analysis to evaluate the LEVEL of your vision, goals and desire. Hey, like I said, this is not for most people. It is a completely different approach to building a MEGA successful....blah, blah, blah...

=====

I pulled it off!

And, **YOU** are going to benefit beyond words (if you can stop saying "wow" and "thank you, thank you, thank you" long enough see what I've put together for you). What's it all about? I thought you'd never ask.

=====

Moving onward...

After you come up with the powerful Angle, you gain the prospect's

ATTENTION **with a bold, benefit driven <u>headline</u>** that snaps your audience out of their preoccupations with power.

An intriguing **story opener** builds the INTEREST and also builds on the whole angle that you're building the entire process around. It compels them to stay engaged and continue ascending the ladder. Not to mention, opens them up to your romancing and starts them wanting your offer.

The **bullet point (benefit list), third party voices and Voice of the message** are the elements that allow you to effectively create the necessary DESIRE and <u>credibility</u> you need to get them to take the immediate ACTION you instruct them to take in your **CTA**.

The **P.S.** (and, of course, the liberal use of **curiosity** throughout the entire marketing message) are tools to pull the prospect back into your story (and offer) just in case they have ADD and skip around.

Got it?

You lead your prospects through those 4 stages with the 9 components in the checklist above. Remember, each of the 4 stages are the foundation for the next one. You can't skip or short-cut steps.

A prospect won't take action if they don't have enough desire for your offer. You have no chance of building desire if they don't have an interest in what your story. And it's absolutely impossible to build interest if you haven't captured their attention to begin with, in the first place, right?

See?

Now, let's talk headlines for a second. The best headlines are benefit driven that packs a "POW" of the boldest promise you can deliver. And a *benefit* is what your offer **DOES FOR** the prospect: What they get. **A winning headline should be built around the ANGLE you've spent the majority of your time developing** (remember, once you've done your homework to develop the right human interest angle it directs everything else in your marketing efforts).

Headlines can promise to reveal some secret. They keep people curious and dying to know more. Headlines deliver news. Promise pain relief.

Try to incorporate any or *all* of the above… Here's some proven fill-in-the-blank templates you can use again and again to quickly and easily create your own winning headlines around your angle (you can also use these templates for your sub-headlines and bullet points):

1. "How to _____"
2. "How I _____"
3. "The Secrets of _____"
4. "The Amazing Discovery of _____"
5. "They didn't think I could _____ but when I _____ they _____"
6. "____ stumbles on to unusual way to _____"
7. "____ reasons why _____ will _____"
8. "How a _____ made me _____"
9. "The truth about _____"
10. "Amazing Free Report Reveals _____"
11. "The Shocking (Yet True) Story Of _____"
12. "Why this information was banned by _____"
13. "___ ways to _____"
14. "Little known (and powerful) way to _____"
15. "I was _____ and now I'm _____"
16. "How _____ provides the almost magic power to _____"
17. "Offbeat, Unusual and Slightly Off the Wall way to _____"
18. "Give me _____ and I'll give you _____"
19. "If you _____ then you can _____"
20. "The List Of _____ You Must <u>NEVER</u> Do If You (When You) _____"

21. "They Laughed At Me When I _____ but when I _____ they _____"

22. "Do you make these _____ mistakes when you _____?"

23. "The Quick & Easy _____ Trick That Eliminates _____"

24. "Young Genius (or Madwoman?) Reveals _____"

25. "You will _____ if you _____"

26. "Special Report: How To Get Anyone To _____ Almost Instantly. And how this report can make you a _____ on the spot"

27. "5 Common Mistakes To Avoid When You _____"

28. "A Breakthrough Approach To _____"

29. "21 Ways To Improve Your _____"

30. "18 Point Checklist For _____"

31. "**FREE** _____: If you _____ then you can get _____ but only for a limited time"

STEP 5: Add Posture and Stir

After completing STEP 1, you'll see just how much your prospect is hurting. And clearly understand all the different areas of their life that are lacking (their bigger pain-points). Where they want (and need) more.

You have the cure for what ails them. So, remember, your offer holds tremendous value for the prospect. Keep that in mind as you craft your value ascension processes. It keeps your eye on the prize (and lets you have some fun with them at the same time).

Make sure they know you are very choosy and careful about who you associate and do business with. Play hard to get. You've got the goods, and you are going to be improving their life, giving them the means to finally scratch all their unscratchable itches. Hey, you don't spend your time with just anyone who comes along. You only work with those you know you can serve best. That's why they've got to qualify to join your pack.

Here's some helpful magnetic tips and tricks:

1. Once you write your marketing message, read it ALOUD and reword any anything that you get hung up on until it sounds *conversational*. Like you're just having a casual conversation with someone. Reading to someone is also helpful.

2. Write how you *really* talk. Tone down the "proper" English teacher language. Be a real person… just be yourself.

3. **Remember, the biggest mistake people make is talking about THEIR company, THEIR products, THEIR wants and desires… but your visitor doesn't care about you, they only care about their selfish interests.** Think about the benefits you provide them. What does it DO for them? What problems do you *solve* (and how are *your* solutions *better* than all the other options available to them)? Why do they need to stop everything and spend time exploring your offer (solutions)?

4. **Problem/pain:** Identify the pain in your prospects life that you can help solve and bring it to their attention. Get 'em stirred up and agitated so they will be ready for your solution when you whip it out.

5. Pile on the benefits until they say: *"Ok, Ok, I'm sold"* – **do this in the form of bullets and/or benefit lists.**

6. Create a **limited offer** (structure it in a way that there are *real* (NOT BS) deadlines and/or warn them why it can end at anytime without warning). This puts the "posture smack down" on them and create a **reason for them to act now** instead of procrastinating. Deadlines are very powerful motivators. The most powerful ones are those that have consequences and rewards if met timely. It creates **legit scarcity.** People hate missing out and being left out.

7. **Summarize your irresistible offer** in the form of benefits to the prospect and **CLOSE, CLOSE, CLOSE!** Tell them EXACTLY what they need to do next to take advantage of the offer. Then direct them to do it now or they'll miss out!

8. **Always use a P.S.** – This is the second most important part of your marketing. Right behind your headline. Most people scan emails, web pages or a letter to see if it's worth their time to dig into it or not. They stop at the end of the message. Which makes the P.S. the perfect place to hook them back into your process with something important to them. You can restate your offer in different words. You can use it to create curiosity and desire to pull them back into your story. You can use it to handle any objections that you know will come up and so on. Just recognize how valuable that portion of your message is and use it wisely.

9. **Always use headlines and subhead lines.** There are some people who want to know every detail of your offer and they will read every word. There are others who are bottom line people and they want to cut through it as quickly as possible. Use the headlines and subhead lines to telegraph your benefits and offer and to create curiosity and to handle both reader types and personalities. Also when you break it up, it's more inviting, easier to read and feels less intimidating.

10. Don't just think about why some will love your offer. Every offer, no matter how great, has it's own set of objections that keeps people from acting. **Make a list of all the reasons why YOU wouldn't respond to your own offer.** If you know why someone *won't* respond, you can handle those issues by framing your story to answer the big ones before they say "no" to you and your entire offer.

11. Don't be afraid of to reveal a small flaw (a "chink" in your armor or in your offer's armor). **Hey, nobody is perfect and your prospect knows that.** Better to let them know you're clear about who you can and can't help. This saves you both lots of heartburn! It makes your creditability and believability soar because now they KNOW you're *not* just out to make a buck. They trust you more because you're walking the honesty walk most only give lip service to.

12. **The ascension process is FRAGILE!** All prospects, no matter the market, all come preprogrammed and predisposed to say "NO." You can loose them without the slightest warning. Which means you've got to make it easier to say "YES" than "NO" – You must take away all their excuses and reasons to cut 'n run from you. Make no mistake, YOUR

PROSPECT IS LOOKING FOR A REASON TO BAIL OUT ON YOUR OFFER. Don't give them one!

13. What can you do if you <u>think</u> you can't write? **Record yourself presenting your offer.** Get it transcribed. Rewrite according to this chapter. See, it's not that you can't write. It's the blank screen that stops us. This short-circuits that fear.

14. Start a "Swipe File" of winning direct response marketing and ads so you always have lots of ideas to pull from. However, don't just collect these files… **Rewrite them in your own handwriting.** Why? Because you'll master the concepts in them and actually *own* the power (instead of always having to borrow it) if you do.

15. Pretend you're a reporter that just "heard through the grape vine" about your offer/story/business. And, as this reporter you decided to check it out. When you did, you fell in love with it! In fact, you loved it so much you decided to do a feature, full page rave article about it. **Write that rave article just as a reporter would.** Tell the full "unbiased" story just like a real reporter would (including any flaws - see #11 above). And at the end of that article, out of the goodness of your heart, you perform a "public service" by telling your readers how they can get their hands on the product or service themselves (like a good movie review). Why do this? Because did you know that content that is editorial in nature (or <u>appears</u> to be editorials) <u>gets 500% more readership</u> than content that is obviously advertising? Powerful stuff.

16. **Passion. Passion. Passion.** <u>Forget being *conservative*</u>. If *you're* excited about your product or service, so will your audience. **Don't expect them to get excited if you're not.** All salesmanship is a transfer of your enthusiasm to the prospect. **Your heart equals their heart. Your passion equals their passion. Your excitement equals their excitement. Your vision of a bigger future equals theirs.** You lead, they follow. Put passion into your message, because otherwise your message gets lost in the sea of shouting clones chasing each other's tails!

17. If a prospect does **NOT** respond it almost always comes down to one or more of these three *crucial* things:

    a. They didn't like **your offer**

    b. They didn't like the way you **explained** your offer

    c. You made your offer to **the wrong people.**

So, before you assume your whole process is "broken" and needs a complete makeover, look at those key elements first. Make adjustments based on those things before you trash it all start all over from scratch. You may be just a few quick tweaks away from breakthrough success!

18. Use third party stories to explain the benefits your product or service offers and to explain why your audience's objections have already been asked and 100% solved. Remember, they will be suspect of you until they do business with you for the first time. However, their BS meters are less likely to get triggered if it comes from an impartial third party who doesn't care if they buy or not. Therefore, whenever possible use the full first and last names of the people (this is much, much more believable). And, of course, consult your attorney for how testimonials are allowed to be used in your specific situation (remember, the education shared in this book is NOT a replacement for professional advice).

Phew!

We covered a ton in this chapter!

You'll definitely want to dog-ear and make notes for future reference.

Now, get ready. Because in the next chapter you're about to discover my secret Profit Prophet Attraction and Ascension weapon. It's made me, my students, and clients millions!

CHAPTER 13:
The X-Factor

This'll knock you for a loop.

A while back I was a guest trainer at a very high priced Information & Internet business training seminar. The main teacher at the event did an email campaign to his big tribe (over 500,000 people). We wanted to demonstrate the techniques live, without a net.

He hits send on his email and over the course of the workshop it brings a little better than $600 in sales for a low price eBook. Which ain't bad considering that it didn't cost him anything to generate those sales.

Not bad until you hear the *rest* of the story...

See, right after the main trainer hit send, he put me on the spot (with a film crew capturing the whole exchange, btw). Live, in front of all the people in the room he challenged me to a marketing duel. I was a little annoyed, but I had no other choice but to accept. Even though I was handicapped because my tribe consisted of *only* 32,000 people (compared to the over half-million people in his), **I knew something everyone else in the room, *didn't*!**

So, I sat in the back of the room and banged out a quick email off the top of my head, while he continued with the lesson. About 90 minutes later (I'm a slow writer), I hit the send button to my list of about 32,000 prospects (not buyers, mind you, prospects)… and, then, settled in to see if I could win this impromptu marketing battle.

Well, you probably already guessed the outcome, right? I kicked ass. And, not by just a little bit.

The results shocked everyone watching (but not me). That spur of the moment, off-the-cuff email to 32,000 prospects ended up with $7,520.00 in sales for the **exact same low priced eBook** that the main trainer did $600 from his email!

What made the difference?

Why did one list of over a half a million people produce only $600 in sales while the much smaller list of only 32,000 prospects produce sales over $7,500.00? And, while you're thinking about that, ponder this: Both campaigns sold the exact same product, using the exact same sales process to sell it, and at the exact same time!

See, as you just discovered all tribes are NOT created equal. How you communicate with, and culture your pack matters a great deal! If you want maximum results and profit leverage, you've got to create a *bond* with your list. Just like we've addressed numerous times throughout, you MUST **establish a <u>relationship</u>** in the minds of your followers.

It's probably the most powerful form of business leverage you have. It's what makes you stand head and shoulders above any competition.

Think about the way you sort your snail mail from your mailbox. You sort it standing over your wastebasket, right? Trying to throw away everything that's obviously junk as quick as you can. Then, what's left, you probably sort into 2 different piles: One that's bills and "official" stuff that you have to get to eventually; and the other pile is personal correspondence from family and/or friends, yes?

And, of those two categories, which pile gets opened first? Like duh! We go for the personal pile before anything else, of course.

It's the same thing with email (and any online communications). Except, multiplied by about a billion! You sort your email standing over a virtual garbage-can (only on steroids because our spam filters *automatically* trashes most junk emails before you ever even see them). The ones that make it through our filters usually get deleted in bulk (or moved to some catch-all folder that never gets looked at again)! All because it's too overwhelming to look at all that shit, right?

So, just because someone has a big list doesn't mean they are profiting. The secret is to make sure your pack *looks forward* to your *communications*.

Key concepts: "Look forward" and "with you." Good marketing feels like a two-way conversation between just two good buds. It's *not* a lecture or a monologue. Just like you're excited to hear from a good friend, you want people to welcome your marketing. Your list becomes very responsive when every interaction with you feels like it's coming from a trusted friend they *perceive* to have a relationship with. Every time your name pops up, they'll set aside everything else because they can't wait to visit with you for a bit. It's the high point of their otherwise ho-hum day. Because doesn't it just feels good when a close friend checks in with you after a rough day?

Which brings us to this: Do you know what your most powerful source of sales will be?

Your best customers will always come from word-of-mouth endorsements from one friend to another (that's why Facebook, Twitter, all social media, blogs, and network marketing are oh so powerful). Think about the last movie you saw or last new restaurant you tried because a friend told you about it. Did they "sell" you on it or did you try it because the suggestion came from *them* and you already value their opinion?

See, when your peeps elevate you that trusted advisor position in their minds, your communications goes into "Must Read" status. It conquers the hardest parts of marketing. Now, although it sounds hard and may seem like brain surgery, it's really *not*. It is actually simple once you know how (and you already know how to be a good friend… you already know how **you** want to be treated and talked to, right?).

However, this is the "X-Factor" that few <u>fully</u> grasp (or leverage to the fullest potential). It is *the* difference. The X-Factor allows you to grow your business **EX**ponentially (quicker, easier and bigger than you probably think is even possible). What you're about to discover is how (and why) you can go up against bigger companies, with large audiences and EAT THEIR LUNCHES with your smaller, more responsive pack!

<u>The secret X-Factor is simply *this*</u>: Utilizing the right automated communication processes that **bonds** (endears) you to your audience. It's how you *systematically* make every member of your tribe feel like you're talking *only* to them on a very deep and personal level. It's how you can meet them in each of their 7 mental conversations and guide them to ascend up the value ladder we already covered in depth.

It allows you to get to know them. And let them know you in a deep meaningful way. They become a part of your inner world. It's like the kind of friend that no matter how much time passes, every time you get together with 'em you can pick back up where you left off without any awkwardness. With this bond, you create a deep connection with your audience which, with the proper steps, converts to trust and respect really fast.

And, when people trust you enough to do business with you *once*, it's much easier to get them to buy *more* of your solutions. Not just once. No. They will buy again and again for as long as you continue to lead them to live a bigger and bigger future (and, assuming, you don't do anything to break that bond).

See, this is how the truly great visionary entrepreneurs build empires. It centers around a concept known as "the Lifetime Customer Value" (or LTCV). The LTCV is the total amount each brand new customer, *on average*, **spends with you over the entire life of ALL her business transactions** with you.

So, if, for example, your average customer buys from you, say, 3 times a year, spends an average of $200, and stays a happy customer for an average of 5 years, what's your LTCV? Each brand new customer you acquire, on average, will be worth $3,000.00 in this example (because ($200) X (3 transactions per year) X (5 years) = $3,000)!

See how it works? Now, most businesses only look at the **first** transaction, *not* the LTCV. Which means they limit their growth by looking for ways to generate more first time buyers at only $200 for the initial sale.

Ok, now stick with me here because this is where it gets good (and also exactly where the X-Factor fits in). Oh, and, by the way, it also happens to be where most entrepreneurs really screw the pooch. Here's why: Because, what if, you bumped the number of annual purchases up a bit (the purchase "*frequency*")? And, what if, for no real extra time or effort you increased the amount of each average sales transaction (add value and raise the price with something like "good," "better," and "best" versions of your offers)?

Let's put some numbers to this for clarity. Say we don't set the world on fire (yet). You're only going to bump your yearly frequency purchases from 3 to 4. And let's say you make a few minor tweaks and your average transaction size goes from $200 to $250. And, with the relationship building processes you've learned here, you're able to keep them engaged and happy for just one more year.

With these small improvements to the 3 key areas, now, what's your new LTCV? Yup! You got it: Each new customer you get is now worth an average of $6,000.00 over the lifetime of your business relationship with them, right? **You doubled your sales from the SAME customer!**

> (And, frankly, those little increases are just the beginning! Because you can add different products at different prices and different buying cycles! What if, over time you built out your funnels to include $500, $1,000, $3,000, and $5,000 value packed offers along with $25, $75, and $100 monthly continuity membership offers in your value ascension processes? Your LTCV shoots straight into the stratosphere!)

So in our quick, conservative example, you doubled business **without getting even one more new, first time buyer,** right? All because you start serving them at a higher level (you do a better job of creating value and building relationship with them)!

Talk about killer leverage.

Now, in every business, there's a natural portion of your customer base that will ascend the value ladder *accidentally*, on their own (meaning: Without the entrepreneur knowing and intentionally designing these Profit Prophet principles into a systemized ascension process). In direct response marketing terms we call these buyers, the "hyper-responsives." They're the raving fans, who can't wait to buy everything you ever release. And they bring your average LTCV way up across the rest of your other buyers.

Generally, if you don't do anything at all, about 4-5% of your buyers will gravitate all by themselves into this hyper-responsive category automatically. However, there's a way you can *substantially* increase that percentage WAY above where it naturally falls. I've been able to increase it to levels of a *consistent* 35+% and I know of entrepreneurs who go as high as a 50+% rate of hyper-responsives.

How? **The X-Factor!**

So, with this background, we'll move right into all the secrets of cracking the X-Factor code for yourself…

Romance 'em, Seduce 'em, Tease & Tantalize 'em... And, NEVER Propose <u>Before</u> The First Date

Have you ever been romanced or courted? Or been the one doing the courting and romancing?

It's the same thing with your audience. You've gotta romance 'em. When you write an email bonding sequence, a salesletter, a script for an Infomercial, short-form TV or radio spot, a podcast, VSL, Newspaper ad, YouTube Video ad, a newsletter, a website, blog, FaceBook or Twitter post, training course, an eZine, etc. — If you want to put the X-Factor power to work for you... **Everything you do needs to strategically deepen your relationship bond with your tribe.**

Maybe you're selling an idea. Or why they should look forward to future communications from you. Or to take advantage of a specific product or service before the deadline.

The point is you're always *marketing*. And, really good marketing communications is simply: **Leveraged and systemized *salesmanship*.** See, your marketing becomes an army of the best salespeople in the world and does the selling for you.

Now, contrary to mainstream thinking, cutsie slogans, stuffed animals, sock-puppets, talking Chihuahua dogs, or any of the other "funny" things do NOT constitute systemized salesmanship! All those things are the equivalent of the pimple-faced boy going right up to the home coming queen that he's never met before and saying, *"Don't worry about these cold-soars. They come and go. Let's go to my car and do it!"*

What are the chances he gets the result he wants?

Here's another less crude example:

Say you're going out on a first date with someone. Would you blurt out, *"Will you marry me?"* on your way to the car at the start of your date? People are simply *not* attracted to desperation. I suppose, even a blind squirrel finds a nut occasionally. However, this approach is *far* from a sure-fire way of producing *predictable* results! There's no way to scale a business up if you're relying on luck or hope.

Guiding your audience to ascend up your value ladder it's a dance of romance. And, romance is a process. You can't rush seduction. That's where all fun lives. It's the life-giving anticipation that makes people want more. Sure you stack the decks in your favor, but you've got to let it unfold at *their* pace! So you tease 'em a bit. Play a little hard to get. That's the kind of relationship *the other person hopes* will blossom into more.

Being the Profit Prophet for your business is no different.

Luckily, you can leverage all sorts of amazing technologies to systemize and automate your business seduction processes in a way where your audience doesn't EVER feel they're just another notch in your bedpost.

You can automate the process that makes them feel safe enough to agree to a first date. Then a second and third. Which leads naturally to dating regularly. Soon they update their Facebook status to "in a relationship." Then, maybe, they start looking for wedding planners.

"Me-To-You"

Now, the key to this kind of personalized (yet automated) seduction is "me to you" communications.

See, intimacy is how you romance their socks (and rest of their cloths) off. However, the concept is as obvious as it is ignorable. It's almost *too* simple because all it requires is for you to **be real**.

Too often we put on airs in business. We put on our "Ms. Successful" and "Mr. Professional" masks and go out to greet the little people. As if we're super-heroes, protecting our secret identities. Publicly we put on our business faces (which is FAR from our authentic selves). Use big words. Speak in glowing, holier than thou, "professional" language. Puff out our chests and say stupid things like *"Our 10,000 square foot state-of-art headquarters houses our Harvard educated team, whom under the direction of our exploratory committee, studies the effects of a proud litany of impressive… blah, blah, blah."*

What a steaming pile of *horseshit*!

Look, be who you *really* are! **Your *authentic* self.** Show the world the REAL you. Flaws and all. Give 'em *all* of you (by the way, how great is this lyric from John Legend's *"All of me"* song: *"…all your curves and all your edges. All your perfect imperfections."*).

Whatever.

The point is: **Do <u>You</u>.**

Remember, your audience is made up of *people*. So speak directly to 'em as the *real* people they are (and the authentic, real person *you* are). With a one-on-one feeling. A conversation *with* them. <u>Never</u> lecture *at* them. Me-To-You means never talking *down* to them. Instead, you will raise them up so they start to make your vision for their bigger future theirs.

Don't be afraid of slang. Speak how you speak in real life. Whatever is normal language for the pack you serve is not only *appropriate* for you to use, it's also *appreciated*! Because when you talk to people in *their* language you trigger the level 4, *"You're Like Me"* conversation in their minds to start automatically. So speak how they do.

You're *not* trying to alienate your audience. And, yet, use dry, general terms (as some giant, faceless company void of personality does), and **that's exactly what ends up happening.**

Even though your tribe is comprised of many different people, your marketing has got to *feel* like it's one-on-one. Don't get stuck in the trap of thinking you have appeal to everyone in your audience, all at once. General marketing trying to sell the whole group dilutes your power because when you try to be all things to all people, you end up being nothing to nobody.

How often do you get emails from "Customer Service Staff," "Customer Service Department," "GreatCo" or any number of faceless groups of people? That sucks!

Remember, you're communing with an actual person. And, <u>you</u> are an actual person. Why blur that line? Especially because people have to buy **emotionally**, first (and, only then will they justify it with the "logic and reason" sides of their brains which gives them the socially acceptable story to tell their family and friends about why they made the purchase).

<u>And, here's the thing</u>: "Professionalism" falls under the logic and reason realm. Now, since logic and reason comes only *after* the emotional buying decision is made, all the professional posturing can only <u>prevent the sale</u>… **but it <u>never</u> creates it.** Because we buy emotionally, FIRST. Period.

Now, the way out of this trap is to create 1 or 2 (but usually not more than 3) ideal profiles of the types of people represented by the rest of your pack. Give them each a name. Write an imaginary story and background about each profile. This is called your "customer avatar."

Here's an example so you can get an idea what I'm talking about:

Jennifer is in her mid 50s. Has grown children. Divorced. Straight. Has lots of friends and family that keeps her busy when she's not working. Loves her two dogs, *Crash* and *Nibbles*. Likes cats but doesn't have any. Tries to eat organic but can't always because it's too expensive. Hates big farma. Supports all things non-GMO. Won't leave in the morning without her huge travel mug of Jamaican Blue Mountain coffee. She smokes weed at night to cycle down. Spends a lot of time with her cyber friends on Facebook because she doesn't like to ever be idle. She wants a relationship although struggles with trust because she's been cheated on by one too many guys.

However, by nature she's very optimistic and tries to always see the positive in life and the good in people. She loves The Secret, astrology, and all things metaphysical. College educated, she's only really known the world of working for a company as a salaried employee her 30+ year professional career. She looks forward to her vacations all year long. Although, she longs to make more money and dreams about starting her own business, she's also resigned to way things are.

Jen doesn't really think she will ever have much more than she does now because she's lived several years in this down cycle. Now she fears that her future will be about the same as it is now (or worse, even smaller). Dreaming for more just hurts these days so she prefers to "keep her feet on the ground." However, what she wants more than financial stability is inner peace and fulfillment… something to give real meaning to her life beyond the surface, funny cat videos and memes on Facebook. She wants control back over her life: To escape the grind; find real freedom; and make a positive impact and leave a legacy her kids (and hopefully, grandkids) are proud of.

###

I could go on and on. However, that's more than enough for you to get the idea of how to create your own avatars (profiles), yes?

You'll find having these short stories about your ideal audience, focuses you in powerful ways. You'll spot all sorts of different story angles that you missed by thinking about your pack as one big giant group.

Anyway, now when you think about your marketing, pull out your avatars and direct your conversations to them specifically. Use all the details from the profile to connect with them (everything, except the specific name or gender you built the avatars around). It's just you and them figuratively sitting down for a private, confidential conversation. Talk with 'em as you would a close friend. In a direct, conversational way. Just you and your old bud catching up on all the latest gossip.

Think about this book.

Haven't I been speaking directly to YOU *personally*? Don't you have a fairly good feel for who Joshua REALLY is? You're probably damn close too because you really have gotten to know me personally through my writing, right?

How well would it work if I didn't talk to you from my heart? What if this was some dry, academic textbook? I doubt you would've made it past the back cover. That's why I'm doing my absolute best to speak directly to you from my heart in a "me-to-you" way. I've done my best to put myself in your shoes as I write this so I can anticipate and answer your questions as if we're hanging out shooting the shit over drinks.

You don't want another boring lecture full of theory by someone who's never actually had success, do you? No, you want someone you trust telling you like it *is*. The straight scoop without sugar coating it, right? An in-the-trenches account of EXACTLY how to *be* a **Profit Prophet** <u>yourself</u>. A show you (NOT *tell* you) what to do step-by-step guide that doesn't pull any punches or leave anything out, yes?

By the way, how I'm speaking to you here is exactly the same voice and approach I use in all my business model and product development. Because I'm crystal clear what you're *really* buying is **me**. My unique approach, perspective, and experiences! I'm pulling out all the stops to build a solid relationship of trust and a value for value exchange because I know if you see a bigger future for yourself through our time here, you're likely to ascend up the value ladder, buy all my other resources and probably hire me to help you scale up your business. (Hint. Hint.) ;-)

See, I'm well aware that if I do a good job of bonding with you and giving you everything I can in my "oh so *Shaffy Way,*" you will feel a kinship with me and hopefully will want to take our business relationship to the next level. You'll buy more if you get good value here (and hopefully fusing my personality into this has made the learning process fun for you). We've formed a real bond together here, right?

You want that for your business and connection with your tribe.

Yes, you want <u>massive</u> numbers of people, but *don't* ever get caught in the trap of trying to communicate me-to-<u>everyone</u>. It's *NOT* about me-to-thousands. Each person that makes up your audience is an individual. They are unique, special and each have their own gifts to share that make a difference in their world. They deserve to be treated, as Jim Rohn would say, *"A meaningful specific instead of a wandering generality."* Which means you make them **feel** like (at least in *their* heart and mind) you are talking directly to them: One-on-one; in a **"me-to-YOU"** way.

<u>A quick warning</u>: This reference dates, but have you seen the movie, *"Stir Crazy"* with Richard Prior and Gene Wilder? In it there's a scene where they go to Jail with hard-core criminals.

And, as they walk by all these crazed killers, sizing 'em up, they do their best to fit in. So Richard & Gene starting "be-bopping" off-beat, saying, *"That's right! That's right! We bad! We don't want no shit, either."* Trying to *act* tough. (https://youtu.be/kNbZcT8RXgE)

The point is, you can't fake it. **You've got to *be* it.** Otherwise, just like the killers in Stir Crazy, your audience will see right through it (and you). And once tagged as a phony, there's almost no recovering. *Period.*

This is the key to creating the hyper-responsive response rates every entrepreneur lusts after. It is the difference between typical mainstream results where a campaign is lucky to pull in fractional percentage point profits. This is the reason why some business struggle and say marketing and advertising doesn't work (because, in a sense, they're *right*: **THEIR** marketing sure doesn't work).

Moving on. The next key of the X-Factor is:

The Bonding Power of Membership, Fraternities and Sororities

Why are sororities and fraternities popular? Why are they long standing tradition for families to be a part of them? What drives the desire to join?

Simply because frats and sororities are *exclusive*, hard to *"pledge"* (get in to), steeped in tradition and if accepted, it's badge of honor you wear that lets the world know **you're a part of the in-crowd** (a member of the "cool kids club").

It's a place you *fit in*. You're *accepted. Superior* from the outsiders because you know something the rest of the world doesn't, right? Plus, all your "brothers" and "sisters" speak the same language because only you guys know what you endured to *earn* your membership and *status* within the pack.

Your mind should be exploding with ideas right now on how to create a similar atmosphere with your audience attraction and ascension processes, yes? How can you create an environment where any *prospective "candidate"* for membership into your pack has to *pledge* and prove their *worthiness* to even be *considered*?

They're getting the opportunity to apply to join your exclusive Profit Prophet fraternity or sorority (and they probably won't have to *jump through the hoops* of streaking naked through the quad, singing "jingle-bells" and "I'm a little teapot" to qualify for *membership consideration* in your *exclusive club*… or will they? ;-)

Just take a look at the key words italicized the last few paragraphs. Grasp the vision? See how powerful it is? Great, then let's take it deeper with...

People want what they <u>can't</u> have

The first resource I ever published back in 1997 was titled, *"How To Make People Stand In Line And Beg To Join Your Network!"* It was all about establishing *"posture power,"* as I called back then. In it I revealed how any MLM'er could turn the tables and make prospects ASK to be sponsored into your Network Marketing downline organization.

The reason it works so well is because of a basic human psychology truth: <u>People want what they *can't* have</u>. People love things that they can't get easily. For some reason, when you tell somebody they can't do or have something, all of a sudden, a deep desire to prove you wrong is birthed.

Use this to your advantage.

It's an interesting dynamic. You've got to use it "gingerly." Don't slap them in the face with it. **You have to say things in a subtle way that makes them try to prove their worthiness to you.**

For example, one of the techniques is *'I can't promise you anything,'* which subtly lets them know, **without stating it directly** that, *'I've got the greatest thing in the world, but I can't promise you that I'm going to be able to help you out with this. If you give me a call, I try to get to you, but hey, please be patient with me because there are 3,762 people that want my attention this month.'*

See, without being too "in your face," it implies you're extremely busy, popular, and you're not sure if you'll even consider them for your cool kids club. **All of a sudden you're hard to get, and they'd be lucky to have you and the thought of you turning them down is unacceptable.**

Next door to wanting what you can't have is this: **Whatever we *do* have now, is yesterday's news because we quickly tire of the things we've already checked off the "must-have" list.**

We naturally want to move on to bigger and better things. What's the next goal we want to achieve because we are unsatisfied with what is now?

Let's say you've always wanted a particular car. Or to live in a particular area. Or a certain status position at your company. It consumes us, right? I gets our full attention. Nothing is more important until it's finally ours.

And, sure, that accomplishment feels incredible. But only for a minute or two. Right?

That's because sooner or later, something else comes along you want even more. We tire quickly and tend to take our past accomplishments for granted. It's the promise of a bigger future that pulls us forward. Because what we have currently, no matter how great, is never as exciting as the even better things waiting at the next horizon. It simply no longer holds the same life-giving mystery, promise and intrigue as it did before you accomplished the goal.

People get tired of what they <u>do</u> have. It's old to them. They <u>aspire</u> to new things. Things they <u>don't have</u>. And it feeds on itself because the actual accomplishment never seems to be as satisfying as the way we built up the having of it to be in our imagination.

It is insatiable.

An infinite circle of never-ending expansion that continues to feed this "wanting what you *can't* have" phenomenon. And, this feeling of never being satisfied drives the growth of our economy.

I think it was Paul Zane Pilsner, an award-winning economist, who first opened me up to this principle. The example he used was cars. Carmakers originally thought that if they made cars that lasted forever (improved their quality instead of the planned obsolesce that was standard back then), they would go out of business. The reasoning was that people would not buy cars if they lasted for 25 years. But in fact, this is not at all the case. **What they found out was that the nature of human desire is that it always wants more.**

Once we get to a certain level, it's no longer satisfying. Doesn't give us life because we aren't moving towards the anticipation of living a bigger future. We want more. Different. New. We want to continue to grow.

If you think about it, it's also why people get bored with their romantic relationships. When it gets stale the imagined promise of something better fuels the desire to trade lovers in for something fresh and exciting. It works the same way with cars, houses, jobs, boats, electronics and really anything else you can think of. Once the excitement of the newness rubs off, we want the next bigger and better model.

Think about it in your own life, I know that's true for me. When I was 20, my dream car was a brand new Ford Explorer. More than anything else I had to have that Ford Explorer. Finally, I got it, and I was so happy. And that joy, excitement and enthusiasm for it stayed strong for about 3 years or so. Then I started getting bored with it. Before I knew what hit me, I was thinking the Explorer was a shitbox. I needed something new. Something better. Sexier.

The same cycle repeated itself when I upgraded to my first, second and third luxury cars. It even went the other direction too because all the fancy cars wouldn't do for off-roading. I "needed" something rugged. Had to have beach toy. So I joined Jeep Ranger club for four-wheeling weekend play time (which, by the way, I don't think ever saw 4-wheel drive again after the first 2 months I owned it).

This behavior is inherent in us all. The "stuff" we are passionate about differs, however, everyone is subject to this phenomenon. Be it the next self-help book, the next novel, the next house, the next pet, the next trick they teach their dog, the next thing they do to improve their garden, the next child they have, etc...

It's human nature. It comes pre-programmed inside us all. And, the aspiring Profit Prophet (that's you), knows to use it to your advantage.

See, our inborn desires are all insatiable. They continue to grow. So when you pick a tribe to lead, guide and provide breakthrough solutions to, they will stick with you. Assuming you continue to grow your vision and stay ahead of your pack's desires, you'll find **the very act of satisfying your audience's immediate wants, needs, and desires actually stokes their fires to want more.**

All because, by nature, they're insatiable. The more we consume, **the**

more we want to consume. Each purchase gives us joy for a fleeting moment. Wealth goes to the sharp Profit Prophet who is first to supply the next new solution when the old one no longer satisfies.

Sometimes people judge this process as "bad." However, the reality is your tribe is going to buy the next solution they want *somewhere*. If you don't fulfill their desires, they will move on to someone who will. They'll find a new pack-leader to follow. *Fact.*

So why not continue to serve and grow with them instead of forcing them to leave you?

You be the one to provide more and more value to your audience by growing your products and services *with* them. As they face new challenges, they want the new solutions you can give them. Your tribe knows they're insatiable. They are going to continue to want more and thirst for more regardless if you're involved or not!

Be the one who gets to 'em first the next time they get the itch.

Period.

The Grass Is ALWAYS Greener Syndrome

Similar, but not identical to the last two topics covered is, *"The grass is always greener syndrome."*

Okay, we just did a deep dive on valuing exclusivity (wanting what we can't have) and also how our insatiable desires makes us take for granted that which we already have. Well connected to those, is the tendency to compare what you have against what others have as being better (or worse) than yours. This comparison is often how we decide how valuable we believe something to be.

On a personal note: I think the secret is to be happy where you ARE; but to keep your aspirations strong so you keep growing. Keep moving towards attainment and fulfillment. And, yet stay grounded and passionate where you are. Fulfilled AND eager to expand!

When you are happy with what is, life flows with a natural ease. But funny thing: When you're truly happy with where you are, it opens the door to even greater possibilities (plus, you make progress a lot easier and faster when you're *free* of desperation and fear-based action).

When you aren't happy with what is, you're focused on the negatives of the situation. This controls our perception so all we look for (and therefore see) are the problems of the current situation (remember back to Book 1?). Life becomes avoiding pain; making decisions based on which hurts less instead of what has potential of bringing more joy, pleasure, and happiness.

If your goal is to accumulate a certain amount of money so you can start living at some future point in time, you're cheating yourself out of living right now. It's a trap because you'll find that money solves a lot of things, but never creates happiness. Won't give you purpose or meaning. Doesn't give you a sense of fulfillment unless you're using it to move yourself towards something you feel is worthwhile.

So, if you aren't happy while you're making your millions, it ain't gonna magically change when you finally hit your mental number (in fact, it makes things worse because you've been putting off truly living life for the lie that promises it'll be worth the sacrifice because reaching your goal will fix everything). Lots of people say, *"when I make $XXX amount of money, then I'll be happy… then I'll have the freedom to do what really makes me happy."* The problem is money, possessions, status, and the such never make you happy. Those are all things outside of yourself; happiness only comes from within.

Now, if you've never made big money before, I can guess what you might be thinking: **"yeah, yeah, yeah, I've heard that all before. I don't buy it… it's easy for you to say that, Joshua, you're already rich."**

Consider this: As soon as you have some money, it WILL be very exciting; and you'll experience what I'm talking about first hand. For me, it took about two years to come down off that high and realize that, "Hey, all this material stuff is great and I've enjoyed it, but is this *all* there is? How come this stuff doesn't drive me anymore? How come I *still* feel empty?"

These days, joy is more important than money for me. Things that feed me spiritually, personally, and make a real impact for others are the things that give me life; that get me gladly ripping back the covers, without an alarm at 5am, raring to go, because I'm so "amped" up about what the day holds that I simply can't sleep any longer. That's what drives me these days. Not the money. However, interestingly enough, when the money *does* come, it's usually in much bigger amounts. And, yet, believe it or not, money is always the *byproduct* of the joy, happiness, and passion we experience along the way… Never the *cause*!

Being a Profit Prophet is a prosperity and abundance *mindset*.

Now, that being said, most of the world doesn't live this way. They're in a continual state of fear-based thinking that drives them to be more responsive to avoiding pain than anything else. Why? Because that's where their attention is focused.

That's why the grass is greener syndrome is something you need to be aware of. Otherwise it'll work *against* your audience attraction and ascension efforts. When used properly, it keeps us all growing and moving forward. Reminds us, there's always more that you can accomplish. Always greater heights.

Onward…

Be Opinionated, Be Bold, Be An Outspoken Straight Talker, Be Yourself, Let People Know You Personally:

But, NEVER <u>EVER</u> Be Boring!

Next ingredient in building the X-Factor bond is to be *opinionated*.

That's right, you *want* to stand out. Be different! People often need a quick (but affectionate) slap to snap them out of their preoccupations and routine trances that captures their attention and makes them ignore your *initial* relationship building attempts.

Because if you never get their attention, you are cheating them out of the opportunity to see if your solutions offer value to them or not. Besides, the shock value of gaining attention by being opinionated, can be used to powerfully guide your audience to ascend to the higher levels of their mental conversations about you (see earlier chapters).

That's because people love (or hate) those who have the guts to stand up for their beliefs. We appreciate people who dare speak their minds without giving a shit who cares, approves or who's toes get stepped on. Fact!

Most people are afraid to speak their minds because their need to be liked and accepted is stronger than their need for independence. They don't want to offend anyone for fear of being tarred and feathered. But secretly, they wish they had the guts to speak out.

Here's the great news on this: Standing up for your beliefs makes your X-Factor Bond stronger and stronger. Plus, you don't have to worry about those who completely oppose your strong opinions (you WANT the friction)! Because regardless if they love or hate you, you've successfully captured their attention in a way that automatically positions the rest of your relationship building efforts.

Those that love you will be inspired by your courage. They'll stand up for you because you have earned their respect. You've empowered them to stand up for themselves! And, who doesn't LOVE someone who encourages and gives them power?

Think about the loyalty Steve Jobs created with Apple. Say anything bad about the company, the man, or any of their products and what happens? Their raving fans spring to their defense as if you tried to sell their first born into slavery! Apple is the most profitable company on the planet (with over $100 BILLION in cash reserves!). And that's because of the amazing X-Factor bond they've created with their customers!

But what about those people you piss off by having the courage to stick to your convictions?

That's the best part: If they *hate* you, they will opt to leave you, which is exactly what you want because they weren't going to buy from you anyway. You'll be well advised to decide the kind of people you want (and will enjoy) to lead to a bigger future. Who will sync up with your style? Who are the type YOU want to hang out with? Might as well appeal directly the peeps you can see *yourself* falling in love with because that's who you'll be serving and doing business with (hopefully) far into the future! You want to find out as soon as possible who your haters are. And do everything possible to turn 'em off so they take their negativity elsewhere! Because they ain't never gonna buy from you anyway. Not never!

(And, yes, I'm well aware of the grammar issues in that sentence, but I don't care because it's what felt right to me;-)

The people who love what you stand for are the ones you're here to help, support, and grow with. If you waste time arguing (or trying to please everyone) you're allowing yourself to get distracted from your Profit Prophet mission.

So give your opinion straight from the heart, and don't be afraid of being outspoken. Don't apologize for your opinion. Be bold. There's no need to defend your position either. You're entitled to believe what you do and because you're not attached to people agreeing with you or not you can remain calm. Never a need to be mean or nasty.

You don't want to ever make people wrong or feel stupid if they disagree with you because everyone is entitled *their* opinion. Because you know that even though haters oppose you, it's only because they are *insecure* (if they were secure, they wouldn't feel the need to attack differing views).

Not you, though. You've got the confidence that comes when you don't need consensus to believe the way you choose.

See, most people wish that their lives were more interesting. By giving voice to what they wish they could, you let them be a part of a "movement" that makes them feel alive and engaged in something worthwhile. Plus, they get to live vicariously through you without worrying who disapproves of them because they're not voicing it themselves. When they come across someone that has the guts to say what they *feel* (but are afraid to voice), you become their hero. You are their champion. They want to be you. Can't get enough of being around your energy. Somehow listening to someone ranting on a subject you're interested in, is funny and exciting. It gets your head nodding in agreement. And, each head nod deepens the X-Factor bond with the tribe you guide.

Just ask Rush Limbaugh, Donald Trump or Oprah Winfrey, opinionated people attract very strong followings.

How about Howard Stern? You either love or hate him. You've probably heard the studies done about how long people listen to his show and why. They report that the average listener that loves him listens for something like an hour, and when asked how come they listen the most common answer was *"to see what he's going to say next."* Now, on the other end of the spectrum you have the people that *hate* Stern. They report that **the average person that hates him listens to his show for something like 3 hours.** And when asked why the haters tune in? Again, their most common answer was, *"to see what he's going to say next."*

Hmmm… ain't that a honker?

Think about what that means. **People that hate him, listen 3 times longer than those who like him?** I'd say that Stern's opinionated approach works gangbusters. Especially since he gets paid based on ratings (and ratings are based determined by how many people listen and for how long)! The more people he draws, the more they can charge for advertising. And the more money Stern makes! Isn't it strange that his haters made him very, very, very rich?

Being opinionated works wonders. Remember, people wish they had the guts to be outspoken, direct and blunt. *They cry out for that freshness in their life.*

Now, I'm <u>not</u> saying you should become a Howard Stern knock-off. No, I'm not. What I <u>am</u> saying is take the concepts he uses to make himself a success and make them your own. Because regardless of if you love or hate him, you've got to understand and respect his marketing brilliance. <u>He knows what his audience wants. When he's on the radio, he does some of the same thing we're talking about. He speaks to people on a one on one basis. You feel like he's one of the guys, like he's your bro.</u>

The world is filled with people crying out for leadership and direction. They want to be told what to do. You *want* to be controversial in your own way. You *want* to be opinionated. Leverage it to the max. You'll find that <u>people really respect that straightforward, bottom line, no sugarcoated approach. Just telling it like it *is* because you can't be bought!</u>

The "Super-Powers" Of Making YOURSELF The Idiot:

This works wonders (and it's so damn simple)…

There are times when people get stuck in limited thinking and beliefs. You'll have to break them out of this mindset before you can help them see the solution. There's a right and wrong way to do this.

Never talk down to your audience when you're trying to snap them out of the lies they've come to believe are actually true. Because, if you do, it'll kill the X-Factor bond you've worked hard to build (and it conditions people to ignore you; and automatically resist EVERYTHING after that because no one likes to be embarrassed or made wrong for what they believe).

Here's what to do instead.

Tell a story and use *yourself* **as the idiot.** Or tell a story where *someone else* is the idiot. However, don't confront them directly. You never want to be the one to make them the idiot. THEY can call themselves an idiot but you can't. In fact, **your job is to let them off the hook** when they are feeling stupid (i.e., give them something else to blame so they can move on with hope of never getting stuck in the same trap again).

Let's make this even clearer. Say you need your tribe to see how procrastination is robbing them blind; how their inability to make a decision or failure to take the right actions, at the right time, will make them go broke, cost them their marriage, and is making life miserable.

If you said, *"Hey idiot, you're never going to get anywhere in life if you don't get up off your ass and do x, y and z, right now! Your wife will leave you as soon as she realizes she married to a looser who's never going to change. If you don't do these things now, you might as well slit your wrists and get it over with because you're dying a slow death anyway."* –

Even though that's probably the wake up call they need, they'll never hear you because you're attacking them. Mentally they say, *"Who the hell are you to judge me? Screw you!"* They can't see you're really trying to help with your brand of tough love.

So how do you get them to do x, y, and z immediately with the *same* kind of urgency, impact, and conviction? Simple. **Make it THEIR idea!** *Get them to tell themselves* those things.

Here's how you could twist that same conversation and create an opening where they will instantly listen (and likely comply without any pushback whatsoever):

"Truth be told, knowing what I know now, I'm surprised it took her so long to dump my sorry ass (but she didn't have to be so vindictive). Today, after years of therapy, I see how I blamed her my failures because she didn't support me enough, but who the hell believes in someone who talks a big game for 10 years without action? Failure would have been better than facing I wasn't man enough to even try x, y, & z! But I had my long list of excuses I used to avoid admitting what a loser, wuss I was; always whining about how the world wronged me. Too bad I had to find out the hard way, no amount of positive thinking replaces positive action! Such a shame, because if I just had the guts to try x, y, & z I could've saved myself the horror of....."

See how it works?

Make yourself the asshole. But in the telling of your story, *they* put themselves in your shoes without you asking (or lecturing them). They will see happened to you and be concerned that the same fate is about to strike them down if they don't learn from your mistakes. Plus, your true story earns you the right to lead them. Now they respect you as an authority because you've shared a very private and personal story that proves you've already been down the road they're traveling, know where it ends, and can save them needless pain, suffering, and heartache!

By calling yourself out, you endear yourself to them and remove all confrontational pressure at the same time. It also removes **the "yeah, but I can't do that because I'm not an expert like you" excuse** because they see you're just as messed up as they are (maybe more so); and if you can do it then they can too with your help. Wake up call delivered *without* smacking 'em upside their head directly.

Something else very subtle happens with this approach. Besides heeding your advice, they'll say to themselves, *"glad that wasn't* ME. *I don't want that to happen to* ME. *I don't ever want to be the idiot he was"* – As soon as they say that to themselves, they almost *have to* follow your advice, because if they don't, they end up calling themselves the idiot! Grasp the power this gives you?

Two warnings about misusing your new "Super-Powers"

First, don't ever make up a story that isn't true (you can tell someone else's true story but don't *ever* lie about your experiences). I promise you'll get caught eventually (plus, it's illegal).

If you misuse this technique you'll destroy the X-Factor bond that gives you all your Profit Prophet leverage (and once you breach that trust, it's usually impossible to recover; it follows you everywhere, as it rightly *should*).

Second, you have a *responsibility* to your tribe to protect, serve and help them. If you manipulate them with lies, now you're looking out for *your* interests, instead of **theirs**. You might pull the wool over their eyes for a bit, but people always see through the fake shit if your intention is to make money over truly helping. **Profit at their *service*, not their expense!**

If I tell them, it's suspect. But if they tell me, they'll fight for it and accept it as fact because it was their idea!"

I think it was Tom Hopkins, famous sales trainer, who said *"If I tell them, they'll doubt me. If they tell me, it's a fact."*

So, if you make an assertion and expect your audience to just take your word for it (before they elevate you to Trusted Advisor status), you'll die an ugly business death. You never want to make a statement and expect your tribe to just take it at face value.

Remember, until they ascend to a level 6 or 7 belief about you, **you're the enemy**. You are trying to get their hard earned money. You are not to be trusted. As protection, their caveman instincts makes them *automatically* resist you.

However, if you use third party stories (like the example from the last section), you meet them where they are, and create an atmosphere where you bring it out of them. It becomes THEIR idea. And, since **THEY said it to themselves, now they believe it; so it MUST BE TRUE!**

No One Ever "Wins" An Argument!

Think about that. There is never a winner of any argument. *Period.*

Anytime you go head-to-head and aggressively (or even softly) try to convince someone they are wrong, both sides *always* loose.

If you don't make yourself the idiot as we discussed, then even if the other person **says,** *"you're right,"* it's usually only because they just want to shut you up. They just said "OK" to end it. However, they walk away from the conversation **feeling** *they* are still right and you are definitely wrong, regardless of conceding. **They almost *have* to because it hurts their ego if they don't at least mentally defend their position.**

This triggers the, **"arguing to be right,"** insanity to kick into high gear. Which is very hard to overcome because now they're *irrationally* defending their position to the death (no matter how crazy it gets)!

Have you ever experienced this from either side? Has there ever been a time when you've been arguing with someone and said to yourself *"screw it, this just ain't worth my energy and aggravation to continue arguing about this. I'm just going to shut up now."* I bet the other person thought "Aha!, I won." But, **actually, they <u>didn't</u> win,** did they?

Why?

You shut down to anything they said from that point forward because you stop listening, right? And more importantly, you probably thought something like, *"Wow, this guy is delusional. He can't be saved from his own stupidity. I'll just nod until he takes the hint and goes away."* They've lost you, right? So, no matter how well meaning his message may be, you're over it (and him). It's like Charlie Brown's parents: They talk but all YOU hear is, **"Wah-Wa-Waaa-Wa-Wah!"** - right?

It fosters a dislike (and even distain) for them if they don't let it go. However, they think they've "won" by proving you wrong. And, yet, neither side wins because the opportunity for a bigger future of possibility ends when we dig our heals in to be right (and prove them wrong).

People Will Work For Money, But They'll <u>DIE</u> For A Ribbon!
* Recognition * Recognition * Recognition *

Remember, your audience thinks *only* in terms of *their* selfish, self-interests. In their minds they are <u>the</u> most important person in the world (or at least the most important person in *their* world).

Everyone longs to feel special. Wants to be *recognized*, praised and feel worthy. To a greater or lesser degree, we all feel insecure in these areas. It seems to be hard-coded into our very DNA! We're starved for approval, acceptance, and belonging. Often the things we feel we deserve recognition for, goes unnoticed and/or ignored.

Everybody wants to <u>feel</u> special. Everybody <u>IS</u> special.

Yet, to a greater or lesser degree, everyone that makes up your audience feels they aren't getting their just recognition. They long for the respect that they feel they are entitled to. It's an inborn *craving*. We tend to be insecure beings. Always getting slighted: Doomed to the shit end of the stick somehow; never getting (or feeling worthy of) the approval we want.

That's why members of your tribe will die for that ribbon (a public pat on the head). People give their lives in exchange for recognition. The lust for approval has been used to manipulate people into doing insane things (think suicide bombers). It's a much bigger motivation than money.

So, knowing your audience is made up of insecure beings, who all crave public approval, respect and recognition… **What happens if YOU'RE the one who bridges that gap for them?** That's right! **They fall in love with you because you fulfill their deepest needs.** Which triggers an instinctive and automatic ascension up your ladder of influence!

Start with what makes you feel special. What fills your approval needs when you want to be acknowledged for your contributions? How do you know you're respected and appreciated? How do you (or would you) like to be recognized? Simply build those things into your ascension processes and your audience will feel empty if they go too long without your guidance.

Here's some quick ideas to get your creative juices flowing:

Send 'em a birthday card. Surprise them with a special personal phone call. Give 'em gifts they aren't expecting (team T-Shirts are great because it lets them brag to the world they're part of a special club). An autographed picture. A special lapel pin. A Mary Kay car. Spotlight them in your newsletter. Outstanding member of the month award. A coffee mug. Put them on a public stage in front of other pack members and recognize them (and give them a platform to share their story so they know people they respect, admire THEM).

Your possibilities are endless!

Be sure you congratulate them, sincerely, from your heart. And do it in a PUBLIC way. Thank them. Appreciate them publicly. Let 'em know they're important to you (in a NON ass kissy way). It's not about false flattery. People see right through that shit (plus, it can give the feeling you're making fun of them).

It's about recognizing people from a _genuine_ place of _sincere_ gratitude so it shows the rest of your pack just how important they are to you personally. After all, everybody in your tribe ARE critically important. They DO mean the world to you. Without them, you don't have a business, right?

Giving public recognition creates value for your whole tribe! And, it's the exchange of value that makes people eagerly anticipate the next solution or breakthrough you supply. You satisfy deep desires that's gone unfulfilled for far to long. While the messages they get from probably everyone (and everything) in their lives is that they aren't good enough, you make them feel special because they're under your wing.

Do you see how this creates immense value in their lives? Instead of beating 'em down, you build them up. It allows them to live a bigger life. And, it's completely _separate_ from your business solutions, by the way. Let that swim around your Profit Prophet mind for a bit!

See, it's an easy way to over-deliver on the value they expect. And, there simply isn't any price high enough to put on making people feel respected, recognized and special! You give them psychological value (which is WAY more valuable than just your products and services).

Hey, a quick aside: The price you charge for your solutions shouldn't have anything to do with your hard costs to produce and provide them. They should be based on the *perceived* value it creates for the buyer. If something costs you a buck to produce, but it creates $10,000 worth of value for that customer, does it warrant a $500 price tag? I'd argue, "YES." Because, what does your costs have to do with the incredible value they get? If they get $10,000 in value and only spent $500, then in their mind they just came out $9,500 ahead, right?

Hell yes it's a good deal for them! *You'd* make that value exchange, wouldn't you? All day, every day! And so would everyone else. Show me how I can write you a check for $500, and if I believe you'll give me $10,000 back (according to my personal values), you better believe, I'm in! In fact, my next question would be, *"how many times can I do that?"* And, interestingly enough, unless you make a point of telling me it only cost you 10 bucks to give me that value, I don't care. **Just gimme my $10K!**

So, please don't get caught up in the cost. Unless you're in an industry that's regulated, the price you charge only needs to be fair for the utility it delivers. A good rule of thumb is to charge 10-20 times LESS than the *legitimate* value it gives the buyer! (Notice, it's about *legitimate* value...NOT overinflated bullshit value.)

Anywho.

Remember, just putting them in a vision of a bigger future of recognition creates MASSIVE value!

Often when I get emails from my tribe, I'll reprint their question and praise them for having the guts to ask it. Or if they've shared a story with me, praise them for having the courage to share their story with me. I'll email the whole tribe and say something like *"the other day I got an email from John Jones and he brought up an excellent point. He pointed out that my last email left him confused a bit. So I re-read it myself. And, know what? He was right! I did NOT do a good enough job explaining it. Please allow me to right that wrong now..."*

See what I did there? You caught it, right?

Actually that does TWO things: First, it gives John the recognition he deserves with a nice public pat the back... So now he feels special and feels a deeper, bonded connection with me.

However, something MUCH more important has also happened. See, this increases the X-Factor bonding effect with my *entire* tribe, not *just* John. Because guess what happens when the rest of the pack sees John's question and my response?

Exactly! It makes *them* crave the same kind of recognition even more, doesn't it? It makes the **whole gang** *more* responsive. It deepens my bond with *everyone* because it makes me more human and relatable. They see that I really do listen and give them what they want. So now when Suzie reads about John she's more engaged, more responsive. Maybe she'll even email me in hopes that I'll recognize her the next time around.

And the deepening the bond cycle continues.

The other people in your tribe also feel like, hey, he's talking straight to me (almost like I'm saying *"hey, Suzie, I expect to hear back from you on your question"*). It comes across that personal to everyone. Just like it's a personal, one-on-one conversation.

In fact, you know it's funny, I'll get tons of emails from people telling me that because of the way I wrote the email they actually <u>felt obligated to respond</u>. Even though it was a mass email… and they KNEW it was a mass email to the whole tribe!

Give 'em "Insider" Information

The feeling to create with your pack is: *"hey, pissstt… cumheeerr… closer… Shhh, nobody knows this and I'm only telling you because I like you, but…"*

Now, I can almost hear your push-back, *"what if I don't have any secrets my tribe wants? I don't know anything like that."* Let's speak to that for a second because it simply isn't true. Stick with me here and you'll see the truth.

First, a secret is only a secret if you don't know it.

If that sounds like a stupid, obvious statement, it's because it *is*! But just like hiding in plain sight makes you impossible to find, the power here is: **You take YOUR insider secrets for granted because they aren't secret to you!** They could be mind-altering and life-changing to someone who doesn't know all you know. However, because it's second nature to you,

you don't think it's any big deal.

Every single apprentice Profit Prophet reading this right now has specialized knowledge unknown by the rest of the world. Think about everything you learned so far in this book. This stuff is all second nature to me. I eat, sleep, and breathe it automatically. It's no big whoop to *me*. But how many breakthrough *"Aha! Moments"* have you had from our time together here so far? My guess is it's been many, right?

See, I'm sharing my unique understanding from my personal experiences. So, even if you're familiar with some of the concepts shared here, <u>one thing is for *sure*</u>: **You ain't *never* heard it the way I've pulled it all together because no one else has my *unique prospective*.**

Same goes for you.

What secrets do you possess? You've got bunches. All you have to do is take a beat to acknowledge and inventory them.

Maybe it's a way of getting superior service at a restaurant. The inside track on an undiscovered perfume that's gonna be big. How to save money. How to get great deals on plane tickets.

Did you go through a divorce and figure out how to keep from getting screwed? Have a great recipe for brownies? A piece of deathbed advice whispered to you that worked miracles in your life for years? A great fishing spot where the fish just jump in the boat? How to talk to your kids so they clean up their room, the first time? How to shave 10 minutes off your workout in a way that gets even better results? Perhaps your aunt from China gave you her remedy for colds that works so well you've never caught a cold again?

Your secrets are waiting for you to stop taking them for granted.

And, oh, sometimes the secret isn't the actual info, <u>but in the way you explain it</u>. So, while they may have heard it before, you have a unique point of view that let's them actually capitalize on it in a way they *couldn't* before. **Reframing things and giving people new paradigms to look through is definitely a big type of valuable inside information.**

Also, you can (and *should*) always **discover <u>new</u> insider tips, tricks, secrets and unusual information! It's fun and simple.** Here's how:

Just spend a few hours on Google, YouTube and/or Facebook and you'll uncover all sorts of stuff you can consolidate, curate, and reframe into valuable stuff to give your tribe. In fact, with 3-5 days of fun research, you can become enough of an expert on almost any subject your audience wants more of from you.

All sorts of incredible info is waiting for you on every subject imaginable: I dare you spend a few hours on a topic you're interested in and not come up with a list of little known gold nuggets that makes you say, *"WOW! I didn't know that. This is some good stuff!"* If you don't come up with at least 30 potential things your tribe will find valuable, your eyes must be closed ;-)

It's not like you're looking for the cure for cancer. Just little known twists the majority of your audience wants your unique perspective on. You can come up with 10, 20, 30, 100 or more of these little gems that can be positioned as your "jealously guarded secrets."

Let's Get Personal

Since bonding is emotional, you've got to get *personal*.

Now, this is the exact opposite of what "common business protocol" dictates. Most people take their personality OUT of their businesses. They write dry memos, academic, institutional marketing pieces that doesn't give the slightest hint that there are *real* people, with *real* feelings, struggling up against *real* problems on the other end.

The result? No bond. No hyper-responsives. No systematic repeat business. No obligation to stick with your company out of loyalty. Which all adds up to tiny (and ever shrinking) profit margins and no *lasting* success.

What follows is an excerpt from one of my newsletters. Look at how I let people into my life. How does this differ from other newsletters and marketing you see? Look for all the different elements we've covered here.

###

The casket was to my left.

I was smack in the middle of a heart-wrenching eulogy in honor of the loving woman who took me in when my mother died at 2 months old.

All of sudden some unplanned words of wisdom just leaped from my mouth. The message even surprised me. It was like God (or something outside me anyway) was whispering in my ear. Somehow it was exactly what the 300 plus people at the funeral (including me) desperately needed to hear at that moment.

It effortlessly poured from my heart.

It was very powerful. I KNOW it was because almost every one of those 300 plus people went out of their way to tell me so. But the most meaningful comment came from a successful entrepreneur and powerhouse speaker. She told me with glassy eyes and a slight quiver in her voice that my message was the answer to a personal crisis she faced.

Let me tell you, it could not have come at a better time for me. You see, the last 4 months have been bittersweet to say the least. Actually, among the toughest, most challenging - yet most exciting, passionate, joy-filled (not to mention absolutely the most lucrative - bar none) - of my life.

Here's just a sample of what I've experienced...

In the last 4 months I was lucky enough to marry the most fantastic woman in the whole world. The bitter part? A week before our wedding her mother died very unexpectedly (actually, this deepened the love and bond between us more than I can ever explain).

Then I got the long awaited news I'm gonna be a daddy and had tears well up in my eyes as I heard her thundering heartbeat for the first time. I helplessly watched 3 grandparents pass away... But built a deep connection and strong friendship with my father-in-law while helping him through the shock and grief of losing his wife. And in the midst of it all managed to squeeze a little business in between.

(That's a laugh... Business has NEVER been better or busier - which, as it turns out, is going to allow a few subscribers (maybe you) a unique opportunity to cash in big time! I've got something up my sleeve that's so amazing - such an incredible technological and marketing breakthrough - that it will make you more money than having the exclusive marketing

rights for Viagra! This is BIG (pun intended). More on this later.)

Life's like that, isn't it? A mixture of stress, joy, disappointment, and triumph. Quite a paradox... often what you think is something really bad turns out to be a blessing in disguise (if you look for the hidden benefit and let it unfold). Whatever. It's probably time I got off my soap box and got down to business...

What's that you say? Before we shift gears, you want to know what I said at the funeral? Hold your horses. I'll get to it. But first...

Check out this next Slice-Of-Life X-Factor example:

Subject: How a 3-year old humbled <u>ME</u>!

Hi Jane,

Have you ever been "schooled" by a 3-year old?

Well, *I* just was!

See, I've been struggling with a business decision for the last week. I've flipped back and forth on it so many times that my neck hurts (and, that's odd, because usually I'm very decisive).

But here's the *REALLY* annoying part...

Here I am, "Mr.Npod" (the successful Net Profits On Demand businessman) and my 3 year old daughter, Aimee, steps in and solves my problem in 5 seconds flat with only 11 simple words.

Sure, WHAT she said was important, but it was the "matter of fact" *WAY* she said it that floored me (I knew this empowerment stuff would come back and bite me in the ass one day).

I don't know. Maybe I should retire and turn things over to her...

Actually, *YOU* might think so too.

THE PROFIT PROPHET

Why?

Because her voice of clarity has lead me to do something that I believe with all my heart will change your life FOREVER....

Actually, I predict her advice will probably be responsible for creating 10-15 new multi-million dollar business model in the next 24 months!

Yes, it's THAT powerful!

Let me give you some background...

###

Here's my semi-famous $7,520.00 email that saved my ass in front of live TV cameras:

###

Subject: Why I HATE Shawn Casey!

hey.

Imagine the nerve! He put me on the spot.

Let me explain. Right now as I write this, I'm sitting in a hotel conference room listening to Shawn Casey, explain the secrets of using the internet effectively. Now Shawn, besides being a master marketer, a successful MLM'er, and an attorney (but I try not to hold that against him... till <u>now</u>) is also one of my very close PERSONAL friends.

But now I'm <u>reconsidering</u> that friendship.

I came to his seminar to support him and learn from him. <u>Now get this</u>: The seminar just gets going and he puts me on the spot in front of the ENTIRE audience... and to make matters worse the entire event is being video taped.

Shawn calls me up in front of everyone and tells them I don't care about my newsletter subscribers. Now, as you guys know, nothing could be further from the truth. And Shawn knows that TOO... which is why he got me so upset when he said that.

"What do you mean?" I politely ask him.

"Well," Shawn says, "you've got newsletter subscribers right now that are dying to learn the secrets of promoting their MLM opportunity on the internet and you've never once told them about my product, 'Mining Gold On The Internet.'"

I was speechless (which as you probably guessed by now is almost impossible for me).

Now, not only was I dumbfounded, I was (and still am) embarrassed because he was absolutely right (I hate it when he's right)...

Do you see all the different ways you can build your X-Factor bond from those last few examples?

However, this is only how *I* do it. It's my personality. So, don't try to be *me*. **You be you.** Let your tribe connect and bond with you (the *real* you, not some fake persona) on a deep, personal and authentic level.

There's one more thing you should know before we put the X-Factor to bed for now. It's really important (and almost always overlooked by even seasoned entrepreneurs).

Without leveraging this X-Factor, eventually you'll find yourself stuck in the same trap almost every business does: Constantly chasing down new customers to keep your ship afloat. Running on that hamster wheel might build you a healthy cash-flow, but it'll never give you the freedom of systemized profits that comes from building equity in a real business model.

Plus, nobody can run at 100 HPH on that wheel without burning yourself out. And when you stop, slow down or get knocked off "the-get-more-first-time-buyers" treadmill, **kiss your success bye-bye!** You're forced to start the wheel from a dead stop again. And, getting momentum on that wheel again gets harder and harder. Takes more and more energy.

Such a shame too. Because focusing solely on *new* business leaves 90+% of your massive profits sitting on the table. And, even worse, when you deploy the things you learned here, it's *much* less work. **These poor burnt out souls end up discarding their customer after only one use.**

One and done. Because then they have to jump back on the hamster wheel to chase down another first-time customer sell and discard.

Stupid, stupid, stupid!

Unless you like fighting for leftover scraps like stray dogs in the streets, after you get a customer to trust you enough to do business with you the first time, deepen that relationship and give them more of what they want.

Life (and profits) BEGINS *after* that first transaction. Easily 80-90% of your total profit potential lives beyond the first few sales (while, the majority of your highest costs always comes *before* your first sale).

Why leave all the easy money on the table to go chasing the hard, expensive money?

Not you, right?

You're gonna serve your tribe beyond their first transaction with you. Continue to stack value on top of value. You're going to leverage the X-Factor (all of Book 2) to provide a continuous stream of stellar solutions to your tribe, aren't you? You recognize how hard you have to work (and how expensive it can be) to lead your tribe to ascend to level 5 where money finally exchanges hands for the first time, don't you? And, you're too smart to get stuck on that hamster wheel, yes?

Perfect.

Well, not only is time to wrap up this chapter, now you also have enough of a foundation to capitalize on the knowledge I'm about to lay on you in our third and final piece of your Profit Prophet puzzle: **Book 3…**

BOOK THREE:

BUSINESS MODEL PREEMINENCE

(Demonstrating And *Delivering* EXPERIENTIAL VALUE To Your Tribe For 10X Prophet PROFITS)

CHAPTER 1:
The "Voodoo" That I Do, You Can Do <u>TOO</u>!

If you're reading each of the three books in order, you already know that by nature, I'm *not* one of those people who can sell ice to Eskimos.

However, just in case you've skipped ahead to this book, it's important you know I'm not a salesperson. In fact, I HATE selling. Old school selling anyways. Cajoling, convincing, and begging people to buy, just plain SUCKS!

Now, here in BOOK THREE you'll discover the "voodoo" that reaps you the Prophet Profits (notice the two Profits have switched places from the rest of all the previous ways it's been referenced). That's because we've finally arrived at the hard-core business building and moneymaking stuff. In this book, you get to leverage everything you learned in the first two books to build (or rebuild) yourself a business of PREEMINENCE. In other words, here's where you put all the Audience Attraction & Ascension voodoo to work for you to 10X your business success.

It's all about building the right systems into your business so you capitalize (and cash-in) on all the groundwork you've laid thus far. It gives you incredible cash-flow AND long term profitability. And it gives you ultimate control over the "Profit Tap" (i.e., the ability to dial-up or dial-down your business volume, on demand... and do it with complete confidence). It gives you a way to increase the equity value of your business WITHOUT relying on lucky breaks (or breaking the bank).

Here comes the rest of the "voodoo" that makes profitable business come to you in a completely systematic, predictable and scaleable way. With the insider info (remember what you just learned about "secrets" a few pages back, right? ;-) I became a cash millionaire in under 2 years (after 30+ years of struggle). You're about to discover the secret of making people, success, and, yes, lots and lots of money COME TO YOU!

Before we get into the meat of the matter, let's talk about the elephant in the room: Her name is *"Voodoo."* Right away, it conjures up feelings of magic and mystery, right? Good. That's exactly why I use it.

However, voodoo is only voodoo because you don't know how it works, right? See, *"voodoo," "magic,"* and *"luck"* are words we use when we can't make sense of things we don't understand. And, yet, with understanding, the same things you use to describe as mysterious voodoo becomes a rock solid reality.

Stumble onto something, and it works by chance, and you call it luck. However, once you know how and why it works... and, more importantly, once you can reproduce the same results again and again... well, now that voodoo is your *scientific* formula, right?

Some call it "magic" when I reengineer a business (or start a new cash flow machine from scratch) in the matter of a few days, weeks or months and all of sudden it's instantly swamped with profits (and usually it's with LESS person to person contact, NOT more).

It's really <u>not</u> mystical at all. In fact, <u>it's</u> <u>completely systemized and predictable</u>!

And so it is with the Profit Prophet "voodoo" you'll discover here in this third book. Mark my words, the first time you experience the kind of breath taking results it brings, you'll pinch yourself to see if you're dreaming because it's going to seem too good to be true. That's what any true breakthrough feels like the first time.

A real game changer.

What is it?

Patience, my friend, patience. We'll get to it in a few. But first we need to make sure you have the foundation necessary to use it (otherwise it'll remain as the mysterious voodoo as it appears now).

Anyway, in this book, I'm going to take you backstage and show you HOW the magic is done. You're about to come inside. You'll see exactly how to build total business preeminence!

> (Specifically, how to design the right business model and marketing that **systematically communicates your vision for a bigger future to your pack; and emotionally engages them so powerfully that it becomes their idea to elect you as THEIR Profit Prophet.** It's all about the structure that serves your pack best; that delivers superior value that they can only get from YOU as their pack-leader. Your business preeminence is all about how you impact them by improving their lives **better than all the other options available to them.**)

So, here we go…

CHAPTER 2:
You Gotta *Go Direct*

First things, first: **Traditional Branding BLOWS!**

In order to build business PREEMINENCE you've got to wrap your mind around "DRM" (Direct Response Marketing). Because that's where your Prophet Profits come from.

So, what, then IS, "Direct Response Marketing"? And, how (and why) is it incredibly different than any other type of "traditional" advertising, marketing or business building methodologies? Well DRM is marketing that justifies its very existence…

It Is Marketing That PROVES Its Profitability With Documented Stats And Results!

It's *measurable*. Direct Response Entrepreneurs know *exactly* how much money they generate in sales based on how much money they've spent to generate that action (sale or lead).

In its most basic form, **direct response marketing is about making a specific OFFER to your tribe (remember back to Book 2) and then MEASURING how many of your audience take ACTION and respond to that offer.**

The ACTION could be to simply request more information (called lead generation). Or the ACTION could be to simply open an email, click a link or start watching a video. Or it could be to call you. Or to purchase a specific product or service. It measures how many in the pack took advantage of whatever OFFER was presented as the Call To Action (CTA).

MEASUREMENT is key. That's because DRM always monitors how much is spent to generate each desired ACTION in the process.

If the desired action is to generate leads, then you would measure how much you spend to get each lead. This is called "Cost Per Lead" (CPL). Likewise, you monitor "Cost Per Order" (CPO) when the goal of your marketing is to generate orders for your products and services.

Simple enough, yes?

So, if you spend, say, $1,000 on a campaign designed to get prospects to "raise their hands" and say they want more information (lead generation); and that $1K gets you 100 qualified leads, then your CPL is $10, right? Because (the $1,000 spent) / (the 100 leads collected) = $10 cost per lead.

Follow?

Regardless if the desired action you want, you always measure back to know exactly what each big action (like sales) OR smaller actions (like ad views, clicks, visitors, and leads) costs to generate on a "per" basis.

So we measure things like: Cost Per View (CPV), Cost Per Impression (CPM), Cost Per Click (CPC), Cost Per Engagement (CPE), Cost Per Lead (CPL), and Cost Per Order (CPO) to name all the major ones.

Measuring each points us to the problem areas to focus on fixing because each of those numbers represent human behavior dynamics and psychology that can be improved.

What Did You Spend, And What Results (Actions) Took Place Because Of That Expenditure?

The concept is very basic. It's based on simple calculator math any third grader can whip right through. And, yet, the implications and the power it gives you is beyond all reasonable expectations!

Now, you've seen all sorts of Direct Response Marketing and Advertising in your life (probably even purchased because of some... even if you didn't directly know they were DRM businesses). You've seen 'em on TV (and YouTube). Heard 'em on the radio. Get 'em all the time in your email. See 'em in your Facebook newsfeed.

How about the 30 minute infomercials that air at 3am? Or those commercials that direct you to call the 800 number before the special offer for the extra acne cream ends? Any kind of an offer that has a coupon code attached to it is a form of DRM (and because of breakthroughs in online tracking technology we can track and measure everything without the audience's awareness).

Anyway, are you starting to get a feel for DRM?

You see, there's a specific offer. Sometimes they're enhanced with extras to make that offer as irresistible as possible... **all to incentivize their tribe to take the specific action the business wants.**

Now, what you might not have known about this type of business building is, behind the scenes, these entrepreneurs measure every single aspect of their list building, lead generation, front end sales, as well as their bigger, "back-end" purchases. They know things about their audience's behaviors in ways you have no idea is possible (unless you're already leveraging DRM).

For example, on TV, did you know that the infomercial marketers, put different phone numbers (CTA's) in each ad they run on each station they run it on so they can monitor not only which station produces the most orders, but also what the cost of the order is from each station they run the ad on?

These marketers know that the cost of generating a sale from one station is cheaper or more expensive than generating a sale from another station. And they are constantly monitoring the results. And they are always "split-testing" ALL the different aspects of their campaigns. Then, based on the bottom line results, they quickly scale up the profitable results and, more importantly, eliminate the losing ones!

> (SIDE NOTE: There was a popular saying by business owners, *"I know only half of my advertising is working… I just don't know WHICH half!"* Actually, it's more like 20% of your advertising produces 80% of your profits. Well, this is exactly why traditional advertising and branding blows! And, why Direct Response Entrepreneurs run circles around everyone else: Because they measure everything and therefore they know the 20% they need to give ALL their resources to… and, at the same time, they quickly cut the 80% that isn't working. They redeploy that 80% to test, find and scale more in their 20% categories!)

So, from all of their advertising, they track and measure WHERE it was placed, how many people viewed it, how much money it costs, and all of the specific actions that resulted along the way. And all of that adds up to the ultimate measurement: how much money you made (or lost) as a result of the marketing.

After small, inexpensive limited tests, you will know for every $1.00 spent on marketing, how much you get back in return (and at what dates). So, for example, maybe at day zero you make $0.80 for every $1.00 spent. And, at day 15, you're up to $1.10. On day 30 it might be $1.50. And day 90 maybe $3.00. And by the one year mark, each initial $1.00 spent on that specific marketing campaign might have generated a total of $15.00!

Now, this might not sound exciting when you look only at it from the $1.00 point of view. However, it'll make your head spin looking at it with even modest numbers! Let's look at what a one-time $15,000 invested in that same example Direct Response Marketing campaign produces. At day zero you've only recouped $12,000, which means you've lost $3,000 at this point, right? However, by day 15, that *original* $15K investment generates you an additional $4,500 in sales (so by day 15 you've passed breakeven and made a $1,500 profit)! At day 30 your $15k investment has grown to $22,500. At day 90 it would be $45,000. And, one year after spending that initial $15K you've collected $225,000.00 in this example!

That's exciting, isn't it?! And, it gets even better! Because that assumes you only invested in your marketing one time AND NEVER AGAIN. What if, in month 2 you invested all of your $22,500 return and put that to work for you in addition to your first $15K investment? Now, assuming your campaign stays consistent, you'll have $33,750 to invest in month 3.

Then what would your gross sales be at the one year mark? Do the math and you'll see it comes out to $978,750.00… from a total of only $71,250 invested over the first 3 months! So, let me ask you a stupid question: With these types of returns, would you stop at month 3 or would you continue to pump more and more into your campaign every single month? The smart Direct Response Entrepreneur keeps reinvesting ever increasing amounts into the business until the point of diminishing returns.

And, she doesn't stop investing all together when her business does reach that point. Nope. She dials it back. And once she finds her business's sweet-spot, she continues to feed her campaigns at that level for as long as they continue to provide acceptable returns.

Since she's REALLY sharp, she's constantly working on her business to increase her customer value beyond only a year… AND… She'll be testing NEW Direct Response Marketing Campaigns to beat her "control" (or replace it when it burns out… or having more than one winning campaign, right?).

We're getting a little ahead of ourselves. The point to take away is: This all starts with…

- **Monitoring And Measuring Your** *Expenses*.

- **Monitoring And Measuring Your** *Actions*.

- **Monitoring And Measuring Your** *Results (profits & losses)*.

- **And the timing of each** (just like our quick example above)

That's marketing that justifies its existence.

And, the best news about all this measuring is that it increases your profitable results at the same time it limits your losses!

See, when you leverage DRM, your business only scales up proven campaigns. You'll NEVER find yourself in a situation where you're spending a gazillion dollars for a 30 second advertisement during the Super Bowl, gambling the entire future of your company, with no indication if it'll drive enough sales to make it work or not. You'd never spend that kind of money without knowing you've got a hard-core, proven ROI (or if you didn't already have a pressure tested, systemized business model to leverage and capitalize on the investments in your marketing and advertising)!

A Direct Response Entrepreneur makes decisions based on documented results. If it makes money, you expand your marketing efforts: Test new ideas, develop new offers, try more, expand into different advertising mediums and new media sources. You roll out your campaign based on the success of the campaign. If it's profitable… Do MORE of that. If it isn't, you <u>stop</u>.

Real brain surgery, right?

It's common sense but even some of the most seasoned folks don't know how to build a business this way. Such a shame because if they did, their businesses would be 100 times more profitable and their losses minimized because it's tested literally in an isolation chamber, in a vacuum, and your loss is always protected.

Understand the concept?

<u>What</u> **is** your offer? <u>Who</u> are you going to communicate it to (the qualified targeted prospects)? <u>How</u> are you going to communicate it to them (the media type)? How well are you communicating the marketing message to your prospect? Are you communicating it to the right people? Are you using all the secrets revealed back in book 2 to systematically guide your audience to ascend up the value (and your influence) ladder?

If any one of those things are wrong, and the others are right, then it's like multiplying by 0, the whole thing falls apart and it doesn't work.

The Lifetime Value Of A Customer:

You can't create PREEMINENCE for your business *without* knowing how to leverage Lifetime Customer Value (LTCV). LTCV is the lynch pin that gives DRM all it's real power.

Now, you've already seen it in action a few pages back in our little example about the gross sales generated on day zero, day 15, day 30, day 90 and 1 year (plus, we discussed briefly back in Book Two). However, no Direct Response Marketing lesson is complete without a deep dive into how the Lifetime Customer Value is the REAL magic responsible for 10X'ing your business success!

Utilize this info properly, and it'll completely revolutionize your business model and increase your profits beyond comprehension.

First off, most businesses think about their customers **transactionally**. That is, they focus on each transaction in isolation. Almost always thinking in terms of only the very first transaction a brand new customer makes.

And, as soon as that transaction is completed, they spend all their resources running off to find the *next* brand-new, first time customer to sell. This is completely *backwards*. See, it's almost impossible to make a profit in today's business climate on that *first* transaction. You might be able to do it in very small numbers, but it certainly isn't scalable.

Why?

Remember back to our deep dive on the 7 mental conversations that your audience ascends through? Well it isn't until they get all the way to the 5th level where they're ready to trust you enough to make that first transaction with you. And because of the skeptical times we live (and do business) in, it can be an expensive proposition.

It takes trust to convince a skeptical prospect to buy from you. **Trust is a by-product of building enough of a relationship with the prospect so they'll risk doing business with you the first time.**

Think about it for a second.

The type of business or product has no effect on your trust building process. It doesn't matter if it's an air conditioner shop, a doctor's office, a dentist, a restaurant, a chiropractor's office, or whatever. Nor does it matter if it's a hard product, like a vacuum, or a soft product, like a software app.

Before a prospect buys from you the first time and becomes a customer, they'll be looking for an excuse to say "no" to your offer.

They're Skeptical From The Onset!

So, it takes time to build that trust. And building that trust is ALWAYS a PROCESS (refer back to Book 2 for the exact process)! Further, **the time it takes to transform that trust into a first sale is <u>longer</u>, and therefore more expensive.** That's because it's the <u>first</u> time your audience is being introduced to you. So they're naturally more guarded. Which means their sales defenses will never run higher than <u>before</u> that first transaction.

However, **AFTER** they buy from you just once, it instantly creates a level of trust that didn't exist before. Which means, once your audience crosses the line and spends at least a little money with... they are 100+X *more* likely to buy from you again. Immediately after that first transaction is completed, they're no longer a "cold" market, they're now a member of your "warm" market. That's why:

The Cost Of Producing The Second, Third Sale, Fourth (And All Subsequent Sales) Ends Up Costing You Less And Less And Less And Less...

Almost all your expenses live in generating the first transaction from a cold market. Whereas all your profit lives in the lifetime of future purchases that first time customer makes after joining the ranks of your warm market.

Let's look at an example.

Say, a roofer injures his back and decides see a chiropractor to help ease his back pain. He asks his friends if they know a good chiropractor. Then probably looks in the yellow pages and/or googles choices, looking for positive yelp reviews. Now he's got like hundreds of choices. So he chooses the ad that has the best testimonials, which also happens to offer a free consultation. He calls and after talking to the office manager, schedules to come in for his free consultation.

After the free consultation, he decides to pay for an adjustment because, after all, he's still in pain. And after the free consult, he trusts them enough to have the adjustment.

Now if that chiropractor is like most businesses, the roofer gets his immediate problem fixed and goes on his way. Unless he has another problem flare up he'll probably never do business with that chiropractor again. In this case, the roofer pays the chiropractic office only one time and that's it.

If, on the other hand, the chiropractor said, *"look, when you're roofing your body is constantly exposed to stress and sometimes that stress can turn into long term chronic problems if they aren't spotted early and reversed with simple ongoing maintenance.*

"We have a special program for hard working physical people just like you where we can help keep your body running in peak condition completely free of pain so you avoid any long term problems. Plus, we're running a special only available to you as a brand new client. Normally this whiz-bang service would cost $100.00/month, but with this special deal it's only $50.00... blah, blah, blah, blah"

See the difference?

This way, they take a one time sale to a first time customer and turn it into ongoing sales and profits... FOR THE EXACT SAME INITIAL EXPENSE!

Instead of making one and done, now they've set up an ongoing stream of future transactions which translates to direct profits coming in on a regular, predictable basis. LTCV looks at what the average customer will spend with your business over the ENTIRE period you keep them as a client by providing them with ever increasing value propositions. It dramatically changes your entire business's competitive advantage because you can do things that your competition can't or won't because they don't have a clue what their LTCV is. Nor do they know things you're learning here to exponentially increase their LTCV!

Now let's take our chiropractic example a step further so you really get what this is all about.

Let's say that on a subsequent visit, our LTCV savvy chiropractor recommends, *"...we've got this special whiz-bang back-brace, that has got this brand new magnetic pulse technology built into it that not only helps heal, but also blocks out the pain at the same time... I've been using it VERY successfully with some of my patients and I think it will work well for you..."*

Of course, our hard working roofer gives the back-brace a try. Again, more profits to the chiropractor at no additional expense. The patient (customer) bought an additional product/service from the chiropractor (Profit Prophet Entrepreneur), because our roofer has decided that *his* chiropractor is now a trusted advisor and won't go against her recommendations.

Next, on a subsequent visit maybe the chiropractor notices that the roofer has flat feet and that his fallen arches are pulling on the muscles in the roofer's back in a way that makes him susceptible to greater injuries. So she recommends to the roofer, *"...this is probably why you're starting to have these back injuries more often. But I have the solution, I can take some molds of your feet right now and have some custom supports made for you to use in your work boots."*

The cash-register rings again, right?

It continues to ring because that chiropractor is now a trusted advisor. And, with the sale of each product and service, guess what? She's adding value, building a stronger trust and relationship, all by helping the roofer live a bigger, pain free future!

You can add all sorts of different products and services into the mix once trust is established, can't you? As long as the offers add value to their lives, you'd be surprised how many different things that original customer will buy.

The best part about this process is with each transaction, the act of buying actually builds more trust! It feeds itself. See, once the trusted advisor level relationship is reached, that's when the Oprah-Effect of compliance without much (if any) push-back happens. It's extremely likely that your pack member will purchase whatever is recommended. And, by the way, with this level of trust, it's not some big sales job. It becomes a part of the very natural flow of the relationship you've established.

So now look back on the way over 90% of all businesses (chiropractic and otherwise) do it; they settle for that first time visit to solve that problem, and they get a little bit of money.

Or sometimes they might have 3-5 products, offered over the course of the first 30-60 days. And, then what do they do? That's right, they focus on finding the next one time customer (leaving $1,000's on sitting on the table). They're like crack heads, looking for their next fix (i.e., their next first time customer). They're focused on finding their next roofer in pain so they can convince them to come in for a free consultation and hopefully get that first, one time sale. It becomes 100% about driving new, first time customers instead of servicing the ones they got.

Stupid!

And, so VERY expensive!

There's no comparison when you look at the transactional, one time vs. the LTCV approach. Figure out what it costs (in time and money) to get that first time customer to buy from you and you'll never ignore the massive profits awaiting you in that portion of your tribe who have already given you at least some money. Plus, usually the first purchase a customer makes is their lowest because they want to start slow to make sure they made the right decision to do business with you in the first place.

After more relationship and trust is established, everything naturally unfolds AFTER the first sale. Compare the amount of money (and the amount of work it takes to convert a cold stranger into a customer) with the amount of profits you make from that first transaction and you'll see it's almost impossible to turn a real profit on the first purchase!

However it costs nothing *extra* for the chiropractor to make the additional sales because all the expenses to generate that first sale is a "sunk cost." They've already spent the ad dollars and whatever the consultation costs to deliver. Those expenses are the same regardless if they only make one sale and done... or if they turn that first time buyer into a lifetime buyer! It also doesn't cost them anything more if they focus their attention on increasing their LTCV!

See the power?

Whatever they've spent to get that new customer in the door and sell them, is a single, fixed, one-time expenditure; it doesn't matter what happens after that point. The front-end expenses have already been spent.

There's No Limit To The Profits This Can Reap For Your Business When You Put LTCV To Work For You

Because, remember, for the same money that they're spending on their marketing, they're now making *more* money. Now, *that's* Profit Prophet leverage.

CHAPTER 3:
The <u>Foundation</u> Of <u>All</u> Business Success

The root of success in ANY business venture boils down to 3 primary functions:

1. **Lead Generation** (SIFT, SORT & SCREEN CANDIDATES);

2. **Initial Sale** (CONVERSION);

3. **Future Sales** (MAXIMIZING LTCV).

Now, it doesn't matter what your business sells. It can be "hard" products (like: Diet pills, office supplies, computer hardware, CD's, DVD's, paintings, etc.); or "soft" products (such as: ebooks, apps, games, seminars, workshops, training, education, software, etc.).

Every single business (bar none), must excel at these 3 activities if they want success. And, if you want to go beyond success to PREEMINENCE, you need to follow the Profit Prophet playbook for these 3 areas.

Lead generation feeds conversions to your first time customers (called the "front-end"). Then, your front-end feeds to the "back-end," which is the ongoing future sales. And, as you now know from the last chapter, the back-end of your business is where the real profit lives because that's how to increase your LTCV, right?

Remember back to Book 2 where you discovered the 7 mental conversations your audience has to ascend through? Well, those levels of your influence all relate to these 3 main functions of your business model. The first four levels happen as they ascend through your lead generation processes. The 5th level mental conversation is what gets them over the hump and creates your initial front-end sale conversion. Your audience's level 6 mindsets sets your back-end future stream of sales in motion. And, when you systematically guide your tribe to ascend to the 7th level, that's how you maximize your LTCV!

See how it all fits together?

Notice how your cold-market must ascend through 4 mental conversations during your lead generation phase. And only 1 for that initial, first time transaction (level 5, as you'll recall). So, this means, the better job you do designing strategic systems for ascending your tribe through their level 6 & 7 relationship with you… THE MORE YOU INCREASE YOUR LTCV! Which is how you can 10X your business success without breaking the bank.

Are you starting to get a visceral feel for just why the first two functions are the most expensive? Your audience must ascend through 5 levels of trust and relationship building before they ever do business with you for the first time. And, depending on each of their past negative experiences, it can take time. Their memories of their past buying decisions governs if they're "tough sells" (or "lay-downs).

Follow?

Either way, you can't rush 'em. Especially during the first 5 levels, you gotta love 'em where they are and show them the possibility of only a *slightly* bigger future. Your offers have to be just big enough to compel them to act, but not so bold that it pushes past the limits of what they currently believe is possible.

Remember, your audience is naturally skeptical. They've been hurt before and don't trust instantly. In fact, right up until the moment they actually give you their money for the first time, they'll be on the look out for how you're going to screw them. Yet, the *instant* they buy, their trust in you takes a big leap forward (unless they felt strong-armed into buying).

The ONLY 3 Ways To Grow ANY Business:

Now, just like the 3 foundational functions, your business's growth is 100% determined by these 3 root things (the 3 *prime* tenants all scalability comes from):

a. **Increase the number of new customer acquisitions** (feed more first-time transactions into the front-end of your business); and

b. **Earn higher prices** (continually increase the value exchange of your business's back-end provides by adding more products and services with escalating prices, increasing the average ticket size of your future sales); and

c. **Increase the purchase frequency** (adding new back-end solutions on a regular basis because obviously a client that buys 15 times a year makes you more profit than one who purchases less frequently).

These are the only 3 ways to grow any business. You might think you have an exception to the rule; however, I promise that if you trace it back to it's roots, it's a derivative of one or more those primary ways listed above.

So, of course, the smart Profit Prophet Entrepreneur gives about 20% of her time to acquiring new customers and the remaining 80% goes to maximizing her LTCV by working on the back-end represented by (b) and (c) above. Because

It's about SYSTEMIZING all 3 of your business's growth

processes… AND doing it in a powerful way so that ALL THREE ASPECTS work together to maximize your overall results! Because, after all, were you aware of these little known things?

- **Did you know your lead generation process can increase (or decrease) your chances of getting the initial sale?**

- Did you know your lead generation process will also affect your LTCV because it can pre-program how much a customer is willing to spend and how frequently they will make future purchases from you?

- **Did you know that your initial customer acquisition process influences your positive or negative word-of-mouth and therefore directly impacts the effectiveness of your lead generation processes?**

- Did you know that HOW you convert (the specific process used) your audience to do business with you for the first time trains your tribe how to respond to you in future business dealings (i.e., sets up their expectations in terms of the frequency and size of their future purchases)?

Most entrepreneurs get fixated on fresh blood, only. Meaning: The only way they know to grow their business is by acquiring new buyers. They get so locked in there, they leave all the easy profits sitting on the table while they continue to run 100 miles an hour on the new customer hamster wheel.

See, most business folk have been unknowingly programmed to think transactional in terms of finding new customers. As soon as they get a new customer, their attention immediately shifts to, *"how can I get another new customer?"* When, instead it should be, *"how can I serve my current clients better, create more value for them, and turn them into lifers?"*

I suppose this trap is kind of natural because when any business first starts, it doesn't yet have any clients to sell more to, right? So in the beginning all we can think about is the fastest route to cash, money. Since we all start from scratch, the only logical move is to generate sales by first acquiring a few initial customers, yes?

They think, *"I'll worry about building my back-end and maximizing after I get things rolling."* While I agree it *starts* there, without a solid **strategic growth plan** (that utilizes all of 3 primary growth options) and gets maximum leverage for your lead generation, front-end AND back-end processes… well, let's just say you're guaranteeing yourself a very long 'n winding road (with many potholes). Without it, it's a crapshoot! Then, if you stumble on to success it's by *accident*, not **by design.**

Since it's like a big spiderweb, where pulling on one strand shifts the whole ecosystem, you'll want to give *some* forethought to your whole business model BEFORE launching. Otherwise, it's likely your business will hit its sales and profit plateaus long before you should (or maybe your business crashes and burns before it even gets off the ground).

You've gotta be at least a *little* strategic in your approach!

You have to decide what your strategy is for generating leads before you can convert them. Why? Simply because one conversion process might work phenomenally well under one specific situation, but fail miserably under another.

Let's say you have a sales process that has one type of lead generation, and you build your lead conversion step to the point it's converting like a champ. Now you're starting to make great money from that one source of leads.

What happens when all of sudden, leads from that one source stop converting as well as they did before? It happens. You didn't change anything but all of a sudden your prospects don't behave the same way they used to inside the system. Now you need to find another lead generation source to have a stable business.

Or, what if you're doing well with one source, but you're getting all you can from it so you aren't able to grow beyond your present level. If you want to scale to the next level, your only choice is adding new lead sources, right?

So you figure *"well, under my current system, for every 100 leads I generate, I make 5 sales. Since I want to make 50 sales a day, all I have to do is go out and find more lead sources because if I can feed my system with 1,000 new leads a day, then I'll automatically generate the 50 sales/day I want."*

But what happens when the new lead sources don't convert the same? You think, *"What's wrong? Why isn't it converting?"*

Your system is <u>not</u> broken.

You've built a conversion system for one specific lead source, but not for another. The new source pulled your business's web in a way you hadn't expected and it produced a different outcome. Follow?

Here's a more obvious example that will make it clearer. Say you have a Steak of the Month Club. You sell high quality dry-aged T-bones, fillets, New York strips, and rib-eyes in your monthly buyers club. And you get all your initial customers from people who subscribe to *"Steak Lovers Magazine"* (I don't know if there is such a publication, I just made it up for this example).

So your conversion process is built around mailing offers to all the subscribers to that magazine. Life's pretty good. The subscribers from *Steak Lovers* convert really high for you but there's only a few thousand of them so you're concerned because you can't grow beyond your present level.

You hear about another "awesome" list that someone made a killing mailing to. They said, "This list of food lovers made me $1 million. You should mail to it, too." You say, "Okay. My system converts like crazy. It makes sales like crazy. With so many more people and my process, I ought to have 10,000 new customers in a heartbeat."

And you start counting your future profits while preparing for the biggest campaign you've ever done.

However, you find out that most of the food lovers on that list are vegetarians (and the guy that made a million from the list had a fruit of the month club). No matter how killer your conversion system is, it ain't never gonna sell meat to vegans. Not never!

Right?

Now, here's a real life example from my own personal experience: I used to run a monthly training program called *"The 2 Comma Club (Secrets to*

Bridge the Millionaire Gap®)" and I built out a killer lead conversion system that was converting, if I recall correctly, at about a 20% signup rate of the people who visited my website. Meaning, for every 100 people who came to the offer page, around 20 people signed up for a free trial.

I offered it to my own "in-house" list of subscribers. About 1,000 people signed up immediately on my first campaign (which meant that at the $52.99/month subscription, I'd make over $50,000.00 a month for as long as they stayed subscribed! Not bad for sending out a few emails to my back-end, in house list).

I thought, *"This is really great. Wonder what would happen if I let some marketing partners promote it on a performance basis for a share of the future profits they produce?"*

I didn't expect they would do as well as I did because, after all, my in house list already knew, liked, and trusted me to a degree, right? However, since these partners already had established relationship with *their* in-house lists, I figured they'd do well enough to make it worth their effort.

So, I allowed a few select joint-venture partners promote the offer and leverage my proven process for 50% commissions on the sales they generated. One company did about 12% conversions. Another did around 18%. I think the lowest was 9-10%. Anyway, in 3 months with approx 5 partner promotions I had right around 4,000 new members on a monthly continuity program!

I thought, *"This is a proven sales system. It's converting. We have this thing handled. I have the conversions. I know what my stick rate is. It's on!!!"*

So I decided to expand beyond JV's into paid media.

I found a company that promised they would put at least one million people in front of my proven offer for only $10,000.00!

I pulled out trusty calculator. The worst conversions the system did was 10%. But let's keep it really conservative. What would happen if it only converted at 2% (not the 10-20% "normal" conversion)?

Well, 1,000,000 leads going through my lead conversion system should, at only 2%, wind up converting 20,000 new subscribers!

I mean, even if it only converted at 0.001% it would still be worth the $10,000 because that would still give me 1,000 new subscribers (and every 1,000 new signups earned me approximately $50,000.00 a month!).

Hell, even if I only got 100 new members, in two months it would pay me back the 10 grand and I'd have still have a $5,000/month positive cash flow after that!

An easy decision, right?

You better believe I wrote that $10,000.00 check on the spot!

And, sure enough, they **DID** deliver me the 1 million leads they promised. And guess how many of the 1 million leads signed up?

Not even ONE!

What's the difference?

The difference was the way that people were cultured to buy.

It was the way they were trained or *programmed* to purchase, as well as the trust factor.

CHAPTER 4: Creating Buying Cultures

Ready for the good stuff?

You're gonna love this. I call it *"creating the right buying culture."* And, it's also where we blend everything you discovered in books 1 & 2 together into Prophet Profits.

So, what's a buying culture?

Well, it's all about psychological conditioning. I like to think about it as mental programming because done right, you create a buying environment in the mind of your prospect using your business model to do it. Because, when you use everything revealed in book 2, it syncs up so powerfully with what your audience is already thinking and wanting. It becomes their idea to gladly move through your process. They call the shots. And it becomes their decision to buy (instead of you needing to sell 'em)!

Let's back up a minute. Remember, we mentally talk to ourselves *all the time!* You do it. I do it. Your Mom & Dad do it too. That means your tribe, prospects, customers, students, employees, partners, and friends all have *constant* conversations with themselves!

These mental conversations are so automatic in most of us that we don't even realize we're having them (which means we can't stop 'em if we don't have conscious awareness of 'em).

We're talking to ourselves all the time.

Pick a person. Anyone. They're having a conversation with themselves right now. That's because every thought we think is really a string of questions.

We think a thought. Which leads to another thought. Pictures pop into our minds. Then we talk to ourselves about the pictures or the thought we just had. Then we think about our *reaction* to that thought. Then another thought in response to the last. More questions. More thoughts. More mental "chatter."

Unless we meditate, we simply can't shut off these thoughts. Our thoughts run us by way of our minds. These thoughts make up the internal mental conversation that we all have with ourselves.

You've got a conversation going on in your mind right now as you read these words. You're questioning if you agree or disagree with my last few statements. Maybe you're stopping to ask yourself if that's really true? Or if you can come up with something that proves me wrong? Just recognize that whatever is going on in your mind right now, simply proves my point!

I know, it's kinda freaky, when you first start paying attention to it all, isn't it?

These mental conversations are going on all the time and what **you've got to remember, whenever you enter a communication situation with your audience, <u>you are entering the conversation that is already established and going in their mind</u>.** (And, oh, by the way, each of your business functions ARE *all* communication situations!)

Read that again. And again. One more time, please. Seriously. It's THAT important.

Now, because our own mental conversations are so loud, we don't usually stop to think about what kind of mental conversation the other guy is having.

Many of these conversations are so habitual, we don't even know we're having them anymore (remember way back to book 1?). In other words, because we've had the same thoughts over and over again on the same subjects, we have to believe they are absolutes. The constant repetition of these habitual conversations have conditioned into what you call *instincts*.

Anytime you enter a familiar situation, it triggers your habitual conversation (thought process) to fire off in your minds. Same for me. Same for everyone.

(What's your knee-jerk reaction if a salesman comes on too strong and says something like *"Can I help you out? Are there any questions I can answer for you?"* – If you're anything like me it triggers your YUCK reflex and you hear yourself say *"No thanks, just looking"* even if you really need help. See, he caused that reaction because he didn't recognize the pre-programmed mental conversations I had based on my past conditioning, right?).

So, you, me, we, <u>everyone</u>: We've ALL been conditioned by the habitual conversations running in our minds all the time. And, to be a master communicator (and influencer)...

You've got to know WHERE your business functions are entering THEIR mental conversations!

If you accurately predict where you're entering their mental conversations (at which stage) and enter it at that exact right point (so they feel you understand what they're thinking at that exact moment), then, they aren't just having a conversation by themselves. You're in it with them!

This level of "kinship" makes people more open. And, the more open they are, the more likely they are to actually "hear" the value of continuing the conversation *with* you (which eventually leads to them taking action on your offers to increase the value they get from you).

Now it's their idea. They WANT to explore what you have to "say" because you entered their mental conversation and didn't push against their current thoughts. See, you either trigger the automatic "OH, YUCK!" or the "HMMM TELL ME MORE" reactions depending on how well you sync up with (or push against) the conversations that are already taking place.

Sync up with 'em the right way and it doesn't take long before they gladly let you redirect their mental conversations because, after all, they really want to see new possibilities in the first place. But only if you enter the conversation where they already are, first!

That's what creating the right "buying culture" means.

REPROGRAMMING THE MIND TO A NEW CONVERSATION!

Once we enter someone else's mental conversation, we can work with them.

We can follow. With their permission we can lead. We can evolve them beyond their normal habitual thoughts.

We can be a friend. Provide an "ear" by showing them we understand 'em. We can make them feel heard instead of ignored. Make them feel validated by simply acknowledging how their mental situations may make them feel.

We can cry with them. Laugh with them. Show them how they can laugh more and cry less with some of our ideas.

You can help them grow, expand, and see new possibilities where they couldn't. Once inside their minds, **at their request**, you gently show them how and why a belief (habitual mental conversations) may be limiting the bigger future they've been struggling to reach.

Here's the *really* interesting part: Because it's in our minds, these conversations are completely *imaginary*. **We've made 'em ALL up to begin with!**

That means that regardless if you acknowledge it or not, these conversations are going to naturally evolve for every single person. Based on our life experiences we decide and try to make sense of life. Our reality (the "rules" we believe to be true about us, our situations, and the world around us) all stems from these mental conversations.

It's how we make sense of our world. It's our perspective.

And culturing (or human programming) is about consciously directing these conversations on purpose (instead of letting the inmates run the prison by allowing each thought to think itself without conscious awareness).

Fostering The Buying Conversation

So what does this have to do with business preeminence?

EVERYTHING!

Recall your 3 primary business processes? Sure you do, it wasn't that far back;-) They are: 1. **Lead Generation**; 2. **Initial Sale**; and 3. **Future Sales**, right?

<u>Here's what you need to know</u>: Your audience will AUTOMATICALLY SHIFT THEIR MENTAL CONVERSATIONS BASED ON WHICH OF THE 3 PROCESSES THEY'RE IN! This means that as your business relationship evolves, their mental conversations do too.

Now we can apply this insight your success. Here's a quick review of the key elements of your strategic plan to 10X your success and create business preeminence. First are the 3 different business development systems required:

1. **Lead Generation** (SIFT, SORT & SCREEN CANDIDATES);

2. **Initial Sale** (CONVERSION);

3. **Future Sales** (MAXIMIZING LTCV).

And you will maximize the lifetime value of your average customer (your

LTCV) by a powerful combination of:

a. **Increase the number of <u>new customer acquisitions</u>** (feed more first-time transactions into the front-end of your business); and

b. **Earn <u>higher prices</u>** (continually increase the value exchange your business's back-end provides by adding more products and services with escalating prices, increasing the <u>average ticket size</u> of your future sales); and

c. **Increase the <u>purchase frequency</u>** (adding new back-end solutions on a regular basis because obviously a client that buys 15 times a year makes you more profit than one who purchases less frequently).

Notice that with each of your business's 3 primary functions (soon to be customer, and eventual raving fan) your audience switches their mental conversations. And, if you want to continue your conversation with them, you'll need to switch right along with them. The only difference is that your tribe won't be consciously aware of the mental conversations… or that they will change as they progress through each of your systems.

However, you WILL be. ;-)

Because you strategically designed it into your business models, you'll be aware of exactly where these shifts take place. You'll stay consistent with each mental shift as they go through each stage of your business process.

See, at each stage, you have a different desired outcome for what happens in that specific process, right? The goal of your lead generation is *not* to try and force them to become an instant lifetime fan. It's too big a jump to ask them to ask them to swallow the elephant whole. You *can* get 'em there, but it's gonna be at *their* pace! If you try to skip, sidestep, or shortcut the process you're going to confuse them… and, remember, **confuse 'em and you'll lose 'em.**

Lead generation is about getting your audience's *attention* long enough to build a little *interest* (usually using curiosity as discussed in depth in the last book). The goal of generating leads is to sift, sort and screen so your ideal candidates raise their hands (i.e., qualify themselves by taking the action required to move to the next stage of the process).

The next business function is converting your prequalified (and pre-sold) lead into a first time customer. And this requires shifting with them into a new conversation called "Conversion." This is *different* from their conversation about attention and interest that took place when they were in the lead generation process.

Each of your business functions not only triggers a brand new conversation, but it's almost a completely different language. The language of lead generation is different from conversion. Front-end conversations differ from back-end ones. Purchasing more frequently is different from a one time only transaction. And so it is with all the elements of your business model: Each is a *different* type of a conversation in a *different* language... because each has its own specific goal to be achieved (and set of mental challenges that must be overcome to achieve it).

Get it?

So when your audience is talking to themselves about if they are curious enough to find out more in your lead generation stage, it's completely different than the mental chatter they'll have when buying for the first time (or making a bigger investment in your higher priced back-end product, higher up the value ladder).

And, likewise, their mental conversations shift to a whole new set immediately after they take the leap of faith to make that first transaction with you. Depending on how good of a job you do on making good on your promises for that initial purchase (and things like follow up, support, fulfillment, new solutions, etc.), their mentality towards you and your solutions will shift yet again.

See, at each stage of your different functions, your audience starts to make up a new story. And that's the story they will tell themselves over and over again. It's how they define the experience they take away from each interaction with you. These stories (i.e., mental conversations) evolve with what they decide each interaction means to them.

They shift about you.

They shift about themselves.

They shift about the level of trust and belief they have in you (your products, services, solutions, etc.).

And they shift about the belief they have about the value they're getting from your business.

> SIDE NOTE: There's two levels of belief: 1. The belief in your solutions working as advertised; and 2. The belief in your solutions working for THEM given THEIR unique situations. They can *believe* your products work AND *still doubt* it'll work for them.

Therefore, the better job you do at identifying the "global" stories ARE for your target market, the more effective you will be at influencing them to move quickly through each of your business's phases. By "global" I mean the common thoughts, concerns, pain, experiences, situations, etc. that enough of your tribe all share (the similar wants, desires, goals, etc. that a good candidate for your solutions share).

For example, you can be sure, one basic story we all tell ourselves is that we're too busy. Which means, a typical conversation your candidate has when he's in your lead generation process is, *"why should I listen to you for even one more second?"*

Actually, it's more like, *"hurry up and say something stupid, like I KNOW you're gonna, because I need an excuse to stop listening to you now and get back my already overwhelming day!"*

Enter their conversation there, answer that mental question to their satisfaction and they naturally want to know more. That's the exact point where they shift to the next conversation. You've got their attention and now they're trying to decide if they're interested enough to consider your offer for the solution.

This is the *conversion* conversation, right?

At this point the mental conversation goes from "why should I listen?" to *"Am I interested enough in this to explore the benefits and value this holds for me? Sounds good on paper but because of all the experiences I've gone through in my life, I'm not gonna fall for this crap again. It's gotta PROVE to me why it's different than every other thing I've already tried and, more importantly, why this solution is so special that it's absolutely going to work for me, where everything else failed and let me down?"*

See the different tone, direction and depth of someone considering doing business for the first time compared to the previous lead generation mindset?

The lead gen. conversations usually revolve around wondering why/if you're worthy of any of their time and attention. Then it shifts gears into why they should believe in you, your solution, and then why they should believe it will work for them (even if it works for you and others).

It's serious business now. The conversations are all about trust, belief, and respect factors. Their guard is sky high because once you have their attention and interest, **they feel vulnerable.** What if they get screwed?

It's about 90% emotional and 10% logic and reason. That's because we won't ever consider the logic and reason of an offer from a stranger we dislike and suspect is a two-faced liar, right?

No way!

We won't buy from anyone we don't feel we know, like, and trust enough to believe them. How do we decide if we know, like, and trust someone?

Aren't those all *feelings*? If you like someone, isn't it a **feeling**?

How do you decide when you really "know" someone? What do you base trust on? **In reality, (regardless of what we proclaim publicly to save face) it's all based on your "gut," right? It all happens emotionally, <u>first</u> (even if you are an analyzer type personality).**

Which means all of your communications to people in the initial transaction conversation has to successfully answer their mental questions about why should they like, trust, and respect you. How can *they* know you well enough to believe the logic and reason of your offer will bring them enough value to overcome their fears of doing business with you for the first time?

And, speaking of the belief and trust, there's actually two levels you've got to acknowledge and answer because they control the buying decision:

The first is do they believe **you**? Are you coming across credible to them? Do they trust you and believe you're telling them the truth at this point or not?

After you acknowledge and enter their conversation about their level of belief in you (and redirect that conversation towards all the reasons why they can and should trust you're telling them the truth), they shift into the second level of belief, *"OK, clearly this guy/gal knows her stuff and I believe the product/service actually works for HIM/HER (and others)… BUT that doesn't mean it will work for ME… now that I believe you, how can I believe this will give me the same benefits I now believe is possible in general?"*

The second stage of your business process will make people think:

- What IS this product?
- **Why will this benefit ME?**
- What makes this offer special?
- **Why should I even consider it?**
- Why is it valuable to ME?
- **Why is it worth way more than what's being charged?**
- Can I get a better deal somewhere else?
- **Why should I care?**
- How will I benefit?
- **Why is this different than all my other options?**

And so on.

Guess what happens after they make the initial buying decision to do business with you the first time?

Right! *Their mindset shifts yet again!* And, what's the next conversation following immediately on the heels of all first time transactions?

JOSHUA SHAFRAN

Buyers Remorse

It's just a fact of business life. Immediately after we make the buying decision to trust someone we've never done business with before, we wonder if we made the right decision. We tend to second-guess ourselves.

Since it's in our human nature, you had better plan for it in your business processes because ignoring it doesn't make it go away (in fact, miss this conversation and it'll kill your profits and you'll never know the *real* reason why your business is flat-lining).

Like clockwork, all the excitement and dreams they had about living that much bigger and better future, is squelched by their fears of **not** having that dream come true. It's not a question of IF buyers remorse will happen because it's an absolute certainty! No big whoop because you've got a plan to again meet them in this mental conversation AND address it to their satisfaction so they don't freak out and cancel, refund, or chargeback on your merchant account, right?

Yes, this takes some work. Sometimes it means not only redesigning your sales and fulfillment processes, **but ALSO redesigning your actual product lines!**

But here's the GREAT news: If you'll do the work to acknowledge and solve their buyers remorse conversations in your business process, you'll get rich faster than you thought was possible because your new customer will gladly make the transition from that scared, first time customer into your biggest advocate! Because by solving their biggest fears, you help them get the full value and benefits from your solutions that they desperately want!

Make no mistake about it, the work it takes to address it, converts to cold hard, bottom-line profits because they will gladly buy more and more from you. They'll GLADLY purchase more frequently. And they'll GLADLY spend higher and higher amounts on those solutions because they know you deliver!

Since 80% of maximizing your LTCV (and therefore profits) is controlled by developing more solutions at higher and higher prices and increasing the frequency of future transactions, handling buyer's remorse in a systematic way is one of the highest payoff activities you can focus on.

Before we wrap up this chapter, here's a powerful *takeaway*: All of your audience's mental stories create the overall buying culture of business processes. And, since no matter what you do, these mental conversations

WILL happen, you can either let your culture unfold on its own or you can strategically engineer your business's buying culture to form according to your vision.

A culture WILL form. The only question is will it unfold with or without your conscious awareness and control over it?

If you don't get active with these mental conversations, you're leaving your success to chance.

Left to develop on its own, the mass mindsets that unfold on their natural accord in reaction to communications without regard for what the other person thinks, feels, and believes may or may NOT support your goal for each stage of your business process. You can't be effective if your audience tells themselves stories about not understanding the benefits your solutions give 'em to improve their lives in a major way.

And, one thing is an absolute certainty: This mental chatter ain't never gonna stop (regardless if you acknowledge it or not). You can take it to the bank that a specific culture (mass mindset) IS going to develop. *Period.*

Will you be the one to deliberately mold and shape that mass mindset… OR… Are you going to let the parade lead itself?

See, the totality (the combination of the mass mindsets) is what develops into the culture that sets the tone for your business! It happens in response (and unconscious reactions) to what you say and how you say it. And, once it gathers a head of steam, this mass mindset takes on a life and gravity all its own!

Remember, regardless whether you *consciously* design and direct it to support your goals or not, a culture and communication momentum *is* automatically *going* to happen.

CHAPTER 5:
What's Reality Got To Do With It?

(The TRUTH About Mind-Control)

Reality is relative. Your definition of what's "real" and "true" is unique to you.

That's why it doesn't matter what's *actually* true about you, your offer, or the value you create; the only thing that DOES matter is what your audience has *decided to believe* is true!

Please read that again. I hope you will really internalize that fact. If you do, you'll find it easy to make success chase you. If not, it'll be impossible.

Fact.

What we decide to believe *is* true. Likewise, what we believe is bullshit, *is*. Both are only mental stories. A belief is just a thought we think so often it's become the habitual conversation we believe to be true. It's only true to the extent that we believe it.

Think about this: All stories, all thoughts, all beliefs, all mental conversations (and *what we decide they mean to us*) are 100% in our minds!

Do you realize that means it's all *imaginary*?

So the story we decide to tell ourselves (which controls what we believe to be true) is 100% made up! It has no basis in "reality" because it's just a conversation, taking place in our minds without conscious awareness.

But it IS *our* reality because *we believe it to be true.* Over time, through repetition, the stories we tell ourselves and believe to be true becomes the codes we live by.

We all have these "rules" limiting us on an unconscious level. Ever buy something and don't know why? Almost like you were in a trance and only snapped out of it when you got your credit card statement? Likewise, have you ever had an instant dislike or uneasy feeling when someone walks by you?

That's your unconscious mental programming hard at work controlling your automatic reactions based on the stories you've been telling yourself are true for you.

Here's how this fits into your business process: **You can help people to assimilate your story within theirs.** When you know generally what people will be thinking at each stage of the process, you can show people how your story (your beliefs about the value they get if they take you up on your offer), supports the code they've already decided is true for them.

You don't fight, argue, or attempt to convince them to change their mental stories. Instead, you show them new possibilities *from inside their stories.* That allows them to reframe, edit, and/or rewrite what parts of their stories mean.

Notice two key things in that last sentence: First, **THEY are the ones doing the reframing, editing, or rewriting, NOT you.** You're just providing the opening they need to see a part of their own story they didn't see before. The new possibilities come from the blending of their stories with yours.

Second thing to notice is **they <u>don't</u> change their stories, only its <u>meaning</u> to them!**

We become *invested* in our stories. We don't give them up easily because our stories are our realities. If they <u>know</u> their world is flat and you try to force them to see it's really round, not only will they hate you but now they must convince you it is flat. Now it's an ego battle they *have* to win at any cost because your perspective is a personal attack to their reality.

When you try to get someone to change a story they "know" to be true (regardless if it's a false truth or not), they'll spin all "evidence" you give them to believe their story even more! Even if your point of view frees them from their biggest life problems, **they'll fight to stay in their story because it's all they've ever known.**

That's because it's *not* a story to them. It's who they believe they <u>are</u>. The story has become a personal identification for them (part of their self-image). Part of how they define themselves.

So if your story threatens to "kill" their story, subconsciously they react as if it's a personal *attack*. You'll never win that battle. *Ever*.

However, if your story doesn't oppose theirs, threaten to replace it, or make them wrong for the code they've been unconsciously living by, they won't slip into <u>"arguing-to-be-right"</u> mode.

The Twin Powers Of Mind-Control:

Mind-Control sounds like voodoo again, doesn't it?

No voodoo here.

Just two base emotions that govern how we define and make sense of our thoughts, beliefs, stories and conversations that all take place in our minds. They are:

1. The desire to **gain pleasure** (to move towards something that we think will give us pleasure, value, joy, etc.)

2. The desire to **avoid pain** (to move away from things we think are going to cause us pain, fear, worry, etc.)

You'll find one or both of those two emotions controlling every mental interaction regardless if we're aware of it or not. **They are the core of how to culture, condition, and assimilate your story INSIDE theirs.**

So, when it comes to the desire for pleasure, think about and answer these questions to start to get a feel for the people who will become your leads, first time customers, and eventually lifetime fans:

- What *appeals* to THEM (not you)?
- What do THEY *want*?
- What makes THEM feel good?
- What do THEY want MORE of (what do THEY feel they're lacking that they really, really want)?
- What do THEY dream about?
- What are THEIR hopes, wishes, and aspirations?
- What do THEY *crave* (like a biological need that they almost feel they will DIE if they don't figure out how to get it)?
- What are THEY *irrational* about (what are they so emotionally driven to have that they don't realize or care isn't logical; what would they defend as being right: like a smoker defends why they need to smoke and a drug addict needs their next fix)?

Get the idea?

Then simply do the same thing for things people in your tribe fear. Look at all the painful things they want to avoid, with questions like:

- What do THEY (not you) *hate*?
- What will THEY fight to keep from feeling, happening, or going through again?
- What do THEY *fear*?
- What's the biggest frustration THEY'RE forced to live with right now?
- What worries keep them awake?

- What mistakes have they made they don't want anyone else to know about?
- What pain and suffering do they want to avoid?
- What constraints hold them back?
- How are they stuck?

The answers to these questions are how you identify the mental conversations taking place in each phase of your business process. It's how they will let you join them. And it's how you position your solutions so they see the full value of your offer.

It becomes their idea to WANT your solutions because they see how it gives them pleasure and stops all the pain and suffering they've been forced to live with.

So it's all about figuring out exactly what their pleasure and pain points are (and will be) at every stage of your business process. This lets you talk straight to their emotions, which triggers their automatic story based responses.

With repetition and consistency throughout your business process, you condition them to combine your possibilities within their story. You're now actively culturing what they believe to be true about your solutions. You're not leaving it to chance.

Put yourself in their shoes. What pleasure and pain points will they have when they are in the first stage of your business process? What experiences have they likely been through that they are bringing to this new experience with you?

Gear all your communications around what they want to gain and show them how they can avoid the pain they *don't* want (or even how the pain they don't want will grow bigger without your solutions). Do this properly at each stage of your business process, and people will stand in line and beg to move themselves up your culturing chain to the next level of your business process.

It's really as simple as that.

With Great Power, Comes Great Responsibility

You now know how to make marketing dynamite. Like all power, it can be used to help or hurt people. *This is too powerful to misuse.* I hope you'll treat this with the utmost respect and **NEVER manipulate people into a decision that isn't in *their* best interest!**

The only reason to be in business is because you believe in your heart of hearts that your solutions produce killer value for others. That you're almost sad if people miss out on the benefits you have to offer them because it'll make their lives so much better with you in it!

You've got to know your solutions will deliver all you promise (and much more). You've got to be confident you really can save them from unnecessary suffering. That you're here to help, serve, and guide. You lead by example. You demonstrate in deed **that you're *worthy* and *deserving* of their trust!**

This is *not* about manipulating people just so you can make a buck off 'em. **It's about growing rich in service of others, NOT at their expense.**

Because there are certainly many fast buck artists out there that do that, and they always leave such carnage in their wake. They churn 'n burn through people so fast because they know it's only a short time before they burn it out because people can be tricked once by the liars but will catch on quickly when they're being used and abused.

The secret to success is growing with your customers *because* they grow! You help them succeed. From their success, they give back to you:

All of *your* money is in *their* FUTURE!

The better job you do making *their* future bigger than it ever could have been without you, your solutions, and leadership, the more money they will gladly give you (and you'll sleep soundly because there's no better feeling than getting rich helping others)!

Remember, it's all about the people you serve and what they decide about you. It's all about THEM and helping to assimilate your vision to improve THEIR life. The money you make is a byproduct of the culture that develops in the minds of the people you're trying to serve. It's what you condition them to expect from you (the level of satisfaction, trust, fun, and so on).

If you don't think about it ahead of time and give some forethought to the three major functions of business, **a culture is going to unfold automatically that may or may not help you (and may actually work against the value THEY get; effectively cheating themselves out of a better life).**

You have to be willing to take a broad view on your whole business model and process.

Be empathetic and put yourself in the shoes of your "suspects" (people you think might be good prospects to work with). Think like they think. Know their wants, fears, concerns, desires, dreams, etc. *better* than they consciously do.

Look at life through THEIR eyes. You need to have a "conversation" with them ahead of time, **in YOUR mind first.** The more time you spend here (even a few days of planning will put you light years ahead), the better you will anticipate their needs; and the more successfully you will serve them; and the richer you will predictably grow!

Ask yourself questions like:

- What would your *ideal* lifestyle look like?

- What kind of business do you want to run?

- Do you want to have a lot of interaction with your customers?

- Is your business model going to be geared to a lot of personal, one-on-one attention?

- Is it going to be geared to a mass marketing system (geared to high-volume sales, but perhaps a lower price point)?

- Will you go for a business that has a $2,000 or $5,000 product that is your ultimate goal, and that's where your profit is? Let's face it, if you make a couple of $5,000 sales a week, you'll suddenly make good money and won't need a large volume of new customers.

- **What do you <u>stand</u> for?**
- What's your platform that helps people?
- Do you have something important to say? What's your passion? How does that sync up with other people's passions, desires, pains, concerns, etc.?
- **What message would you be happy to share with the world even if you never made a dime with it?**
- How can you break your vision down into bite size chunks for each step of your business process?
- How will they react to your message at each stage of your relationship building process?
- Are you overwhelming them with too much, too soon. Are sharing things they won't be willing to hear, explore, and believe until you've established deeper levels of trust?

You can't be all things to all people. You can't sell 100% of the world.

So the first step is to get clear about you and your message. Dig in to what's ideal for you *before* you look at what's ideal for your tribe. Because then you can be true to yourself and speak truthful from your heart directly to the people you can really help.

Once you know where and what you stand for, you can figure out who can (and, more importantly, <u>*can't*</u>) help.

You want to design your business process to talk to the people you can help (but most of us waste all our time worrying about those who don't sync up with our solutions in the first place). Trying to sell everyone winds up with lower conversions. Focus only on figuring out the 5% (or whatever it is for you) of the people who will dig your solutions once they're cultured the right way.

<u>**Don't**</u> **waste your time trying to figure out the 95% who ain't never**

gonna do business with you even though they really "need" it.

Anyway, once you know the kind of business model and structure that's ideal for you, you know how to address the 3 parts of your process. You'll end up with a completely different strategy depending on your ideal vision and business you want to run.

Most people get caught up in "just doing" – taking massive action to go out and build their business empire. And, massive action is vital, but only AFTER you know what you stand for and the KIND of business you want to build. That will dictate the business model you put in place, **and the ensuing culture.**

For example, let's say your business sells high priced solutions. Say, a $5,000 sale. If you're just starting out, you're going to have to find people who have the desire and ability to write a check for a $5,000 solution.

Logically, it takes a deeper relationship to sell solutions starting at $5K. You have to find the right audience. Then you'll have to educate them so they know what you have to offer. And, you have to *demonstrate* the value they get in a way that they decide the $5,000 is a fraction of what they get from you in return! That'll take more time than selling $50 solutions, won't it?

So that all becomes a part of your culturing strategy, right?

A $5,000 sale versus a $50 sale is a much more relationship-oriented thing. They have to see all the value. There's more hand-holding.

Since that buying process is likely to take a longer time, you'll spend more time vetting your prospects so you don't waste time with people who won't ever do business with you, wouldn't you? After all, you'd want to make sure you're talking to the right person that fits within your ideal vision *before* you ever enter into the conversion conversation with them.

It affects how you go about building trust, right?

The Mental Conditioning Process

Let's review.

As, you no doubt already figured out, you need several different culture plans. This is how you meet people where they are and lead them successfully through the 3 fundamental business functions of your process.

1. Your lead generation culturing plan.
2. Your conversion culturing plan for new first timers.
3. Your buyers remorse culturing plan for getting them to stick.
4. Your relationship and value creation plan for creating lifetime fans.
5. Your culturing plan for how to show them the benefit of increasing both the frequency and average ticket sizes of the transactions they want over the life of your business relationship with them.

ALL Desires Are Insatiable

One more very powerful aspect of human nature before moving on.

Your conditioning and culturing process had better use the insatiable nature of human wants effectively otherwise your customers will leave you too soon even if they get maximum value from your solutions.

Let me explain.

After a customer gets the initial value they wanted, their satisfaction is only *temporary*. Soon they're gonna want more value (no matter how good it was, eventually the magic ether wears off and they're going to become uneasy unless you're right there with the next part of the value they'll want).

We are constantly expanding and growing. The more you help your customers grow, the more they will see new horizons they didn't see and want to explore them. It's a never-ending, perpetual motion machine: One where the better you serve your clients, the more they want.

We never ever actually get to the horizon because it's always in front of us, in the distance, right?

It's not that you're not helping them get to new levels, seeing new things, achieve new accomplishments and get to new places… **because you are**. However, once they get there, recognize they see new horizons they want to explore. Now they want to go even further.

Now that they're standing on the shoulders of what was once the floor for them, it won't be long before where the former ceiling becomes the basement and they're looking at breaking through a new ceiling.

If you don't help them go to their next level of temporary satisfaction, they will find someone who WILL! They're gonna give their money to someone who gives them the value payoff they want next.

You now have an opportunity to serve them and help them go even further and take it to an even bigger level.

But only if your solutions (and communication processes) keep pace with your customers' insatiable nature!

CHAPTER 6:
Selling Sucks, Marketers Are Manipulators & Capitalism Is Evil

(And Other LIES Keeping You
From Reaching Full Potential)

Remember the chapter on reprogramming the mind to a new mental conversation?

Truth is, you probably need to do a little reprogramming on your own mind BEFORE you will ever have the business success you're presumably reading this book to find.

I learned this the HARD way. Remember back when I shared:

> "... *I HATE selling. Cajoling, convincing, and begging people to buy, just plain SUCKS!*"

Here's the thing: I had to redefine "selling" in my own mind before I stopped sabotaging myself at every step. Because how can I hate what I'm doing and not expect people to pick up on it? It was actually programming people NOT to do business with me. It repelled my success!

Today, I LOVE selling, marketing, and believe capitalism is the only true doorway to freedom. And, today, the reason I love these things ain't because I'm a sellout. No. It's simply because before I had a false belief about them.

The first 15 years I spent in pursuit of success, I felt like I was doing something *"to"* people that was *"bad."* Because why would they fight me if I was doing something good, right?

What took me years to get is what people were fighting against was my *approach* to sales and marketing. It was my faulty definition of salesmanship being based on convincing and pushing people into doing things against their will. *That's* what I hated. *That's* what sucks! *That's* what people rebel against.

However, as soon as I *internalized* the material we've covered in depth, things changed… And changed FAST!

That's when I realized, *"Wait a minute. It's my job to serve people. My job is to show people all the new possibilities they aren't aware of. My job is NOT to defend, convince, or justify what I know with all my heart will serve them. I can't control and force anyone to see what I see or believe what I do.*

"All I can do from my side is to do a good job of educating, counseling and explaining what I have to offer, the problems it solves, and how it's helped me and others. If they see it, great. If they don't, that's great too because I truly don't care if they buy or not. I'm not attached to WHAT they decide.

"In fact, I don't even give a rat's ass if they see or agree with me because I no longer base my self-worth on their validation! I know what's right for me and I'm strong and confident enough in that knowledge to let others make up their own minds. Someone else's actions no longer proves or disproves my worthiness."

From that moment forward, I never again got mad or faulted anyone for *not* buying.

You see, *being* a Profit Prophet is about presenting great solutions to people who want (and have the capacity) to take advantage of them. Often they *won't* know the solution even exists. They need the patient education and vision for their bigger future that only I can provide. They need to know what the solution is, how it works and the problems it solves before they'll move forward.

After that, though, **the ball is in their court.** THEY get to make the next move. THEY have to decide to take the action to move forward.

Selling *isn't ever* anything you do TO people. **It's something <u>THEY do to themselves.</u>** Your job is simply to do the best job possible presenting it in a way that lets them see all the facts so they can make an *informed* decision if it's right for them or not.

It's about powerful communication and teaching skills. NOT manipulation. The better you are at communicating, the more likely they will see the bigger vision you have for their life. Which naturally leads to the sale as the inevitable outcome because now they see what you see for their future. And, now they understand how your offer gets them what they want (and/or helps them avoid what they *don't*).

Anyway, the whole point of this brief chapter is to help you recognize there are some mental conversations driving you that may not support your desires to 10X your life, influence and business success.

In fact, the thing standing in the way of becoming a Profit Prophet may *not* have anything to do with your business process at all. It might just be *in* you! Slightly shift your own mindset and you could be shocked, just like I was, by how fast business starts chasing you (which is exactly why we started your journey with book #1).

Don't worry, I'm not gonna get all preachy and off on a rant about personal development here (you can re-read book 1 for a powerful, down to earth way to reprogram your limiting beliefs into empowering ones).

I know you want the hard-core moneymaking strategies, tactics, and secrets from the front lines of business, so I won't get all "wooie-wooie" on ya.

However, in the name of full disclosure and helping you by all means necessary to LIVE the results you want (instead of it remaining "voodoo" to you), I have to bring this subject to your conscious attention.

What you decide to do with (and about) it, is completely up to you (hey, does that sound familiar? HAHAHA)!

Personally, if I were you, I'd spend 80-90% of my time on in this area. I wouldn't stop until I was sure I found and rewired enough of my stories working against my success. But that's just me (I *do* have the added advantage of being able to look back on my journey and see how critical it was for me even though I was resistant to it in the beginning).

If you want some help discovering what your unconscious mental limitations are, and more importantly, a fast, easy, and fun method that melts 'em away, I recommend going to **ShadowSuccess.com** (that's how you can keep up with all the new solutions I come out with… and also find out how you can hire me to help you implement these Profit Prophet methods to experience true business preeminence).

Didja see what I did there?

Cool. I knew you would. You're sharp;-)

Model it in your own process.

(Don't model the words, but rather, model the mindset that wrote them.)

Onward...

CHAPTER 7:
Shadowing Giants
Of <u>Preeminence</u>

Have you heard of a *little* company called Google?

What do companies like FaceBook, Amazon, Woot.com, Google, and Apple all have in common (besides the license to print money)?

Give up?

They all have amazing corporate cultures that put their customers first. I don't know for sure, but I'd be willing to bet they don't think of their customers as customers; they probably consider them family.

Several years ago I toured Zappos' corporate headquarters with several members of my team. I was blown away by their corporate culture. They value free expression and never-ending learning. They build people; empower their employees; and it extends directly to the relationship they have with their customers.

Zappos' work environment is fun and uplifting; and so is the buying experience they create for their customers. And, none of it is accidental! You can tell they've spent the majority of their time thinking about the culture they want.

No wonder Amazon purchased them for over a billion dollars!

"How about 'dem Apples?"

Can you tell one of my favorite movies is *"Good Will Hunting?"*

I love the line when Will asks the pretentious, overinflated Harvard stuffed shirt, *"Do you like apples?"* When ego man replies, *"yeah,"* Will holds up a napkin says, *"Well, I got her number. How do you like 'dem apples?"*

Whatever.

Now, no study of culture, marketing, trail blazing or game changing business success could ever be complete without the Mack Daddy of them all, Apple Computer.

They have the absolute most loyal customers! Not only do they stand in line and beg to buy the latest iPhone, iPod, iTouch, or MacBook… They also take it *personally* anytime someone says the slightest bit negative about Apple, it's products, or Jobs. They rush to defend Apple's honor as if you just called their sister a dirty whore! It's beyond all rational behavior, right?

No wonder, at a time when all big business is struggling to stay afloat, Apple is now the #1 most valuable brand in the world (dethroning, Google, the former king).

Did you know **Apple's cash reserve now exceeds $100 BILLION dollars?** Think about what that means for a second.

That's **NOT** the stock value of the company. It's NOT their *gross* sales. And, it says nothing about current sales or their future market share based on their crazy growth rates. That's just the actual cash they have on hand!

Now, maybe you're not interested in building a billion dollar company. However, there are still some *awesome* lessons we can take away from

Apple's strategy and apply to your personal Profit Prophet goals.

Think back to when Steve Jobs *first* came back to Apple. Jobs had his work cut out for him because Apple's management really screwed the pooch, right? Apple's brand and reputation was the lowest ever.

After inventing the icon driven, intuitive computer, the CEO who ousted Jobs managed to turn Apple into a joke in the PC computer world. That's what Steve faced when he stepped back in as CEO. How'd he change things?

He refocused Apple on what they did best: Changing the game! He immediately got back to playing THEIR game instead of playing, *"Keeping up with the competitors."* Also, with the same ruthless clarity, he reminded everyone about the game Apple was *never* going to play again because it wasn't the vision they stood for!

With that clarity, Steve started looking for how to best serve his ideal tribe who would love the solutions only Apple could give.

Enter the super cool, iMac. A one-piece, flat screen desktop computer. Affordable for all it was and did, but far from the bargain basement prices the rest of the industry was fighting for scraps to win. They focused on giving people who could afford it a much better computer and user experience.

Then what? Steve looked at the whole digital music trend. They applied their same strategy of a higher priced, but better and super cool to MP3 players. And they released the first generation iPod based on what they knew people wanted.

Did you catch that?

Knowing their strengths, Apple created value for people. Suddenly they moved beyond computers into pioneering new ways to *distribute*, listen to, and enjoy music.

Apple's culture (and profits) expanded because it listened to what its audience wanted and figured out how to best serve *their* tribe (not trying to make money selling products to people that weren't a good match for their unique products and services). They didn't sell another MP3 player. They sold an *iPod!* Which came with Apple's coolness culture built right in! Exactly what their pack wanted and expected, right?

There were tons of much cheaper MP3 players you could buy, <u>but *none* were an iPod</u>! iPod's took over the entire market even though they were 10 times more expensive!

From the success and popularity of the iPod, Apple entered a brand new frontier of digital music management and distribution which lead to the release of their free software platform, iTunes. The next game-changer, iTunes, was a cross platform application that worked on both Windows AND Macs. This "little" strategic move introduced Apple to a much bigger universe because now Windows users could buy iPods and manage them without needing a Mac!

iPod sales exploded and, more importantly, Apple expanded their tribe's reach. For the first time avid *"PCs"* got their first taste of the "Apple Experience" (the coolness culture), right? Apple discovered they didn't need to convince people to buy Mac computers to tap the huge customer base preferring Windows.

Next, Apple moves into music publishing and distribution. It turns iTunes into a store that resides on your computer (they didn't even have to go to an online store or website to buy music)! Now all iPod customers, who are already using iTunes to manage all their music, could buy directly inside the iTunes application.

Brilliant!

Now they're selling music without CDs, without records, and without any kind of physical product. It's downloaded directly to iTunes and easily loaded on your iPod. No muss, no fuss.

A whole new industry was born. It starts to take over. They get major market penetration. Not only that, now musicians who can't get a record company to sign them and produce an album can instantly "self-publish" their own records in the iTunes system and Apple does the selling and distribution for them! **A win for Apple and the musicians BECAUSE it's a win for the customers!**

Apple gets a greater selection of music to distribute (plus now they're making money with every song download instead of only from computer and iPod sales). Musicians get their albums published and distributed for free and make a much higher commission than with a traditional record label! And the customer gets a much larger selection of instant music, at a cheaper price and now have thousands of albums stored in something smaller than a *single* CD!

Next, Apple continues to follow their customers. Expands their culture, and enters *another* new realm, right? (And, all they're doing is listening to what their customers and future potential customers want!)

See how the customer leads the show?

Apple looks at what unique solutions they can provide to serve those customer "requests" better than any other company, bundle it within their coolness culture brand, and people stand in line and beg to buy it because it's exactly what they'd been wishing for!

Anyway, what's next?

Apple adds video to the iPod. Then AppleTV and now they're in the video distribution game, right? The same thing they did for music distribution, they're now doing for TV, movies, and DVDs!

Next, it's the Nano. A smaller generation of iPod's, not as bulky. Eventually you can even shoot video with it so now you don't even need a video camcorder because your Nano does it all in a tiny package about the size of a pack of gum!

What's the next logical progression for Apple from there? Right,

Introducing the iPhone.

They used this technology to build the same kind of simplicity they're known for in their operating systems and software, and turned it into a phone. They simply followed the people; and gave them what they want.

They tied iTunes into the iPhone. Now you can download your music directly to your phone! Today, we take this simple ability for granted, but just a few years back it was IMPOSSIBLE!

In six months Apple sells their first million iPhones and introduces the world to a TRUE smart phone that was user friendly with the coolness culture built right in. They were brilliant with the launch.

Can you see how it's just a part of the 3 fundamental parts of the business process we already talked about in depth? They figured out how to sell more to the people they had, more frequently (because now they get paid every time someone downloads a song)... AND they've also expanded their reach into a much bigger pool of new first time customers because they extended their coolness culture brand to PC users, right?

Think about *this*: iTunes and iPhones are effectively little cash registers for Apple that we carry around in OUR pockets! But Apple's far from done. The *real* brilliance is their App Store as far as I'm concerned!

In my opinion, this is what cut off Microsoft's head. Nobody realized it when Apple first unveiled the App Store, but I believe that was the beginning of the end for Microsoft. It was an amazing shift.

Because the same thing they did for distribution for artists and musicians on iTunes, they now did for programmers and developers with the Application Store.

See, Apple gave developers a distribution channel and said, *"We now have millions of iPhone users. There's no sign of it slowing down. We want to give our users the best selection of mobile applications. If you will develop the best at low prices, we'll give you direct access to our millions of affluent iPhone users; and the more useful you make your apps, the more our users will want them."*

And, guess what? They give the developer 70% of the sales! Wow, 70% commissions!

Apple does all the processing, customer service, selling, distribution, etc. and cuts a check to the developers every month for 70% of whatever Apple sells through the App Store.

Now developers are creating cool games and apps, selling them cheaper than ever (like less than $5 bucks) and are getting rich!

A friend of mine told me about a developer he knows who sells a game he created, *"Pocket God,"* for $0.99! People love this app and because it's only a buck, lots of people buy it. The developer "only" gets paid $0.70 per download so it doesn't sound like he's getting rich, right?

WRONG!

Guess how many *daily* downloads he averaged the last couple of *years*…

Two hundred? – nope, not even close…

Seven hundred? -- still cold!

Ten thousand downloads every single day for something like 700+ days!

Really.

He's averaging 10,000 downloads a day, every day for a very long time! Now, take a second to do the math: 10,000 downloads per day at $1/download is $10,000.00 A DAY in gross sales… of which $7,000.00 PER DAY goes directly to the developer who put the thing together years ago (it probably only took him a couple months to program and he's STILL getting paid every day)!

And that's just ONE example of ONE application… now there's MILLIONS of applications in the store!

Because what do OTHER developers do? They say, *"I'm not stupid. I want to get rich. I want to make millions of dollars. If some stupid little fun game like Pocket God can make me a millionaire several times over, in cash very fast, where am I going to spend my programming time?*

"Am I going to spend time on the PC Microsoft platform developing programs for them under their brand, or am I going to do it here with instant distribution where I get to keep 70% of the sale? I get to control the price points, and I don't even have to process any of the credit cards."

Now, keep in mind, Apple does all the billing, servicing, accounting, and distribution of the applications. For the developers it's a *"set it and forget it"* situation with an unheard of 70% profit margin without all the headaches and expense of running their own business!

So, what do you think happens next?

Right! The absolute best programming talent in the world moves to Apple's distribution channel!

Notice the real brilliance of Apple's strategy is all about serving their customers better. Better apps for little or no cost. The customers are always in the drivers seat because the apps are only successful if it's something the iPhone (and now iPad, iCloud, and Mac Lion) users want and find valuable.

Apple has set up an environment that fosters creativity and innovation. As a result, the developers are churning out some of the most fun, creative, and breakthrough apps that do blow away the users (and they're getting very rich, very fast in the process). The most brilliant programming minds in the world have all turned their attention towards value creation for Apple's clientele. Because they only have to focus on the development, they provide their app solutions faster, too!

This allows Apple's app store (and entire company) to evolve at a speed no competitor can seem to keep up with (Google has tried but at the time of publication they are still in a far second place to Apple). Their user experience gets better and better. Brilliantly, Apple has created a true partnership with both their users and developers to do whatever they can do to evolve their business model in a way that serves that partnership (and, obviously, benefits them greatly as a byproduct).

Because what happens when Apple figures out ways to make life better for the developers and incentivizes them to serve the user even better?

The customer spurs technology by looking for solutions to problems and the things that they want. Technology spurs the developers to help provide those solutions and opportunities.

Then something _very_ interesting happens.

Apple created a semi-open-source platform. Meaning, as long as the developers play by Apple's rules to serve its users in the best way, they are free to develop any crazy idea their minds can dream up. No limits. They can do anything on any subject. There are now millions of different apps with the chance of being downloaded.

And, lots of them are free.

Why? Because it builds a following for the developers and their future application releases. Plus, Apple evolved again and figured out how to incentivize developers to give away their best apps for free when they announced iAds!

iAds is Apple's mobile advertising platform that allows for fun, cool interactive ads to be built right into the apps (think Google's AdWords & AdSense on steroids beamed directly to millions of people); **and Apple pays the developers 60% of all the ad revenues generated from ad placement within their apps!**

Now all a developer has to do is build the best apps they can, build the iAds platform into it, and give it away for free. The better their apps, the more users will download their apps for free; the more users, the more times the iAds are shown and the more money the developers make in service to Apple's users!

Brilliant! *F'ing Brilliant!*

But the innovation evolution doesn't end there.

What do you think happens when other programmers see what their peers innovate?

They look at what they're doing and build on it, right? They say, *"I never thought about using the technology that way. I can do it even better by adding this clever twist no one ever thought of before."* Then they develop it; and Apple and all their developer peers watch closely so they can stand on *their* shoulders to support and keep the evolution expanding at warp speed.

That opened up a whole new ballgame of different types of applications that were now possible and developers could build on.

Other developers are watching what other developers are doing.

Apple is watching what they're all doing and what the customer wants. They're developing new software and hardware for it.

That's how Apple decided the format and timing to unleash the iPad on the world (it's also how they came up the iCloud & their new Yosemite Operating System).

On the surface, the iPad seems like it's just a big iPhone or iTouch, but it isn't. Why?

Because with the extra screen space (and new operating system), Apple created a new environment for their brilliant stable of developers to come with new and better apps that won't work on smaller screens!

Being a "Gadget and Gizmo" guy, I'm usually one of those nuts who stands in line for each new innovation Apple releases. However, when the iPad first came out, I had zero urgency to get one because my iPhone already did it all (or so I thought). Yes, I love to get new shit first, but I personally didn't see the value in it. I thought I'd probably buy one in a year or two, if ever.

That was until a friend showed me some of the great apps he had on his iPad! Once I saw all the cool programs, tools, toys, applications these brilliant programmers built for it, that required an iPad to work, I *had* to have one! I saw the advantage of having that touch screen for those programs. I saw the ingenious apps for it which made me see how much bigger it's value was than my "crummy" old iPhone (not because of the hardware, but because of the apps being developed for it)! I saw its potential; where it was going to go…

And we're just at the tip of what's possible and what's being developed!

Out of ALL Apple's product launches, the iPad hit a million units sold faster than any other! Of course, it came with Apple's awesome coolness culture brand built into it, but I believe what made it such a best seller (in record time) was the way they extended their culture to the developers. Think about why I wanted one. It *wasn't* the *"thingy,"* it was the apps!

For example, you can get a full system of programs that work better than Microsoft Office for under 20 bucks (when Office costs over $500.00)!

Yes, we've spent a while on Apple, but think about how it pulls every single aspect of The Profit Prophet way together (all 3 books are represented in this deep dive into Apple)! Think about their users. Apple knows its users are the secret to their success. Think about how great a job Apple has done at getting inside their users' minds to create a never ending stream of more and better solutions that appeals to more and different people. Think about how Apple has evolved by following those mental conversations. Think about Steve Jobs' vision for leading (and how he passed the torch to ensure it survived his death).

Now every time Apple launches anything, they sell millions of units almost instantly. Think about Apple's profit margins on music, video, and app distributions (yes, they "only" make 30%, but they don't have *any* of the R&D time or expenses; so while each individual distributing through Apple makes the lion share of their products, Apple gets a cut of the *whole* ecosystem)!

In effect, Apple gets paid handsomely to sell us a store that sells us more of the stuff we LOVE! We buy all their solutions because they follow OUR insatiable desires for more and better (for that ever expanding, bigger future)! They've carefully crafted a buying culture that makes us excited to quite literally stand in line and beg to buy their next solution.

And we can't wait to do it because Apple has conditioned and programmed us with such great anticipation for what they're gonna do next.

Granted, all this didn't happen overnight. They sure didn't have this culture planned out 20 years ago, but guess what? It evolved. Their culture allowed for flexibility! And they were smart enough to listen and evolve their business model with their users growth. No wonder they have business preeminence!

There are all sorts of lessons here for you (no matter what you're doing specifically). So, what ideas can you take from Apple's brilliance and apply to your business process? Take these ideas and concepts and adapt them.

Ask yourself: How can I take these ideas and apply them on a small level to what I'm doing? How can I make my solutions so powerful and cool that my tribe will fall in love with us for giving them access? How can I increase the value people get from doing business with me? How can I come up with the next thing my pack wants? How can I add to the current solutions they love, and use anticipation marketing to educate them about it in a way that makes them want the next new solution so badly they can't wait?

It's a very different way of looking at things.

That's how "impossible voodoo" translates directly to your bottom-line profits. It's the core of this Profit Prophet "voodoo" (and why it's so damn powerful)! It's why and how I was able to help grow a client almost 10 times in only 18 months. BV (Before Voodoo;-) the business was at $2 million in annual sales; and less than a year and half after I started helping them, it jumped to $19 million a year!

That's because they had great elements already in place. All I had to do was help them develop an integrated strategy where each part of the process supported the overall new Profit Prophet culture and direction we decided to head towards. With a better lead generation and conversion process, they exploded! The culture, systems, and processes I developed for them required them to evolve their business model a bit so they could develop a culture where all three pieces were congruent.

However, that's what exploded them from $2 million to $19 million a year in less than 18 months.

That's the power of this stuff.

In the next chapter I'm going to give you two specific culturing and conditioning case studies: One where I was the one being trained (so you can see exactly what really went on in my head at each phase of the process);

And, the second case study was exactly how I engineered a complete turnaround from the worst possible circumstances (overcoming a negative mindset that had been allowed to develop and gather momentum, which took on a life of its own).

Use both studies as an invaluable guide to you creating your own business preeminence...

CHAPTER 8:
Inside Two Case Studies

(Both Sides Of The Culturing Fence: BEING
Programmed & DOING The Conditioning)

Our first case study is one where I went from hardened skeptic to raving fan myself.

A couple of years ago, I switched lawn care companies. I was dissatisfied with the way the old landscaping company took care of us. My lawn looked ok, but the plant beds, weeds, driveway, etc. was a mess. For what the old company did, they were dependable (i.e., they always showed up every week, and cut the lawn, but they never went the extra bit to make our place look stunning). Not top notch. We hired them to weed and trim once but they did a half-assed job.

So the conversation in my head was, *"The lawn looks okay and they've been reliable for the weekly mowing. I feel a certain amount of loyalty to them because they have been doing it for five years. They do a good job mowing the lawn, and they come every time, but the rest of the property isn't looking good. I really want my property to look good because I don't want my house to look like it's in foreclosure like all the other houses seem to look like today."*

For a bit, I trimmed the bushes myself and tried to convince myself that I liked doing it. I really don't, as evidenced by the fact that weeds are overgrowing the beds.

The only thing that looked good at the house was the actual lawn. Because the rest of the landscaping looked bad, the house looked bad. There were weeds growing up in the driveway, through my pavers. And it's a huge circular driveway with a ton of pavers. So with all the weeds growing in between them, it started to look more like a garden than driveway.

My ego got involved. I didn't like the way I felt when I came home. I didn't like what it looked like when people drove by. I stopped inviting friends and family over. Soon, my mental conversation shifted to, *"Maybe I can find somebody to just do the cleanup. What's that going to entail?"*

No sooner did I ask myself that did I shift my thoughts again. Now I started making up a story about how, *"That's a lot of work. How do you find somebody who's not going to rip you off? They're going to see my big ass house, and all of a sudden the price is gonna inflate 10 times what the job's worth. It's going to take them forever. They're not going to have the eye for detail that I have. It's going to be a pain in the ass and a lot of work to make sure it gets done right."*

By the way, notice, this has nothing to do with anything other than the story I made up and decided to tell myself over and over. **All of that took place inside my head.**

So I bit the bullet and called up a friend of mine who is a Realtor, manages a lot of properties in the area, and has a property management company. I said, *"Who do you use who isn't going to rip me off? Who would you recommend?"*

He gave me a name.

I called his guy, begrudgingly, and had him come out to give me a quote. The quote was, of course, higher than what I expected (then again, everything in my head should cost three cents instead of hundreds).

But since my friend vouched for him (and because he brought a flip book of all the other properties he'd done recently), I decided to give him a shot. He told me what I wanted was such an easy job he could fit it in the following week while I took my family away on a cruise. I liked the idea of all the work being done while we were out of town and I had this mental image of the look of joy and surprise on my wife's face when we got home!

Lo and behold, he did a stellar job. He got it done. He had the eye for detail. My house looked killer again! My wife was overjoyed when she saw it. My neighbors all came over to compliment us on how great the property looked. I had pride in my home again!

Now what I thought at first to be overpriced, was now a deal! It ONLY cost $1,600 to feel this good. *Now* it was worth it. *Now* I saw all the work. *Now* I made up a new story that justified the price in my mind. *Now* it was worth every cent because I got the emotional charge and fulfillment I wanted.

But I still had the other lawn service in place, doing the weekly upkeep. Immediately, I started thinking about what it would take to KEEP my property looking THIS good *all* the time? I didn't want to slip backwards again.

So I talked to the new landscaping guy: *"give me a price quote for what you would charge to do all of this. I love the way this looks now, but I know that I'm not going to keep it up and stay with it. I want it to always look as good as it does right now, and I don't ever want to have to think about it again. I want you to have to think about it and keep it looking this good. What would that cost me?"*

Of course, he gave me a price quote that I thought was ridiculous to keep it looking like that. The conversation instantly shifting in my head to *"I just paid you all this money. How hard is it going to be to keep it looking like this?"*

Long story short, I continued to have these ongoing conversations with myself but took no action. My mental stories made me put off doing anything because I was too busy arguing with myself. So I didn't call him back.

But, of course, the inevitable happens, and my landscaping started slipping again. Did I want to continue to pay that kind of money? That's a lot of money to have to pay every year. Then a few months later, he called me to follow up and said, *"Did you get the price quote that I sent over?"* I said,

"Yes, but as great a job as you did, that's just not what I have in the budget." He said, "What do I have to do to earn your business? What price can you afford?"

I told him, and he said, "If that's what it takes to get your business, I'll do it for that. Maybe if there are some months where I have to do some extra work, you can give me extra money for the hours I have to put in." I was thinking, "Yeah, whatever."

He started doing the work, and now I started seeing his eye for detail and the amount of time he put in. Now all of a sudden, in my mind, again he's more than worth the price. I felt guilty for paying him the reduced price. I wanted to pay him what he originally asked.

Now let's break it down to the three elements of business.

Incidentally, I had to fire the other company, which was something I didn't want to do because I felt loyal to them. I had to let them go, and I was wondering what was going to happen. It turned out that it was just fine, and it worked out to everybody's benefit. No hard feelings (even though the story I made up and told myself initially was one of the things keeping from taking action).

First, notice all of the mental gyrations I went through was/is really just the process of building enough relationship to trust, right? I'm sure you're recalling several situations you went through similar mental gymnastics, yes?

Compare what I went through (and *your* own pre-buying, buying and post-buying experiences) with a prospective new member you'd like to join your tribe. They don't yet trust you, your offer, your process, or solutions, do they?

- What crazy stories are they likely to make up?

- What will they blow out of proportion because they don't want to face it directly?

- What will they think in the lead generation part of your business process?

Once they get over everything in their pre-buying (lead generation) conversations, what kinds of new stories will they be making up as they consider doing business with you for the first time?

My conversations during the lead generation step were all about how bad my house looked. All the pain of my present situation, right? My pride was hurt. The house looked like shit. But I felt guilty for wanting to switch (yes, I know, it's not logical I shouldn't feel guilty when they didn't do a good enough job, but I still *did*, and it affected my decision making process because I struggled with my "loyalty conversations"). Plus, there was the pain of finding (and breaking-in) somebody new who was trustworthy and wouldn't overcharge me.

What if your ideal prospect wants your offer, but feels like they can't buy because they're committed to a different product, service, person, or company and would feel guilty if they switched?

See, if you don't account for that possible conversation in your prospect's mind: NO SALE! You won't get the sale (and you'll never know the *real* reason had *nothing* to do with you, your offer, your solutions, etc.).

If you want to make business chase you, you've got enter that conversation. And, remember, the stories are *going* to shift automatically as soon as they shift to the next stage of your business process. Even if there's no time lapse from the time they qualify themselves as a lead and considering buying your first solution, **the stories they will begin telling themselves will shift to all their past buying experiences that haven't worked out the way they hoped.**

Back to my landscaping experience.

After I decided I wanted to get my property looking good again, I had to find the right guy and get him to come out for a bid, right?

I didn't take action to look for a new solution until the pain got bad enough that I couldn't take it anymore. Even though I got a referral from someone I trusted, I still had trepidation about if this guy *really* was trustworthy.

- Is he really a good guy?

- Is he going to be a good guy for *me*?

- Is he going to overcharge me?

- Is he going to do all these things?
- Will he be timely?

Blah, blah, blah… right?

Now I'm no longer a prospect. Now I've qualified myself as a lead by calling him to set an appointment for him to bid on the job, right? His job now is to show me the value in hiring me and justifying the $1,600 price tag so I'll write the check to get it done, right?

So, what did my mental conversations shift to then? My concern was, *"Is he going to do all the things I want to have done, or is it going to be partially done?*

"Am I going to have to chase him? Is it going to really look good? Is he going to have a better eye for detail than I do? Is this something he can get done timely?"

I wanted to surprise my wife with getting it done. I wanted to have it done while we were away. I talked to him on a Thursday, and we were leaving that Saturday morning. Timing was important to me and he knew (and used) it to justify price and create urgency for me to take immediate action.

The whole time we were out of town, I wondered, *"Is he really going to do everything? Or am I gonna be pissed when I get home because I paid top dollar and it didn't get done to my satisfaction?"*

That was the <u>new</u> mental conversation. See, hiring the guy was not just about spending the money. If I decide to make this purchase, what are all the things it's going to mean to me?

I kept playing these mental scenarios out based on my past experiences. **It's the exact same thing for you and your prospects too.** They will constantly second-guess themselves until they make each positive decision forward. Then they will wonder, *"Did I make the right decision?"*

I gave him 50% down but continued to have doubts. *"I just wrote a check for $800. Did I do the right thing? Was this the right move? I'm going to be going out of town, and I'm not going to be there to answer any questions. What if he breaks a window with shears and I'm not there to fix it or to yell at them?"* One of the things that put me at ease was that he had a flipbook of all the other jobs he had done. He showed me the before-and-after pictures.

He had confidence in how simple this whole process was. As we walked the property he kept telling me how easy and simple the job was that I wanted done. It was going to be a piece of cake, and he was going to do this and that, so that put me at ease. He evidently knew the conversation or his intuition knew enough of the conversation, because he handled all of it with the different pieces of his presentation because it satisfied and quieted all my mental conversations.

We're ALL Haunted By The "Did I do the right thing?" Ghost

Remember, the instant that the sale is consummated, buyers' remorse kicks into high gear. No matter who you are, there's an element of, *"Did I make the right decision?"* It becomes the central conversation as soon as they buy.

Your job is to _confirm_ the fact that they DID make the right decision.

I know a lot of businesses don't think this way, but in my mind the best way you can confirm that they made the right decision is to help them _consume_ that product. Get 'em started with it so they get involved and a momentum of future ongoing sales results.

Consumption is the only way they'll get the full value from the transaction. Tell them that they made the right decision. But don't just TELL 'em, get them involved to actually do something to interact with that product.

For me with the lawn service, the consumption part of the experience was when we came back from our trip and drove up to our property and saw the 47 bags of stuff piled up and how good the property looked. It looked killer!

All of our neighbors came over as we unloaded the truck and made a point of telling us, *"Wow! Where did you find this guy? He worked around the clock. He was there with tweezers. Your property never looked so good."* All of that reinforced my purchase decision:

Yes, I made the right choice.

I hunted him down to give him the other half of his money before unpacking my suitcases because I wanted to make sure that he got paid. I felt like I got the steal of a deal because I started "consuming" my purchase. I loved the way it looked. I wanted more. I was talking to him on the phone and said, *"I need you to give me a quote immediately. As good as this looks right now, I want it to look this good forever."*

Which began the next phase of his business process: Ongoing future sales. The $1,600 was a one-time sale but for most it would have been the first and <u>last</u> sale. He gave me a price quote,

"I can come and just do your lawn cutting, and it's this price. Or, I can come on a monthly basis and do your lawn cutting and keep your lawn looking good, and it's this price.

"Or, you can call me, and anytime you call me I'll come do it, and it's this price per basis. Or, if you want me to do the weeding, the shrubs, the trimming, the trees and all this, it's this price. Or, if you want me to do it on a monthly basis, it's this price.

"Or, if you want me to do the whole thing altogether, it's this price."

All those additional products and services are now MY idea; now I WANT them.

He didn't sell me, **my consumption of our initial transaction did!** Now I'm a raving fan of his services and his work. I'm ecstatic. The interesting thing is that it took me another 2-3 months to make that decision.

However, now that we're in full swing it's the best money I ever spent. Every time I drive up, now I'm proud of my home. It's a showplace again! People are driving by, stopping, and looking again.

People walk by all the time and ask, *"Is this <u>your</u> house?"* and my beaming reply, **"yes, it IS <u>my</u> house!"**

There's no price you can put on that feeling. It's priceless. It feels great. He made me look so good, right?

Oh, and, of course he got like 5 new clients from me because we're ecstatic to help him and our friends and family. I recommend him to everybody now because of my positive experience with him. **Plus, doesn't each person who hires him, reconfirm MY great decision? It's a signal I *DID* do the right thing because other people agree with me, right?**

Think about where my mental conversation was about him at the beginning. Now, I am a fan. Whether he knows it or not, I am. But in the beginning, my mindset was really skeptical because I didn't trust him at all yet.

How do you identify it?

Good question. You get a good feel for it. You put yourself in the customer's shoes. "Play" prospect. "Play" customer. What are they feeling? What are they thinking? What are their fears? Concerns? If they move forward to the next step of your process what new concerns will that bring up for them? What would you be concerned about in their shoes at each point of each of your processes?

I've been fortunate that I always work in businesses that I can identify with and know who that ideal prospect is, what their life looks like. I try to get in touch with that first.

Oftentimes, that helps me. Of course it helps design the marketing but it also **helps me re-engineer products. That's where some of the best product ideas come from, by getting in touch with the pack's psychology.**

If you don't know them, the best thing to do is to do some homework. Do some research.

Ask them. They'll tell you.

Shifting gears to other side of culturing fence (our programming case study):

If you don't know what people are thinking, take your best guess so you get the process started and then test your hypotheses out by asking them.

(Remember back a few chapters where we talked about tracking and measuring everything? This is exactly how you discover how close your guesses and hypotheses are. The numbers tell your whole story on well you are syncing up with the mass mental conversations your pack are having with themselves. The better your conversion numbers, the better you're addressing their imaginary stories in a way that gets them past it.)

Anyway, come up with three different approaches to test for your lead generation and get in the game. Measure your results. Make adjustments to your marketing based on those results. Test some more. Measure some more. Keep going until the numbers work good enough to move on to your next business function.

This removes the hope and guesswork from your business building and scaling.

Here's a case study of how I did just that:

Several years ago, I shut down my businesses and took a couple years off because I was burned out. I stopped all communications with my in house list. For almost two years I went from constant communications to nothing at all.

Even prior to shutting down my operations I hired someone to manage the relationships for me (*don't* do that). It turned out he didn't know how to build trust and relationship. He just threw promotions at my list without concern for value or their mindset. It became ridiculous. The promotions were not well thought out.

It ruined the culture I worked so hard to establish before hiring this guy to manage it for me (lesson learned: never outsource your relationship building strategy). So the love they got from me (and the value and the connection that they felt for me) was missing for almost three years.

Then I started to get active again and wanted to share some of the new breakthrough ideas, concepts and solutions that I'd been developing. So I was faced with starting from scratch. Or try to re-establish the relationships I had with the 65,000 people on my list. It seemed stupid not to, at least, attempt to rekindle the relationship with my old tribe.

My question was, how?

I didn't know what they'd be thinking exactly. I could guess, but I didn't know for sure. So I started by putting myself in their shoes, assuming the worst (never assume the best because you won't be able to anticipate all the potential obstacles and possible outcomes).

I'd be thinking, *"Who's this Josh guy? I don't remember ever being on this list. It's been so long since I've heard from him. I never subscribed to this."* Another could be that they were just angry with me because of all the sales promotions that had gone on with no real communication or content. Yet, another possible mindset the portions of the tribe could share was true concern about where I was, what was going on, and what was happened.

So, I decided to test the waters with a trial balloon communication to see what would happen. I started by saying, *Remember me?"* sheepishly.

I put it out there and said, *"If you're like a lot of my friends, you've probably wondering what happened to Joshua? You've probably been looking for me on the side of a milk carton."*

I didn't know for sure, but I had to start somewhere and invite them to tell me what they were truly thinking. I asked, *"How do I start to enter that conversation so that I can start to direct it?"* I emailed them a couple of times. Then I decided to set up a blog so I could engage and interact with everyone, publicly.

I figured, this way, I could let people vent their frustrations and share what's on their minds. And at the same time I'd get a real good idea of the worst-case scenario mental conversations they have concerning me. **I can never address the conversations directly unless I truly know what they are.**

By giving them a forum to vent and to say whatever they want, two things happened:

One, *I learned what those conversations were without asking them.* They weren't shy about telling me. All I had to do was listen.

Two, **I let them** *'drain their abscesses,'* **instead of allowing the pressure to build up** without addressing it.

See, each member of my tribe had varying degrees of a festering, blistered abscess, all puffed up, painful, and annoying, called "past experience." When they get to vent and moan, when they get to let it out and express themselves; **the very act of doing that relieves the pressure**

on that abscess. It drains all the pus out of it. That takes the burn of the sting away. **So they got to say whatever was on their mind.**

Before I really entered their conversation, I took a stab at what I thought their conversations might be. I wrote about that in my first blog post. Just gave them an honest assessment of everything that happened, gave them the raw, real story, in my open, transparent, non-defensive and authentic way. I took full responsibility for my decisions and actions.

I invited them to comment on my post and share their feelings and feedback. I braced myself. And, you know what? To my genuine shock, 80% to 90% of the comments were really positive.

I sure wasn't expecting that kind of support. I didn't know what to expect before I started. There were almost 500 comments within a few days. My post hit a chord with them, and they wanted to tell me what was going on. Out of the 500 comments, I'd say 80%-plus of them was positive, saying, "Congratulations for identifying what was going on for you and why you disappeared. Thank you and welcome back."

Then there was 20% or so that were maximum wrath, negative. You know, the type of people who just can't wait to piss in your corn flakes no matter what (even if you give them a bar of solid gold they'd find a complaint about it, like it's too heavy or something stupid like that because they get off being "wronged").

But, here's the key to draining the abscess. I did NOT censor the negative comments. On the contrary, I needed them. So, I let all the negativity stay up on my blog. **When you culture a conversation you don't judge it or make people wrong for having it, you simply enter it wherever it is. Never get caught up in defending your position, you just want to find out where they are.**

It's *their* conversation.

It's what's going on in *their* minds. They're entitled to think, believe, and make up any story they want. I feel privileged that they were willing to share their feelings with me. The ones I felt could benefit from a little reframing by understanding more of the story than they did, I answered with respect, honesty, and full transparency (and full disclosure).

One of the common (and more than fair) comments I got was, *"You're going to have to convince me that you're truly being authentic and this isn't just some ploy."*

What they said was, *"Convince me. Prove to me that I'm wrong."* What I said to them, because I thought about it ahead of time, was that I wasn't going to get caught up in this game of trying to defend myself. I didn't make excuses for the past; nor did I justify my actions. I simply let them know what happened and what I was working on now.

I made the decisions I made because I made them, and at the time it's what was right for me. Now I'm back. I just wanted to share with people that I'm back, what I'm doing, the solutions that I'm coming up with, and how I'm doing it. It might have some value to them. And it might not. I was crystal clear on that ahead of time that **I wasn't going to get emotionally involved if they started attacking me (which, some of them did).**

My response was simply, *"I understand how you feel. Yes, the past situation is what it was. I can see how you would be guarded; I would be too. I respect that. All I can say is to stay tuned, see what I have up my sleeve, and see what I'm going to do. If you like it, great. If it serves you, great.*

"However, I have no intention of trying to convince you of anything or prove my case to you. I'm not in the changing-minds business. I'm in the changing-lives business. If you've already made up your mind, then nothing I can do or show you will have a positive outcome for you because you'll argue to be right in the decision you've already made.

"Either way is okay with me, but I have no intention of trying to convince you of anything. I'm simply going to share some ideas with you that have had a huge impact on me and others. If it's not your brand of vodka, so be it. If you don't like the program, you should change the channel because you're not going to find the value and satisfaction you want here. Life's too short to spend your time with people you don't enjoy."

That became the tone from a very genuine, authentic place deep inside me. Because that was 100% how I felt. I wanted to serve the people in sync with me. And I also wanted to serve those who weren't by making sure they didn't waste any more of their time "hanging out" with me in the future.

People started to get it. So beyond my blog posts and commenting with visitors I decided to produce a video to create more of a feeling of interaction, intimacy, and relationship with the people who *did* align with me. It created a brand new level of trust and transparency. And became the foundation of the new culture I wanted to establish from that point forward. In the video, I featured different people's comments (both the positive and negative ones). I used it as an opportunity to build culture even more.

I knew the new culture was firmly intact when about a week into the process, almost all the negative people had decided to move along to someone willing to fight with them. But there were still a few "Negative Nelly's" left, but here's what started to happen: The tribe had my back. They took up for me. See, the peeps who liked this new culture, took it upon themselves to squash the negative posts and comments when they popped up.

Some guy wanted to 'drain his abscess' and blame his anger about his lot in life on me. He focused on a grammatical mistake I purposely made in one of my posts. He said, *"By the way, Joshua, it's 'sordid', not 'sorted'."*

I used 'sorted' on purpose because one of the things I was going to be teaching people is how to get clarity by sorting things out. So I wrote 'the whole sorted story' on purpose, knowing the cliché was in fact, 'sordid.' It's amazing what people choose to get upset about, ain't it? When someone wants to be pissed, any excuse will do;-)

So on the feedback video I said, *"Yes, you're right, I know the saying is 'sordid,' but I purposely used 'sorted' for a reason that you'll find out in a little bit."* But even after all that, one guy fires back, *"It's 'sordid', not 'sorted.' It's called English. You should look into it sometime."*

Having already said all I was going to say on the subject and staying true to my decision to not defend, justify or prove my case, I ignored the comment (but still allowed his negativity to be voiced in the comments). I wanted to see how the rest of the community was going to respond to him because that would tell me if I had done my culturing job properly or if more work was needed.

Sure enough, somebody posted, **"It's called 'class.' I'll spell it for you: C-L-A-S-S. You may have gone to one or two in college, but you certainly don't have any."** That's when I knew the culturing process was heading exactly where I wanted.

Now, notice I couldn't have set a brand new culture and direction in motion without asking people to tell me what was going on for them. The only way to enter their mental conversations where they are, is to not be scared to face negativity or criticism. I needed everyone to vent, to get it all out of their systems, if we were ever going to have a chance to get past it.

That's what it means to identify and enter the conversations they're already having with themselves. You can't make their stories wrong (but nor do you take any of it personally). As you clearly see from this case study, I didn't have to make myself wrong or beg for forgiveness.

You *never* sacrifice what you stand for.

You're just looking for people who appreciate your style, tone, and approach to business and life. By staying true to yourself and knowing what's going on in their minds, you speak directly to the people you *can* help and encourage those you can't to move along.

You *can't* direct the conversation unless you enter it at the right point AND then, with consistency (and conditioning), gain a level of familiarity with them where their automatic reaction isn't to immediately shut you down (and tune you out).

That's what it takes to make people stand in line and _anticipate_ doing business with you.

It's about the diamonds, not the coal.

In the lead generation part of the process you might be focused on trying to "say" the right things so it pleases everyone and everyone moves to the next step. This is a mistake.

You should celebrate the 60-80% who opt-OUT and decide NOT to move forward with you. That's because your success comes from the 20-40% who do get the benefits of learning more about you, your story, and offer. If you've designed your process properly, the people who do qualify themselves as leads will be the only ones worthy of your time and attention.

You can't beat the time saving automation of a well thought out marketing system. I always celebrate in the people I DON'T get because the process is sifting, sorting, and screening people for me! Not everyone gets in. That's because my tribe is a very exclusive club. I owe it to the people I CAN help, the ones who DO qualify, to give them everything I can give. And, I can't do that if I'm wasting time trying to please people who aren't ready to be helped at the level my solutions provide. **I ain't trying to win a popularity contest!**

Marketing does that heavy lifting FOR you.

Sure, you want to maximize your results, but only with the people who are true prospects for your solutions. You're looking for the fully formed diamonds, *first*. Then, and only *then*, consider opening the marketing funnel a little wider to *less* qualified people. Yes, there will be many diamonds in the rough but focus on mining the easy money first and augment with the rougher diamonds *after*.

Besides smacking of desperation (which isn't attractive at all), trying to "get everyone" is an amateur mistake of tripping over dollars to pick up a lousy penny! Because now, you don't know who (and what) is the highest and best use of your time. An hour spent chasing someone who will never be a customer is time you can't spend with someone who will love, appreciate and want every single thing you offer in the future!

Even if a prospect is the perfect diamond for someone else, they may be a big lump of coal for you. If you waste time trying to turn them into your diamond, now you're in the begging and convincing business. And, no matter how hard you polish that piece of coal, it ain't never gonna sparkle. Nothing you can do will change coal's nature and magically transform it into a diamond.

Sorry.

On the other hand, if your marketing weeds out the lumps of coal so you never even see them, now your confidence stays high because you're spending all your energy and effort polishing your diamonds (and, as time allows, a few diamonds in the rough here and there).

And, it IS in a diamond's nature to sparkle! They WANT to shine. They WANT to be adored. They WANT to be shown off. They WANT to feel special (they DON'T want to be stuck with the lumps of coal).

Know what?

You're actually doing the people you don't want a favor! By quickly helping people realize that your solutions (and/or offers) aren't a fit for them right now, they can move on to find ones that are. They will appreciate you for not blowing smoke up their asses. Which leaves the door open for the future possibility, if their situation changes (or if yours does, i.e., you come up with a new offer or solution more suited to their mindset).

And, because you dealt with them openly, honestly and transparently, there's a chance for future interaction and potential business together.

Get it?

If your process does a better job at turning *away* the people you can't serve as it does to attract those you can, you'll cruise all the way to the bank! Plus, you'll love it when your process sifts, sorts, and screens your coal away *for* you because now you can have fun "playing a little hard to get" with your diamonds because they want your solutions to make them sparkle and shine brighter than they ever have before.

And, as we covered in depth in the X-Factor chapter of Book 2, "playing hard to get" makes people want it even more. It builds greater value because it's human nature to want what we can't have. If things come too easy, we don't value them.

We appreciate something that's exclusive because it means not everyone gets accepted into the club, but we won our VIP status the hard way (and everyone knows it's a privilege to be an insider).

(Think Seinfeld's, *"No soup for you!"* Soup Nazi. YouTube it if you don't know what I'm talking about. It's a funny exaggeration of the exact same mindset you create in your business development processes.)

You can only create a culture of exclusivity if you know what *appeals* to your diamonds.

Your diamonds won't feel special if your process allows any old rock to ascend up to the higher levels, right?

CHAPTER 9: SHHSSSH, It's A <u>Secret!</u>

I'll let you in on a little secret about this book.

It's a culturing tool for me, isn't it? It's a part of my business strategy and process, right?

Haven't you gotten to know me in the process of learning all about my Profit Prophet Methods? And, isn't this book very likely the first time you've done business with me? Well, this book is strategically designed as the "front-end" of my business model.

Or maybe you've gotten so much value from my other front-end solutions (which are all full of the same culturing process) that this isn't the first time we've done business together. Maybe this is your second, third, fourth, or, or, or... Maybe, just maybe you're a lifetime Joshua Shafran fan.

One thing's for sure: Only diamonds will consume the book to this point. Only the best of the best will discover the insider info I'm revealing right now, right?

All my solutions (front-ends *and* back-ends) are carefully designed to provide incredible value, BUT ONLY TO THE AUDIENCE I CAN BEST SERVE. They all are strategically developed to give (and enhance) the exact buying culture to maximize my business's LTCV at your service, not expense.

And, consider this: After learning all that goes into creating a Profit Prophet culture, do you have a much deeper appreciation for the value that I bring to the table when I work directly with clients? What if I approached you for one of my higher priced solutions and you knew none of what I've educated you to here? It would be a tough road to "convince" you on why both my *"do it with you"* and *"do it for you"* solutions are a steal at the high prices I charge for them, right?

I mean, even though this book gives away millions of dollars of my real-world, in-the-trenches business development experiences, isn't it also in effect the equivalent of a 2 week intensive boot camp that facilitates you selling yourself on the value of working with me in a deeper way than just through these pages? Imagine that? Besides delivering superior value, it's also a 300+ page education presentation on all the reasons why you should continue to do more and bigger business with me!

Plus, does this book automatically build authority and credibility for me and my business? Does it stand out from everything (and everyone) else? It creates an almost unfair competitive advantage for me because of the way it's positioned, doesn't it? Sure I have competitors in the marketing and business development spaces. However, the Profit Prophet WAY can't be accessed except through my tollbooth!

You see, this book is a part of my automated processes. Although, I'd love to sell a million copies of this book, I'm NOT hanging my financial future on that happening. However, since I'm a Profit Prophet, this book will very likely produce millions in "back-end" LTCV. That's because this book IS my "front-end" (it's just the beginning of the value ladder).

Now, I have no idea what my actual LTCV will wind up being for every book buyer because I'm just getting started with this new front-end... and, yet, based on the models I've created before (and all the cool stuff I have planned for the back-end solutions I'll be adding), on average, I know I can get the LTCV into the $1,300/book buyer range because I've done it before. And, actually, I'm shooting to get the average LTCV into the $3,000.00/book buyer range over a 3-5 year period! Yes, it's a big vision. But I'm up to the challenge. ;-)

So, what if I "only" sell 1,000 copies of this book. That's $1.3 Million with an LTCV of $1,300! Or a cool $3 Million with an LTCV of $3,000! And it gets really exciting when you consider that my business plan is designed to feed my front-end for this model with an average of 500 books per week. Which is a *weekly* gross between $650K and $1.5 Million depending on my LTCV, right?!

Are you starting to see the real power of leveraging the Profit Prophet blueprint you're holding in your hands right now?

It doesn't take millions of new front-end customers to make millions from the backend. That's the value of taking action on this information!

Onward.

Now that you're on the other side of the journey, can you see how I've put into practice everything I have been preaching? Do I have a mission? Is my vision for your future bigger than yours was before you started? Do you know where I stand on life? Have I connected with you on a deep personal level even though we've probably never met in person?

Can you see the Profit Prophet is WAY bigger than selling some books? It's about building my own version of Apple's coolness culture and brand. It's about making a *real* difference. My mission is to provide powerful guidance that leads my tribe to 10X their life, influence and business success! It's about truly helping people live the *balanced* success that's been eluding them without backsliding into self-sabotage.

Can you see how some strategic planning in the beginning makes it easy to eat any so-called competition for lunch? See how it's easy to stand head and shoulders above the crowds when you decide to put The Profit Prophet to work for you?

How can you model my strategy and adapt it for your business? Remember, it's not about copying my exact front-end and back-end processes. You're not building my business, **you're writing your own Profit Prophet story!**

You be YOU.

It's about understanding the strategy behind what, how, and why I've built what I have, the way I have. If you can see the underlying principles, you can use my process and culturing model to **build one <u>unique to you</u>.**

Even if, no scratch that... ESPECIALLY if selling books isn't a part of your business process at all.

See, my biggest business breakthroughs have come by looking at completely different industries and figuring out how to adapt and adopt their success to my unique situations.

Just like my business has nothing to do with computers, mobile phones, or the music business like Apple, they give me inspiration and ideas to apply to vision and mission. I'm building the Joshua Shafran culture not the Apple culture. I can't be Apple or Steve Jobs.

But I CAN follow their example as a teaching model to focus me on how to create a similar loyalty for my business model!

Same thing for you and creating your own unique brand of business preeminence...

CHAPTER 10:
Overwhelmed Much?

Hey, don't try to swallow the elephant whole.

It's gonna take a little practice before you get good at building your own culture. But you CAN master these Profit Prophet skills to the point they're an automatic and an effortless part of who you are without any conscious thought.

Take any skill you now have and trace it back to before you mastered it and you'll see clearly there was a very specific *process* you went through to learn it.

Walking, for example.

Today, I bet you don't think consciously "okay, now I've got to bend my right knee, raise my right leg, lean forward, put my right foot down on the ground, etc..." It's just as natural and automatic for you as breathing. Yet, as a baby, it wasn't automatic at all. You had to learn to walk through a very specific process.

It starts with the process of first learning to crawl, right?

Crawl... Walk... Run...

That's always the process of mastering anything (and each major piece of the process can always be broken down into smaller pieces). **Each step in the process leads to the next step.** You simply can't skip crawling and go straight to walking or running.

In fact, it's <u>impossible</u> to walk or run without <u>first</u> mastering the "crawl" process. All your success (in everything) starts by crawling.

<u>And, let's face facts</u>: There's a HUGE difference between just *teaching* you the Profit Prophet Blueprint in this format and giving you the <u>ongoing</u> support, resources and coaching it takes to reap the maximum value from this material.

Look, would you ever dream of reading a book on brain surgery (or taking a month long crash-course seminar on it) and then start operating on people?

Of course not.

Because the only way to become a world-class surgeon is to master the skill bit-by-bit through a combination of book learning and supervised application in the real world.

Here's the key you need to know: **there's a gap between <u>gaining</u> the right knowledge and being able to <u>apply</u> it profitably in your life (mastery of the skill).**

That's why, as great as this information is, it's not gonna implement itself! It ain't gonna leap off the pages by itself and do it FOR you. The key to your success from this point comes down to **how quickly you can <u>consume and digest</u> this info and capitalize it for yourself.**

And how you digest this book is <u>critical</u> because Lord knows how desperately you like to already be leveraging these Profit Prophet processes… to have them built out perfectly and installed in your business in one fell swoop! However, I suggest you set your sights on *"acceptable progress."*

Notice the underlined word above? *Progress.* If you focus on progress, no matter how little, you're always moving forward. Celebrate every win, no matter how small because it's progress. Don't worry, your wins *will* get bigger and bigger.

Here's another hot implementation tip for ya: Only *you* get to decide what progress means to you. Progress towards your goals that satisfies *you* is all that matters. And, since you're the one who gets to make up the imaginary story about what *"being satisfied with your progress"* means, why not make a really empowering story? Why not set yourself up to be REALLY satisfied with your progress right from the beginning?

Zig Ziglar said it best, *"Inch by inch it's a cinch. Shoot for a mile, it's a trial."*

I know you're excited and eager to have all these breakthroughs implemented and working for you. However, before I turn you loose, let's talk strategy for a minute or two. Remember this Chinese proverb?

"Tell me, I'll forget.
Show me, I'll remember.
<u>Involve</u> me, I'll understand."

Involvement holds the key to mastery and therefore your Profit Prophet effectiveness.

(By the way, now that you have the insider knowledge revealed here, can you figure out the culturing role and the reason for reinforcing that proverb? It's *strategic*. ;-)

Look, I'm confident in the outstanding job I've done here educating you how to leverage my Profit Prophet methods to 10X your life, influence, and business success (hey, if I can't recognize myself, then no one else will ;-).

But sometimes education isn't enough. We've got to get you in the game. Without getting *involved* nothing else makes a difference. That's why I **created ShadowSuccess.com, to involve you in your own success.**

(Hmmm, I smell *more* culturing voodoo afoot, how's 'bout you?)

In fact, Shadow Success's mission is to provide you with a *facilitated* learn-by-doing framework so you can quickly and easily *move beyond understanding* to **getting** the results you want. Because, let's face it, understanding sucks if you're not *also* making progress towards your goals, right?

If you've never experienced the kind of fast progress you can make when a supportive community has your back, you're in for a very pleasant surprise! Not only is there safety in numbers, but also you gather amazing gravity when you join forces with likeminded doers, who, like you, are also in the process of implementing The Profit Prophet blueprint themselves!

Anyway, regardless if you decide to **join the shadow success team (go to <u>ShadowSuccess.com</u> for details)** or decide to go it alone, it's CRUCIAL you involve yourself in the process because you want to leverage your new Profit Prophet skills to reap real, measurable results.

The goal is <u>not</u> to make you <u>smarter</u>. You've done the hard work of overcoming inertia to make it this far. IMHO, you owe it to yourself to keep your momentum rolling forward.

One more thing. It's important: Sometimes it's tempting to compare and judge your progress against others (or your idealized picture of perfection). That's the kiss of death of momentum.

Please, please, PLEASE don't judge your success against anyone else's. Again, only YOU get to define what progress means to you.

Develop *your* strategy. Set *your* goals. Follow the plan that's right for *you*. **And then, <u>don't stop until you get where you're going</u>!**

So what if it takes you a year (or longer) to put all this in profitable motion? Who cares if someone else does it faster or appears to make more? If it takes you five years to accomplish your plan, no big deal; the important thing is you did it! You honored your commitment to yourself!

That's what matters.

Hey, I'll let you in on a personal secret: It took me over 10 years of intense trial and error to bridge the millionaire gap for the *first* time. Of course I didn't have this powerful blueprint that you do (I had to figure all this stuff out all by myself in the school of hard knocks because I didn't have anyone to shadow directly). However, which do you think was more important to me, that it took 10 years of hard work, or that I did finally do it?

I'll tell you something else, too: The first time you go through the Profit Prophet process will be the hardest (and take the longest). But after that, it gets easier and easier, faster and faster. That's because once you break through, your skills are a part of who you are. In fact, I've had months where the very skills you've discovered right here *made millions*!

So, *nobody* gets to tell you the right path; nor how long it should take you to travel it. *You're the only person who knows what's right for you.*

Push yourself hard enough so you don't get lazy but not so hard you get overwhelmed, confused, or frustrated. You know if you're selling out on yourself and need to push through your fears. Likewise, you know if you need time to regroup, refocus, and recharge.

If you need a break, by all means, take one! However, instead of "vegging" out, why not make your breaks about recharging your confidence batteries so you don't slip backwards or lose momentum?

You set your rules. So why not set yourself up to win? **Whatever YOU SAY is right for you, IS what's right!** *Period.*

And, please, even if you think you deserve it, don't *ever* beat yourself up for lack of progress. That only drains your confidence and keeps you stuck in the lack of progress cycle (and now you feel *worse* which makes it even harder to move forward). Where you are right now is simply where you are. It says nothing about you, your worthiness, or the progress you can decide to make from this moment forward.

You have a brand new moment right now. And another one *now*. And *now*.

What you decide to spend your moments doing controls your future outcomes. Using your moments to beat the snot out of yourself with guilt, anger, blame, worry, etc. might be what you're used to doing, but it won't bring you the freedom you want.

Ever.

Remember, it's a PROCESS. A journey you haven't ever taken before. So cut yourself some slack. Don't be so hard on yourself.

You're **going** to make mistakes along the way. That's the way it works when you're learning to crawl, walk and run. You *have* to make mistakes because there's always a gap between learning and *doing* (it's something you've never done before so of course you're going to have a learning curve).

Try to minimize 'em but don't be scared of them because they will direct you to the ultimate outcomes you want. Embrace your obstacles and you'll overcome 'em a lot faster than fighting against them (plus, when you get where you're going and look back, often you see it was the biggest "mistakes" and challenges that brought you to your greatest successes).

I hope we get the chance to know each other personally over at

ShadowSuccess.com (there's a ton of fun, support, and a few surprises too). The entire community benefits when you share your successes, progression, challenges, and innovations (who knows, maybe you'll even be featured in one of my future books).

(Now that you're a fellow "voodooer" didja see what I did there? Fun times;-)

Regardless, don't be a stranger. Seriously, I'd love to hear from you. (And that ain't no line of B.S., I really do welcome your feedback – both positive & constructive).

Here's To You And YOUR *Unique* Profit Prophet Story!

Take care.

Joshua Shafran,
Your Profit Prophet Coach

P.S. Extra credit (and bragging rights) goes to anyone who emails me with the correct reason why I included this P.S. here. Be sure you note the page # where I explained it in your email.

Good luck!

WHAT CAN "SHAFFY" DO FOR YOU?

(AKA, WHO THE HELL IS JOSHUA SHAFRAN AND HOW'S HE QUALIFIED TO BE YOUR PROFIT PROPHET?)

You might not know Joshua Shafran's name, however, you probably DO know his work because he's the brains behind a number of Online & Offline Business Breakthroughs, Marketing Innovations, Personal Development Systems, and Experiential Training Solutions that are now industry standards. He is also the founder of the "Cby3 $25,000 Business Challenge," "Prosperity On Demand," the "Income For Life" business development process, "The 2 Comma Club," the "Net Profits On Demand Formula" (and WAY too many more business models and profit systems to list here).

Shafran is also a best selling author, expert facilitator and a very successful entrepreneur. However, you need to know that long before Joshua turned teacher, he was busy leaving his mark on the front lines of the hard-core business world. His proven track record of bottom line results makes him one of those rare teachers who speaks from actual worldly EXPERIENCE, NOT academic, unproven theory. Often called "a reclusive master" because of his loving, yet almost ruthlessly focused approach to BALANCED success, Joshua is at his best when he's breaking down complicated, hard to grasp concepts into insanely PRACTICAL (and immediately actionable) systems for delivering predictable and duplicatable results for those who shadow his success.

His business credits total into the $100's of millions, including a start up he helped grow from zero to over $50 Million in sales (why industry insiders nick-named him "The $50 Million Dollar Man"). Just a few of Shafran's many Profit Prophet Breakthroughs (PPB) helped turn a $2 million dollar company into a $19 million dollar business in 18 months. Far from a one-trick-pony, Joshua has successfully applied his unique experiential training and development approaches globally to tens of thousands of people from all walks of life, helping them personally, professionally and spiritually.

Blessed with insight few can match, Joshua has the uncanny ability to unlock business's (and life's) "complex" mysteries by tracing everything back to its fundamental root level. This core understanding and mastery is how Joshua creates new paradigms of empowered action faster than the speed of your problems.

Like a chess master who sees checkmate 25 moves away, Joshua is blessed with incredible strategic vision: He zooms out to the 100,000 foot big picture view; helps you see all the steps in between where you are now and your desired end result…all from inside the problem itself!

PLEASE <u>DON'T</u> CALL HIM A GURU:

Although Joshua Shafran is "the go-to guy, the Guru's go to" (or rip off) when they need fast business and marketing results, he refuses to be called a guru himself! He prefers "Doer" or "Duru" because he believes a good teacher must first BE the teachings they teach (i.e., lead by example). He says:

> *"How can I, in clear conscience, tell someone to do something I've never successfully done? The world needs REAL leaders willing to freely share the truth of their successes AND mistakes. We don't need another expert, consultant, or guru trying to make a buck reporting on other people's regurgitated experiences (with no way of knowing if it works because they've never dared to risk failure by proving it works in the real world)."*

VISIT SHADOWSUCCESS.COM FOR EXCLUSIVE OFFERS

www.ingramcontent.com/pod-product-compliance
Lightning Source LLC
Chambersburg PA
CBHW020942230426
43666CB00005B/125